# THE CHILDREN'S BREAD

## And the Debate Of Whether A Christian Can Have a Demon

SECOND EDITION

BY

MARK CHASE

PUBLISHED by
PARABLES
*Earthly Stories with a Heavenly Meaning*

The Children's Bread and the Debate of Whether a Christian Can Have a Demon, Second Edition
Mark Chase

Published by Parables
November, 2021

All Rights Reserved. No part of this book may be reproduced or utilized in any form or by any means, electronic or mechanical, including photocopying, recording, or by any information storage and retrieval system, without permission in writing from the author.

Unless otherwise noted, all Scripture quotations are taken from the Holy Bible, New King James Version®. Copyright © 1982 by Thomas Nelson. Used by permission. All rights reserved.

ISBN 978-1-951497-85-9
Printed in the United States of America

Readers should be aware that Internet Web sites offered as citations and/or sources for further information may have been changed or disappeared between the time this was written and the time it is read.

# *THE CHILDREN'S BREAD*

## And the Debate Of Whether A Christian Can Have a Demon

### SECOND EDITION

### BY

### MARK CHASE

To my beautiful wife Jana.

God has used her mightily to bring His healing, wholeness, and peace into my life.

*Calma, paciência, sem chorar!*

Mark Chase

# Contents

| | |
|---|---|
| Acknowledgments | 4 |
| Foreword | 5 |
| The Six Objectives of this Book | 6 |
| Notes | 7 |
| What Do Actual Deliverance Ministers Think? | 9 |

## Part 1
## Foundations

| | | |
|---|---|---|
| 1. | Important Definitions | 29 |
| 2. | The Debate | 49 |
| 3. | Lies of the Devil | 105 |

## Part 2
## The NDMC Arguments That Are Used
## To "Prove" That a Christian Can't Have a Demon

| | | |
|---|---|---|
| 4. | Objection #1: Light and Darkness Cannot Dwell in the Same Vessel | 123 |
| 5. | Understanding Man's Tripartite Nature Resolves Objection #1 | 139 |
| 6. | Objection #2: The Body is the Temple | 167 |
| 7. | Objection #3: A New Creation in Christ Can't Have a Demon | 175 |
| 8. | Objection #4: A Christian Can't Be "Possessed" by a Demon | 187 |

9. Objection #5: My Denomination Says     213
That Christians Can't Have Demons

## Part 3
## Scripture That Shows That Deliverance
## Is for the Children of God

10. The Syrophoenician Woman's Daughter    233
And the Children's Bread

11. The Man in the Synagogue and the    243
Daughter of Abraham

12. The Psalms of David    251

## Part 4
## Two Strong Pieces of Biblical Evidence
## That Suggest that Christians Can Have Demons

13. Paul's Messenger of Satan    259

14. Get Behind Me, Satan!    273

## Part 5
## Conversion vs. Deliverance, the Promise vs.
## The Possession & Challenges for the NDMC

15. Conversion and Deliverance Are Two    285
Separate Events

16. The Promise vs. the Possession    303

17. Six Challenge Questions Posed to the NDMC    329

     A Note on Supersessionism    332

     Index    335

*Mark Chase*

# *Acknowledgments*

I am grateful to June Anika Packer, Ruth Freeman, and A. Allen for offering to read the manuscript and make suggestions.
I am thankful to Artur Rodrigues for helping with the diagrams.
I appreciate Sandy Henry and Patrice Gaillard for helping with the Haitian Creole text. And thank you, Tri Suseno and Wolmer Anjos, for providing critical input for the Second Edition.

Finally, I thank all of those who have encouraged me to share the revelation that God has given me about the need for deliverance and healing within the Church.

*The Children's Bread*

# Foreword

Mark Chase has done the Body of Christ an immeasurable service with his book *The Children's Bread*. For many decades I have had to repeatedly confront critics of deliverance and exorcism regarding the matter of Christians having demons. It is one of the most divisive issues among followers of Christ.

This contention is clearly unnecessary, as Scripture and common sense unequivocally prove that Christians can be demonized. The arguments for this position are effectively set forth in Mark's book. It is must reading for all 21st Century Christians, and especially those in ministries of deliverance. With advanced degrees and a background in public education, Mark masterfully uses his training as a teacher to set forth why his position is supportable. He methodically explains his beliefs with a respectful understanding of those who differ. At the same time, he shows the flaws in their thinking.

Mark's views aren't provincial and illustrate an understanding of all the ways that the deliverance process plays out. I especially like the way he points out that too many ministers under-utilize their spiritual authority, and then pass judgement on those who do boldly confront demons.

I knew Mark when he came to my seminars as a lay person and watched the Lord gradually draw him toward his present calling in full-time ministry to set captives free. I am pleased that he and his lovely wife Jana are personal friends and fellow soldiers in this fight for souls. The church needs Mark and this book to continue waging war on the kingdom of darkness to bring freedom to those whom Satan has bound.

–Bob Larson
*Spiritual Freedom Church*
April 2020

*Mark Chase*

# The Six Objectives
# Of This Book

1. To pinpoint the precise group of individuals that maintains that Christians can't have demons.

2. To demonstrate how it is theologically reasonable for a Christian to have a demon.

3. To demonstrate that the concept of a Christian having a demon does not violate Scripture and is actually supported by it.

4. To demonstrate the overriding Biblical pattern that *God delivers those who belong to Him.*

5. To demonstrate that deliverance is also for the nonbeliever. God delivers nonbelievers from demons as a sign to confirm His word.

6. To serve as a reference of terms and concepts that have been developed by my ministry, Invicta Ministries. These terms and concepts are used and expounded on in the curriculum of our online school of deliverance ministry, Invicta University.

# Notes

### Narratives

In this book, I give examples of deliverance stories and situations that create teachable case studies. These may be anecdotal or made up, or they may be a combination of the two. When a story comes from real life, names and other details have been changed.

### Pronouns

As my ministry is not politically correct, nor is my ministry bound by the spirit of political correctness, I may sometimes use "he," or I may sometimes use "she." Other times I will use "he or she." Please do not read into this as there is no deeper meaning.

### Born Again

In this book, when I say "born-again Christian," I am referring to spiritual Christians. I am referring to those who have genuinely repented of sin and sincerely confessed that Jesus is Lord. These individuals bear the fruit of the Holy Spirit. They fear God and seek to be obedient to His word.

I use as synonyms of *born-again Christian*: "Christian," "converted," "conversion," "saved," and "believer." As I use these terms in different contexts, please do not think that I am using different terms in order to qualify different kinds or levels of Christians. I mean all these terms as equal. I also use the antonymic forms of these words such as "non-Christian," "unsaved," "nonbeliever," etc. I mean these terms as equal as well.

*Mark Chase*

## *Intended Audience*

    This book's intended audience is twofold: First, it is for the individual who is earnestly seeking the truth about whether a Christian can have a demon.

    Second, it is meant to be a reference for the serious student of deliverance ministry and especially for students enrolled in Invicta University.

    Finally, this book is *not* for the casual spiritual warfare enthusiast, nor is it for the reader who is in search of additional spiritual warfare prayers.

# Can a Christian Have a Demon?

## What do actual deliverance ministers think about this question?

Mark Chase

Deliverance Minister: Edra Hays

Ministry: Do What Jesus Did Portland

Location: Portland, Oregon, USA

Contact info: dwjdportland@msn.com

Age in 2020: 81

Year Began Doing Deliverance Ministry: 2000

**What do you think about the question, "Can a Christian have a demon?"**

I think that this question is not relevant to those of us who are versed in bringing deliverance to people who suffer from the demonic. We don't need to ask this question. Really, it is a question for the uninformed.

I also think that this question disempowers Christians and puts them in the position of being a victim. When Christians believe the misinformation that Christians can't have demons, they are unable to take the authority that God has given them to command the enemy to go from their lives.

Finally, I do empathize with people who have the viewpoint that Christians can't have demons because there was a time that I felt this way too. I wasn't wrong on purpose, but I had

*The Children's Bread*

never been taught the reality of the word of God and I hadn't begun this ministry until later in my life.

    I pray for all the Christians out there that need deliverance but don't get it because of this question. I hope that the Holy Spirit releases the true answer to this question to those who feel the need to debate this question in the first place.

*Mark Chase*

Deliverance Minister: Sam Alcime

Ministry: Gospel Power Deliverance Center

Location: Jean-Rabel, Haiti

Age in 2020: 65

Year Began Doing Deliverance Ministry: 1997

**What do you think about the question, "Can a Christian have a demon?"**

    Késyon sa sé yon késyon Mwen konnen ki fè légliz la mal paské mwen wè anpil moun nan légliz ki bézwen gérizon éspirityèl. Moun ki di krétyen pa ka gen démon, sé mou'n ki pa konnen ministè délivrans, oswa sé moun ki jis pa pran swen pou wè manisféstasyon dyabolik. Satan renmen diskisyon ké yon krétyen pa ka gen mové l'éspri ou demon. Satan ri krétyen ki pa kwè yo ka gen mové l'éspri yo, ou démon.

    Pifo lidè krétyen yo ap viv nan réfi. Yo konnen gen yon bagay ki pa maché byen, men yo pa vlé pran tan pou chèché konnen pwoblem nan. Priyorité yo sé sali, men yo pa konsidéré ké krétyen yo toujou bézwen viv sou tè sa a. Yo kwè yon fwa moun yo konvéti, oubyen né de nouvo, tout bagay réglé. Réyalité-a sé yon istwa diféran.

## *The Children's Bread*

Mwen konnen krétyen ka genyen mové l'éspri, paské mwen sé youn ki té délivré anba mové l'éspri. Mwen té konvèti depi laj douzan. An tem dé téyoloji, mwen sé yon fondamantalis konsèvatif. Men, lavi m' té toujou tet anba ak anpil blokaj. Mwen té fondé yon légliz ki té fini pa divizé. Zanmi m yo té levé kont mwen san rézon. Mwen té kon genyen mové rèv ak asélman séksyel nan rèv yo. Mwen tap mandé sa ki ap pasé pou mwen konsa. Mwen té priyé ét té fè jen, rété san manjé, mwen té kon priyè anpil, mwen té fè anpil jen pou karant jou de fwa, mwen té fè jen pou 21 jou twa fwa, ét mwen té fè jen tout pandan set jou. Men, mové bagay yo té toujou nan lavi mwen. Mwen té kon n priyè senp priyè délivrans pou lot moun, men, mwen pa t' réyalizé mwen té gen mové l'éspri nan lavi mwen tou.

An 2010, mwen té vin konprann pwoblem nan: Mwen té genyen mové l'éspri! Mwen té jwenn yon ministè ki té kon n fè délivrans avansé. Mwen té wè yon mové l'éspri manifésté sou yon pastè. Lè mwen té tandé ki jan mové l'éspri a té ataké pastè-a, mwen té vin pansé, sé mem pwoblem sa yo mwen genyen tou. Sé sa kité fe'm vin réyalizé mwen genyen démon. Aprè sa yon moun té pryé pou mwen, ét sé konsa mwen té délivre anba démon yo. Oui, yon krétyen ka genyen démon.

Aprè moun té wè ki jan mwen té pasé nan délivrans pou rétiré démon yo, anpil té komansé vin jwenn mwen pou èd. Li enpòtan anpil pou krétyen yo wè lot krétyen pasé nan délivrans. Anpil krétyen pa konnen yo gen démon sou yo. Anpil krétyen pa konnen yo malad paské yo pa alé nan doktè. Nou mem ki travay nan délivrans, nou tankou doktè médikal, éksépté nou résévwa fomasyon pou jwenn épi éliminé maladi éspirityèl.

Nan Ayiti, pa gen twop moun ki kwè ké krétyen pa ka gen démon. Nan ékspéryans mwen kap travay nan sant délivrans mwen an Haiti, 80% pousan krétyen -yo admèt yo bezwen délivrans.

I know this question hurts the church because I have seen many people within the church who have a need for spiritual healing. I think people who say that Christians can't have demons are either outside the ministry of deliverance or they just don't care to see demonic manifestations. Satan loves the argument that Christians can't have demons. Satan laughs at Christians who don't believe they can have demons.

Most Christian leaders live in denial. They know something is there, but they don't want to take the time to see what it is. Their priority is salvation, but they don't consider that Christians still need to live on this Earth. They believe once people are born again, everything is settled. The reality is a different story though.

I know that Christians can have demons because I have been delivered from demons myself. I became a Christian at age twelve. In terms of theology, I am a conservative fundamentalist. But my life was always upside down. There was setback and blockage. I founded a church which went through a split. Friends would turn against me for no reason. I had nightmares and sexual harassment in my dreams. I wondered what was happening to me. I was praying and fasting. I prayed a lot. I fasted forty days twice. I fasted twenty-one days three times. I did seven-day fasts. But the bad things were still in my life. I was praying simple deliverance for other people, but I didn't realize that I had demons myself.

In 2010 I found out what my problem was: I had demons! I found a ministry that was doing more advanced deliverance. I saw a demon manifest in a pastor. When I heard how the demon was attacking this pastor, I thought, "This is the same problem I am going through!" That was when I realized that I had demons. Later someone prayed for me and that is how I got my deliverance. Yes, Christians can have demons.

After people saw me go through my deliverance, more Christians started coming to me for help. I think it is important that Christians see other Christians going through deliverance. Many Christians don't know they have demons. A lot of Christians don't know they are sick because they haven't been to the doctor. Those of us who work in deliverance are similar to medical doctors. Except we are trained to locate and eradicate spiritual sickness.

## *The Children's Bread*

In Haiti, not too many people believe that Christians can't have demons. From my experience working in my Deliverance Center in Northwestern Haiti, I think that at least 80% of born-again Haitians admit that they need deliverance.

## Mark Chase

Deliverance Minister: Donnie Williams

Ministry: Liberation Freedom Ministry

Location: Atlanta, Georgia, USA

Contact info: www.liberationfreedomministry.com

Age in 2020: 58

Year Began Doing Deliverance Ministry: 2005

**What do you think about the question, "Can a Christian have a demon?"**

The question of whether a Christian can have a demon is a scheme of the devil himself. Satan created this question to create a stumbling block for God's children to receive the healing that they need. The enemy claims victory every time Christians choose to debate this question instead of just receiving God's promised healing.

I have been in the ministry of inner healing and deliverance for 15 years and have cast out evil spirits from many Christians. In fact, of all those I have ministered to, I would say that 90% of them were born-again believers.

## The Children's Bread

The Holy Spirit has made healing available, but Christians need to receive this healing. Spending time questioning whether a Christian can have a demon just blocks the Holy Spirit from working.

### Mark Chase

Deliverance Minister: Jay Bartlett

Ministry: Jay Bartlett Missions

Location: Los Angeles, California, USA & Vancouver, British Columbia, Canada

Contact info: www.jaybartlettmissions.com

Age in 2020: 49

Year Began Doing Deliverance Ministry: 1988

**What do you think about the question, "Can a Christian have a demon?"**

In more than 32 years of global missionary work, in nearly 75 nations, on six continents, it's one of the top questions I get asked.

I think the question of whether a Christian can have a demon is a superb question…IF the end result is that our brothers and sisters get set free from evil spirits. But, if the end result of the question is that Christians spend time arguing about it and refusing to accept the truth, then it becomes a win for the enemy. If Satan can keep Christians bickering, then he knows there are fewer Christians that can rise up to oppose him.

## *The Children's Bread*

In the deliverance ministry, we see Christians who have demons. This is undeniable. Now, this question needs to be examined in light of what the Bible says. I believe that Mark Chase does a good job of that in this book.

Yes, Christians can have demons. I have cast out demons out of more than 20,000 people over the last three decades. Most of those who have received deliverance at my Supernatural Jesus public meetings, Personal Sessions, and during my Extraordinary Home Encounters have been Christians.

I have raised the dead on three different occasions. Some Christians have an easier time accepting this testimony than the fact that Christians can have demons!

*Mark Chase*

Deliverance Minister: Omar Figueras

Ministry: Iglesia Jesus el Libertador (Jesus the Liberator Church)

Location: Miami, Florida, USA

Contact info: www.jesusellibertador.com

Age in 2020: 61

Year Began Doing Deliverance Ministry: 2001

**What do you think about the question, "Can a Christian have a demon?"**

La pregunta o debate de si un cristiano puede tener un demonio o no, representa una gran pérdida de tiempo en mi opinión. Creo que es un debate más bien para las personas que no practican el ministerio de liberación que para nosotros obreros del Señor.

Llevo casi dos décadas ministrando a cristianos y a no cristianos. Y para responder el debate de si un cristiano puede tener un demonio o no, mi experiencia personal ha sido muy práctica. He ministrado a diáconos y a pastores y en su humildad y honestidad hemos encontrado demonios escondidos en dolores ocultos y en mucha vulnerabilidad. Por lo tanto, mi opinión es que un verdadero cristiano sí puede tener un demonio.

The question or debate of whether a Christian can or cannot have a demon represents a great waste of time, in my opinion. I think it is a debate that is more for those who do not do deliverance ministry than for us workers of the Lord.

I have ministered to Christians and non-Christians for almost two decades. And to respond to this debate about whether a Christian can or cannot have a demon, my personal experience has been very practical. I have ministered to deacons and pastors, and in their humility and honesty, we have found hidden demons in hidden hurts and in a lot of vulnerability. Therefore, my opinion is that, yes, a true Christian can have a demon.

*Mark Chase*

Deliverance Minister: Ezequiel de Souza Ferreira

Ministry: Instituto Yahweh Shalom

Location: Curitiba, Paraná, Brazil

Contact info: www.institutoys.com.br

Age in 2020: 49

Year Began Doing Deliverance Ministry: 2005

**What do you think about the question, "Can a Christian have a demon?"**

Esta pergunta é perfeita para as pessoas que só querem debater e brigar. Ela é perfeita para as pessoas que não querem conhecimento e não querem se aproximar da verdade. Pessoas só querem impor o que elas pensam.

Este debate só cria mais confusão. Para saber a resposta desta pergunta, é necessário ir à Palavra, que é cheia de revelações de Deus sobre libertação.

Eu trabalho com evangélicos que querem ser livres de demônios. Muitas destas pessoas praticavam fornicação, drogas, adivinhação, espiritismo, curanderismo, idolatria, Candomblé e Umbanda. Agora eles querem ser livres para servir Jesus. Eu prefiro somente fazer o meu trabalho em vez de debater se Cristãos podem ter demônios ou não.

This question is perfect for the people who just want to debate and fight. It is perfect for the people who don't want to know and don't want to get close to the truth. People only want to impose what they think.

This debate only creates more confusion. To know the answer to this question, it is necessary to go to Scripture, which is full of revelations from God about Deliverance.

I work with evangelicals who want to be set free from the demons. Many of these people used to practice fornication, drugs, divination, spiritism, shamanism, idolatry, Candomblé, and Umbanda. Now they want to be free to serve the Lord Jesus. I prefer to just do my work instead of debating whether Christians can have demons.

## Mark Chase

Deliverance Minister: Paul Cooprider

Ministry: Pulling Down Strongholds

Location: Lakeland, Florida, USA

Contact info: www.pullingdownstrongholds.com

Age in 2020: 83

Year Began Doing Deliverance Ministry: 1968

**What do you think about the question, "Can a Christian have a demon?"**

I think this question is the biggest deceit in the church today. It gives Satan everything he needs to mess with our lives. Most of the time, I do not bring up the subject.

Out of thousands of deliverances that I have done, I have only once cast demons out of a sinner. Everyone else has been Christian. We don't cast demons out of sinners because of Matthew 12:43-45. The demons will come back seven times stronger. In the early church, they didn't have to teach people that Christians had demons. They all knew it. Think about it. If you are Satan, who is your target?

Once, during the Lakeland Revival of 2008, there was a woman in the front row. During worship, she had her hands up in

## The Children's Bread

the air. There was no doubt for me that she was a Christian. At a certain point, this woman asked how it was possible for a Christian to have a demon. I asked her to wait for the answer to her question since I was about to start mass deliverance prayer. As I prayed, this woman started coughing and gagging on floor. At the end of the mass deliverance, I asked her, "Did your question get answered?" She replied, "Yes."

When something leaves you in Jesus's Name, you will have no more doubts on this subject of whether a Christian can have a demon.

*Mark Chase*

# Part 1

# Foundations

*Mark Chase*

# Chapter 1

# *Important Definitions*

I have coined new terms and have created definitions for these terms in order to clearly identify the one group of individuals that maintains that Christians can't have demons. These terms are utilized throughout this book as well as in the training materials of my teaching ministry, Invicta University.

**Session Deliverance**—Deliverance that most commonly takes place during an *appointment* with a deliverance minister. This appointment can be a one-on-one deliverance session (in my ministry, we call these Deliverance Encounters). Or, this "appointment" can take the form of a *scheduled* public meeting or seminar where the advertised purpose of the meeting or seminar is to minister deliverance from evil spirits to attendees.

During Session Deliverance, a deliverance minister ministers to the person receiving ministry (the PRM). Session Deliverance almost always involves the deliverance minister leading the PRM (we say it like *"prim"*) through repeat-after-me (RAM) prayer.

The primary purpose of this RAM prayer is to break and remove demonic legal rights. It is done with surgical precision and is usually specific to the PRM's particular case. RAM prayer consists of declarations to repent of sin, to renounce sin, to forgive others, to break un-godly soul-ties, to break curses, to pull down ungodly strongholds, and to make other confessions made in the Name and authority of Jesus Christ.

After this RAM prayer, demons are confronted, interrogated, and then cast out. Most often, demons are cast out via the *forceful command*; however, there are other ways that the deliverance minister projects Holy Spirit power to accomplish the expulsion of demons. See Chapter 2 for more on the forceful command and the projecting of Holy Spirit power. The fundamental principle of technical Session Deliverance is summed up in two sequential steps:

**Break and remove the legal rights→Cast out the demons**

Because Session Deliverance involves RAM prayer that must be declared by the PRM *in the Name and authority of Jesus Christ*, it is particularly suitable for the *Christian* PRM. In fact, Session Deliverance *requires* that the PRM be able to speak in this authority. Only Christians can make legally binding declarations in the Name of Jesus (Acts 19:13-16). As such, Session Deliverance is excellently suited for Christians. And in terms of the deliverance minister, only the born-again Christian has been deputized to minister in His power and authority. Only the born-again Christian can speak and act in the authority of Jesus Christ.

*The vast majority of PRM's that come to receive Session Deliverance are Christians.*

Another key feature of Session Deliverance is that demons are deliberately provoked to manifestation, and then they are interrogated. Interrogation of demons consists of questioning by the force of the Holy Spirit and always centers on obtaining case-relevant information only. This relevant information includes such things as the identities, functions, and legal rights of the demons that are to be expelled. Typical interrogation questions include:

- What is your name? What other demons are there?
- Do you enforce a curse? Do you have legal right?
- Are you putting sickness on her? Who does the migraines?
- Do you hold on to any broken parts of her heart?

*The Children's Bread*

Because Session Deliverance involves the systematic and technical process of breaking and removing demonic legal rights before the unclean spirits are confronted and cast out, Session Deliverance falls under the class of *Technical Deliverance*. All forms of Technical Deliverance are especially suited for Christians only since only Christians can speak and declare in the Name and authority of Jesus Christ.

Technical Deliverance is the greater class of deliverance. Under this greater class of Technical Deliverance are four forms. These four forms are Session Deliverance, Self-Deliverance, Authority to Act Deliverance, and Territorial Deliverance. Of these four, Session Deliverance is the most commonly conducted within the deliverance ministry.

Observe the following graphic of Technical Deliverance:

*Mark Chase*

# Technical Deliverance

- Concerned with breaking and removing legal rights before attempting to expel demons
- *Repentance* is the foundation
- Deliverance that is, first and foremost, for *Christians*
- Utilizes the *forceful command* and or other *projections of Holy Spirit power*
- Conducted by a *Christian* who knows his *authority in Jesus Christ*

Primary Purpose:
**To Heal the Church**

## Session Deliverance

- Led by a deliverance minister
- Takes place during a scheduled meeting or appointment (although it is conceivable for an unscheduled encounter to take place as well)
- Typically involves RAM prayer
- Typically involves the *interrogation of demons*
- Typically involves Deliverance Counseling and Inner Healing

### Deliverance Session (Private One-on-One)

- *Private sessions* for individuals, couples, families, etc. These are called Deliverance Encounters, Marriage Encounters, etc.

## Self-Deliverance

- Technical Deliverance prayer and *forceful command* conducted by oneself over oneself

## Authority to Act Deliverance

- Technical Deliverance prayer and *forceful command* conducted by one who has *spiritual authority to act* over the one who is receiving the prayer. The one who conducts Authority to Act Deliverance repents on behalf of, breaks the curses over, and commands the demons to go from someone who is under his own *spiritual authority to act*
- For example, a mother over her young child, a husband over his wife, etc.

### Deliverance Session (Public Group)

- *Public sessions* such as seminars, services, *mass deliverances*, public meetings, *deliverance crusades*, group sessions, and prerecorded media

## Territorial Deliverance

- Technical Deliverance prayer and *forceful command* over some *geographic territory* such as land or an improvement on the land. The one praying Territorial Deliverance prayer must have *territorial authority* over this area—either because he has a legal right to occupy it, govern it, or conduct church operations within it, or because the one who does have this legal right has delegated his authority to the one who will conduct the Territorial Deliverance.
- Territorial Deliverance also includes Technical Deliverance prayer over some *nongeographic territory*. There are two kinds of these: *tangible territories* such as vehicles, things, possessions, animals, and even food. And *intangible territories* such as accounts, contracts, corporations, businesses, ministries, digital files, websites, social media, plans, appointment calendars, degrees, jobs, careers, relationships, families, and marriages.

v.3.0 © *Invicta Ministries*

## *The Children's Bread*

Session Deliverance is excellently suited to minister to *Christians* who have demons. This is so for three reasons:

1. Session Deliverance deals directly with the sins that are in the PRM's life. These sins can separate the PRM from God's presence, *and* they can give demons legal right to remain. Only Christians can comprehend the nature of sin, and only Christians can place sin under the Blood of Jesus. The deliverance minister assists the PRM in doing this first by conducting appropriate Deliverance Counseling to make the PRM aware of her sin. Then the deliverance minister leads the PRM in well-placed RAM prayer to confess sin, renounce sin, repent of sin, declare forgiveness, break curses, pull down ungodly strongholds, sever ungodly soul-ties, etc.

2. Session Deliverance succeeds in placing the Christian PRM in exactly the right spiritual position she needs to be in so that God can move to deliver her. This spiritual positioning is achieved as the deliverance minister conducts Deliverance Counseling as well as assisting the PRM in effectively dealing with sin, as described above.

3. Session Deliverance utilizes the Christian's God-ordained authority over demons (Matthew 10:1, Luke 10:19, etc.). The deliverance minister guides the PRM in exercising this authority through precisely directed RAM prayer to repent, come out of agreement with, break the curses of, bind, loose, cut off, torment, interrogate and cast out demons— all in the Name and authority of Jesus.

In two separate Scriptures, Jesus alludes to Session Deliverance when, instead of just sovereignly casting out the demons, He first paused to ask questions and get more information.

For example, Jesus *interrogated* the demon that indwelled the *Demoniac of Gadara*:

*Then He asked him, "What is your name?" And he answered, saying, "My name is Legion; for we are many."* Mark 5:9 (NKJV)

And Jesus sought information before proceeding with deliverance during the *Healing of the Epileptic Son*:

*So He asked his father, "How long has this been happening to him?"* Mark 9:21 (NKJV)

While the precise definition of Session Deliverance is not "in the Bible," I consider Session Deliverance to fall under the umbrella of Jesus's "greater things" that every Christian has been given authority to do:

*Most assuredly, I say to you, he who believes in Me, the works that I do he will do also; and **greater works than these he will do**, because I go to My Father.* John 14:12 (NKJV)

In addition, the ministry discipline of Session Deliverance is protected by the words of the Master Himself. This is because, during Session Deliverance, demons are commanded to leave in the Name and authority of Jesus Christ.

In the story of the *Unknown Exorcist*, Jesus said that whoever works the *miracle* of casting out devils in His Name should not be forbidden to do so:

**38** *Now John answered Him, saying, "Teacher, we saw someone who does not follow us casting out demons in Your name, and we forbade him because he does not follow us."* **39** *But Jesus said,* **"Do not forbid him***, for no one who works a miracle in My name can soon afterward speak evil of Me.* **40** *For he who is not against us is on our side.* **41** *For whoever gives you a cup of water to drink in My name, because you belong to Christ, assuredly, I say to you, he will by no means lose his reward."* Mark 9:38-41 (NKJV)

Seven distinguishing features of Session Deliverance are:

1. Session Deliverance almost always takes place during an appointment with a deliverance minister. This appointment can be one-on-one, or it can be a public deliverance event, service or seminar, or other types of scheduled public group meetings.

2. Session Deliverance utilizes RAM prayer in order to precisely break and remove demonic legal rights such as curses. RAM prayer is a key feature of Session Deliverance.

3. Session Deliverance involves the interrogation of demons. This interrogation is done to obtain critical information regarding demonic identities, functions, and legal rights. Demons answer the deliverance minister's forceful questions under the duress of the strong compulsion of the Holy Spirit. Interrogation of demons is another key feature of Session Deliverance.

4. The fundamental principle of Session Deliverance is first, break and remove the demonic legal rights. And second, cast out the demons. Breaking and removing legal rights before expelling demons is the crux of Technical Deliverance.

5. Session Deliverance is for Christians. It is excellently suited to minister deliverance to Christians since, during Session Deliverance, sin is dealt with. In addition, only a Christian can speak in the Name and authority of Jesus Christ. In some Session Deliverance appointments, the PRM receives the Lord and is born again *during* the session. At which point, he or she can now legally make binding spiritual declarations in Jesus's Name. The primary purpose of Technical Deliverance, of which Session Deliverance is a form, is to minister healing to the Church. Technical Session Deliverance exists to bring the healing of the soul and the deliverance from demon spirits to Christian believers.

6. Session Deliverance also removes legal rights through *inner healing,* which is the healing of the wounded or fragmented soul.

However, the topic of inner healing is beyond the scope of this book, so it will not be discussed in detail here.

7. Session Deliverance involves Deliverance Counseling.

> ## *If Session Deliverance is for Christians, then what is happening when a non-Christian receives deliverance from demons during Session Deliverance?*
>
> Session Deliverance is excellently suited for Christians. This is so since legally binding spiritual declarations in the Name and authority of Jesus are typically made. The most significant of these is the breaking of curses. When it comes to making legal declarations in Jesus's Name, only the Christian has the authority to make it bound in Heaven. Only the Christian has been given authority to bind and loose, confess that curses are broken, and take authority over demon spirits.
>
> So, what is happening when a non-Christian receives deliverance from demons during Session Deliverance? This certainly happens in real life since not everyone who makes an appointment with a deliverance minister to receive Session Deliverance is a born-again Christian.
>
> A non-Christian can go through the motions of repeating the deliverance minister's RAM prayer to break curses, but it will not be spiritually legally binding. Therefore, when non-Christians do receive deliverance from demons during Session Deliverance, one of two things has happened:
>
> 1. The PRM was born again during the session and now has the legal authority to make legally binding declarations in the Name of Jesus. In other words, the newly born-again PRM now has *authority in Jesus Christ*. Deliverance ministers frequently lead the PRM in prayer to repent and confess Christ as Lord during Session Deliverance. In this way, good deliverance ministers are also evangelists!

> 2. The non-Christian PRM received what is called *Power Encounter Deliverance*. Power Encounter Deliverance does not require that the PRM be born again. Power Encounter does not require that the PRM be able to make spiritually legally binding declarations in the Name of Jesus. Power Encounter deliverance is a form of Sovereign Deliverance and is discussed later in this section.
>
> ### *Inner Healing*
>
> As an aside, keep in mind that during Session Deliverance, both Christians and non-Christians alike can receive *inner healing*, which is the healing of the dissociated soul or mind. Inner healing does *not* require that the PRM be able to speak in the authority of Christ. This opens up wonderful possibilities for non-Christian PRM's to experience the healing power of Jesus during a session of deliverance!
>
> ### *Deliverance Counseling*
>
> Finally, every PRM—born again or not—can also benefit from the teaching, preaching, guidance, coaching, spiritual counseling, and encouragement of a trained and gifted deliverance minister.
>
> At Invicta Ministries, the above elements make up what we call *Deliverance Counseling*. Deliverance Counseling serves to *position* the PRM to most effectively receive her healing and deliverance during session.

Session Deliverance is one of the four forms of Technical Deliverance. The other three forms of Technical Deliverance are Self-Deliverance, Authority to Act Deliverance, and Territorial Deliverance. Once again, see the Technical Deliverance graphic above in order to see this in chart form.

*Self-Deliverance* is conducted when a Christian believer speaks to break and remove legal rights and then commands his or her own demons to go. In Self-Deliverance, the PRM becomes his or her own deliverance minister. While Self-Deliverance is not as easy or as effective as receiving deliverance prayer from a trained and anointed deliverance minister, it is useful as a supplementary tool.

*Authority to Act Deliverance* involves praying Technical Deliverance prayer over an individual whom the one praying has *spiritual authority to act*.

*Territorial Deliverance* involves the breaking and removing of demonic legal rights from geographic places or things and then commanding demons to leave these places or things.

Students will learn more about all four forms of Technical Deliverance within the Lectures of Invicta University.

**Deliverance Minister**—A deliverance minister is a born-again individual who routinely and frequently engages in Session Deliverance.

A deliverance minister sits with Christians (and occasionally with non-Christians) during private one-on-one encounters and in group settings to engage in public Session Deliverance.

He is an anointed and highly trained spiritual technician. He is disciplined, compassionate, knowledgeable, Biblically literate, organized, and of sound mind. The deliverance minister is a true servant of God who spends the majority of his ministry time delivering *Christians* from demons.

First and foremost, he relies on his Biblical knowledge and his ability to wield God's word as a spiritual sword. Second, the deliverance minister relies on the power and guidance of his Helper, the Holy Spirit. Finally, the deliverance minister has a thorough understanding of the emotional, behavioral, relational, and spiritual realms in order to professionally execute his work.

Deliverance ministers know that their spiritual authority is in Jesus Christ alone, and they are never "limited" to just technical Session Deliverance. The deliverance minister is fully capable in the arena of sovereign Power Encounter Deliverance (see next section) whenever the situation calls for it.

Every experienced deliverance minister clearly understands

that born-again Christians can indeed have demons on the inside and have the need for deliverance from these demons. In fact, there is not one legitimate deliverance minister who believes that Christians *cannot* have demons.

The deliverance minister understands God's heart relating to deliverance. He understands that it is His people who He delivers. The deliverance minister knows and understands the overriding Biblical principle that:

### *God delivers those who belong to Him*

Five distinguishing features of a Deliverance Minister are:

1. Deliverance ministers routinely and frequently engage in Session Deliverance.

2. Deliverance ministers understand how and why Christians can have demons.

3. Deliverance ministers are anointed, knowledgeable about God's word (the Bible), and highly trained to deal with the emotional, behavioral, relational, and spiritual realms.

4. Deliverance ministers are born again and fully understand their authority in Jesus Christ.

5. Deliverance ministers are fully capable of engaging in sovereign Power Encounter Deliverance when the Lord directs them to do so.

**Evangelistic Deliverance**—Evangelistic Power Encounter Deliverance (Evangelistic Deliverance, for short) takes place during evangelistic labors. Unlike Session Deliverance and its technical removal of legal rights, Evangelistic Deliverance is far simpler. It involves straightforward forceful commands or other projections of Holy Spirit power to loose and expel demons from their victims *regardless of any legal rights that they might have.* God decides according to His good pleasure who is to receive this kind of deliverance.

Evangelistic Deliverance usually takes place at gatherings where the chief purpose is to preach the Gospel to the unsaved. These are events that are not advertised as being primarily deliverance events. Instead, they are events that are held in order to evangelize those who are not yet born again.

*Those that receive Evangelistic Deliverance are typically people who are not yet born-again believers.*

Evangelistic Deliverance could take place on a humble street corner, at the local park, inside a church, at a tent revival, or at a Gospel crusade in an 80,000-seat soccer stadium.

Individuals who receive Evangelistic Deliverance did not typically plan on receiving deliverance from demons. Instead, they understood that they were going to hear a message about Christianity and the salvation of Jesus Christ.

Evangelistic Deliverance rarely involves RAM prayer to remove legal rights, although the evangelist could ask an individual or the entire assembly to repeat certain declarations like renouncing sin.

An example of Evangelistic Deliverance could be the following: A street preacher is proclaiming the Gospel in a city park. Suddenly an unsaved hearer in the audience begins manifesting a demonic spirit: "You can't have him. He belongs to me!" The street preacher commands, "Come out of this man in the Name of Jesus!" The demon is expelled from the man, and everyone sees it and is amazed by it. The street preacher just demonstrated God's power over Satan. The purpose of this type of demonstration is to confirm God's word:

*And they went out and preached everywhere, the Lord working with them and **confirming the word through the accompanying signs**. Amen.* Mark 16:20 (NKJV)

Another example of Evangelistic Deliverance could take place during crusade evangelism. Sometime over the course of his sermon, the evangelist decides to demonstrate God's power by ordering demons to flee. He then begins making general forceful commands for demons to be expelled from everyone under the sound of his voice.

The evangelist commands, "In the Name of Jesus, every demon in this place must go!" I have personally witnessed the late Reinhard Bonnke employ this type of Evangelistic Deliverance very powerfully at a crusade meeting in Miami, Florida. In this case, Evangelist Bonnke directed his expulsion commands toward the whole assembly of crusade attendees and not at a certain individual or group of individuals. Many of these attendees were probably unconverted seekers at this point. As a result of these general forceful commands, people—certain people as ordained by God—received deliverance from evil spirits. This is Evangelistic Deliverance.

Evangelistic Deliverance is under the subclass of Power Encounter Deliverance since it is an encounter of power between the Holy Spirit and the infinitely weaker demon spirits. It is under the greater class of Sovereign Deliverance.

*Evangelistic Deliverance is sovereign since God carries it out whether demons have legal right or not.* God just overrides whatever ground the demons have and expels them. God acts sovereignly, according to His good pleasure, to deliver whoever He has ordained to deliver. God does this to confirm His word. We see the concept of "God's good pleasure" expressed in Scripture:

*For it is God who works in you both to will and to do for* ***His good pleasure****.* Philippians 2:13 (NKJV)

Therefore, during Evangelistic Deliverance, God delivers whoever He chooses to deliver for whatever reason He chooses to deliver them. He moves sovereignly to make a *public spectacle* (Colossians 2:15) out of the enemy—all according to His good pleasure. This is the sovereignty of God. Evangelistic Deliverance is a miraculous display of God's might. It is sovereign, and it is one of two types of Power Encounters.

Observe the following graphic of Sovereign Deliverance:

# Sovereign Deliverance

**Primary Purpose: To Confirm God's Word**

- Legal rights are not considered before demons are confronted and cast out
- Deliverance that is primarily for nonbelievers; however, Christians can also receive it
- A raw encounter of power between the Holy Spirit and infinitely inferior demon spirits
- Takes place according to *God's good pleasure*

## Power Encounter Deliverance

- God does as a sign to confirm His word (Mark 16:20, Hebrews 2:4)
- Conducted *intentionally* to cast out demons
- Conducted by a *Christian who knows his authority in Jesus Christ*
- *Interrogation of demons* is not utilized, or is minimal
- Utilizes the *forceful command*, rebuking, laying on of hands or other *projections of Holy Spirit power*

### Evangelistic Power Encounter
(Evangelistic Deliverance)

- A *Power Encounter* that takes place during evangelistic labors
- The primary recipients are the unsaved

### Non-Evangelistic Power Encounter

- A *Power Encounter* that takes place anywhere outside of evangelism
- It could even take place during *Session Deliverance*, especially with an unsaved PRM

## Spontaneous Deliverance

- Deliverance that is mostly unplanned and is received spontaneously when a person is in the strong presence of the Holy Spirit
- For example, during worship, baptism, holy communion, touching an *anointed object* (Acts 19), or at *radical conversion*

### Proximal Deliverance

- Deliverance that is received spontaneously across a *Godly soul-tie*
- For example, a wife receives deliverance via *Session Deliverance*. Then her husband spontaneously manifests some sort of deliverance or breakthrough

## Supplicatory Deliverance

- Deliverance that takes place when an individual implores God to deliver himself or someone else
- Paul attempted this three times (2 Corinthians 12)
- Parents often pray this kind of deliverance for their adult children

© Invicta Ministries

v.3.0

## The Children's Bread

Evangelistic Deliverance is a type of *Power Encounter Deliverance*. And all Power Encounter Deliverance is under the major class of Sovereign Deliverance. While Sovereign Deliverance is primarily for the unsaved, Christians can also receive it. However, Evangelistic Deliverance will most typically be received by those who have not yet made Jesus Lord.

Five distinguishing features of Evangelistic Power Encounter deliverance are:

1. Evangelistic Deliverance takes place during evangelistic labors.

2. Recipients of Evangelistic Deliverance are primarily unsaved people selected by God according to His good pleasure. Recipients of Evangelistic Deliverance typically were not seeking deliverance, nor did they know that they were going to receive deliverance.

3. Evangelistic Deliverance primarily uses simple, forceful commands to cast out demons. It does not involve the technical breaking and removing of legal rights.

4. Evangelistic Deliverance is practiced by some NDMC's (the concept of the NDMC is discussed in the next section).

5. Evangelistic Deliverance is a type of Power Encounter Deliverance. All Power Encounter Deliverance, including Evangelistic Power Encounter Deliverance, is under the major deliverance class of Sovereign Deliverance.

The other type of Power Encounter Deliverance is the Non-Evangelistic Power Encounter. These Power Encounters take place outside of evangelism. For example, at my public deliverance meetings, sometimes I do not know if an individual is born again or not. The individual may or may not be manifesting a demon. Sometimes, the Holy Spirit leads me to skip over the technical breaking and removal of legal rights and simply issue the forceful command. If this individual receives deliverance as a result, then he or she has received Non-Evangelistic Power

Encounter Deliverance.

Here are two examples of Non-Evangelistic Power Encounter Deliverance:

• A non-Christian receives deliverance from demons during Session Deliverance, such as in the example of my public meetings above.

• A Christian who is trained in deliverance observes a stranger manifesting a demon in a public place. The Christian does not know if this stranger is a Christian or a nonbeliever. However, at the prompting of the Holy Spirit, he approaches this stranger, issues the forceful command or some other projection of Holy Spirit power, and casts out the demon out of the stranger.

You saw on the Sovereign Deliverance graphic above that there are four forms of Sovereign Deliverance:

1. *Power Encounter Deliverance* (of which there are two kinds: *Evangelistic Power Encounter Deliverance,* and *Non-Evangelistic Power Encounter Deliverance*
2. *Spontaneous Deliverance* (discussed in Chapter 15)
3. *Proximal Deliverance* (discussed in Chapter 15)
4. *Supplicatory Deliverance* (discussed in Chapter 13)

**Non-Deliverance Ministry Christian**—A Non-Deliverance Ministry Christian (NDMC) is a Christian who *does not engage in Session Deliverance*. This is the primary identifying feature of an NDMC. An NDMC is a Christian. He might be so by title, or he might be genuinely born-again.

Next, the NDMC does not believe that Christians can have indwelling demons. As a result, the NDMC is opposed to the concept that Christians need deliverance in the first place. And by extension, the NDMC believes that the ministry of deliverance is unnecessary within the Church. Some adamantly dogmatic NDMC's would even declare that it is heretical or even blasphemous to consider that a Christian could have demons.

Another typical trait of the NDMC is that *most NDMC's practice no type of deliverance ministry whatsoever*. Of course, he does not engage in technical Session Deliverance, but he most likely does not practice any kind of Sovereign Deliverance either.

Although rare, there are *some* NDMC's who do engage in Evangelistic Deliverance. For example, the great evangelist Reinhard Bonnke, who I mentioned earlier, did do powerful Evangelistic Deliverance at his crusades. However, Bonnke did not conduct Session Deliverance that I am aware of, and I am quite sure that he did not believe that Christians could have demons either. (In Chapter 9 of this book, we will see what Evangelist Bonnke's successor Daniel Kolenda has to say about whether Christians can have demons.) It is rarer still to find NDMC's who regularly perform Power Encounters outside of evangelism.

Finally, the term "NDMC" doesn't necessarily refer to an individual person. When I am teaching my students of deliverance, I might refer to an individual, a website, a book, a ministry, a church, a theology, a seminary, or even an entire denomination as an NDMC.

Six distinguishing traits of the NDMC are:

1. The NDMC does not engage in Session Deliverance.

2. The NDMC most likely does not engage in any form of deliverance ministry at all.

3. The NDMC does not believe that Christians can have demons.

4. The NDMC correlates *demonization* with a lack of salvation. Demonization means having an indwelling demon in mind (soul) or body. "To be demonized" is synonymic with "to have a demon." The NDMC holds to the belief that if someone is demonized, then he is not, and could not, be saved.

5. The NDMC is a Christian, either by title or is truly born again.

6. There are some NDMC's who do conduct Sovereign Deliverance, such as Evangelistic Deliverance, but these are few and far between. Even fewer NDMC's practice Power Encounter Deliverance outside of evangelism.

## Notes About the NDMC

I want to make it clear from the outset that the NDMC is not the enemy. Satan is the enemy, not the NDMC. Any deliverance minister who ridicules, maligns, or attacks the NDMC is opening *himself* up to demons. Born-again NDMC's are brothers in Christ. This is so, regardless of the fact that they don't do deliverance or think that Christians can't have demons.

The fact that an individual is an NDMC does NOT mean that he is not a genuine Christian or that he is unsaved. Practicing Session Deliverance, or any kind of deliverance, doesn't save anyone. Repentance of sins and confession of Jesus Christ as Lord does.

Practicing Session Deliverance, or any kind of deliverance, does not make deliverance ministers better than other Christians who do not conduct deliverance. We mustn't fall into the temptation of spiritual pride. We must never believe that we are somehow superior to other Christians just because of the supernatural ministry and revelation that God has given us. God uses many NDMC's to do mighty works for the Kingdom of Heaven and are to be respected as such.

In my ministry and throughout this book, I use the term "NDMC." When I use this term, I am by no means implying or intending any disrespect or break in fellowship with those who I have defined as being NDMC's.

**My goal in using this term is simply to drill down and define the precise group of people who maintain that Christians can't have demons.** It is my goal to bring this whole issue of Christians having demons out into the open. Of course, it is also my hope that NDMC's will see their oversight and realize that born-again Christians can indeed have demons and that these Christians need deliverance from their demons.

We are all called to different ministries. God is calling many Christians into the ministry of Session Deliverance to heal the

Church. However, many are not being called into Session Deliverance, including many NDMC's.

All that being said, every Christian is called to deliver those with demons—in some way. This is part of the Great Commission according to Mark 16:17. If a Christian believer refuses to do *any* deliverance, he may be in disobedience.

*One of the premises of this book is that only the NDMC believes that Christians can't have demons.* Everyone who has ever attempted to convince me that Christians are immune from indwelling demons was someone who never sat with people to conduct deliverance, to begin with. And those who do not sit with individuals to conduct deliverance are NDMC's.

In other words, those who do not "sit with" individuals are those who do not conduct Session Deliverance. And those who do not conduct Session Deliverance are the NDMC's. Only the NDMC's believe that Christians can't have demons. Anyone who sits with people to conduct deliverance ministry knows that Christians *can* indeed have demons and subsequently need deliverance from these demons.

If you are interested in learning more about the concept of the NDMC, my teaching ministry, *invicta.university* offers additional in-depth teachings on this topic. Invicta University also offers professional certification to graduates of our online teaching program.

*Mark Chase*

# Chapter 2

# *The Debate*

This book addresses, and hopefully settles once and for all, the popular question that is frequently asked and debated in intellectual North America and Western Europe:

**Can a Christian have a demon?**

My wife Jana and I hope that by this book, we can stop this unprofitable debate of whether Christians can have a need for deliverance and just get on to bringing the healing and deliverance of Jesus Christ to the precious, hurting members of His Church.

It is my view that it is terribly arrogant to promote the misconception that Christians cannot have demons. To me, it is tantamount to declaring that Christians cannot have sinful emotions such as anger, lust, or fear. It is like saying that Christians do not sin. The Bible affirms, however:

*If we say that we have no sin, we deceive ourselves, and the truth is not in us.* 1 John 1:8 (NKJV)

I say North America and Western Europe because, in other parts of the world that are not so oppressed by the spirit of intellectualism and theological pride, this question is really a non-question.

In developing countries around the world (think Central and South America, the Caribbean, Africa, and Eastern Europe), pastors who work on the front lines of preaching and teaching the Gospel of Jesus Christ know that deliverance, which is the resisting and the casting out of demons, is not just for the unsaved. It is for anyone who needs it. They don't try to predetermine who is to receive God's miracle gift of deliverance. They know that deliverance is for the nonbeliever and the Christian alike. It is for anyone who has demons. How do they know?

First of all, these pastors from the developing regions of our world quickly find out find that many of the born-again members of their own congregations (the ones who are already converted) need deliverance! They see this clearly when their own congregants manifest demons during their services. As a result, these pastors do what needs to be done. They cast out the demons.

Next, pastors from developing countries are generally more humble than their North American and Western European counterparts. Since they generally have less materially, they are more thankful for the salvation that God has given them. And now, in gratitude, they want to be obedient to the Great Commission as outlined in Mark 16. This means that they long to do what Jesus commanded them to do, which is to preach the Gospel to all creation, drive out demons and lay hands on the sick.

In his book, *Free in Christ* (2000), Argentine deliverance minister Pablo Bottari, who served under Carlos Annacondia, once confronted people who were debating about whether Christians should be working miracles today. He challenged them with the question, "What are you—servants or lords?" (page 25)

Bottari meant that if you are a lord, then do as you see fit. However, if you are a servant like we all are under King Jesus, then just obey. Do what the King says to do! And what does the King say to do? He says to preach the Gospel, drive out devils and lay hands on the sick.

Pablo Bottari also knew that Christians need deliverance:

## The Children's Bread

*When we minister deliverance in crusades, 90 to 95 percent of those who need help are believers.* (page 60)

Pastors from the developing regions of the world get the servant-Lord concept much more easily than we do here in North America. They know that they are servants and not Lords, so they don't question every command in the Bible. They don't try to make Scripture conform to their own theological preferences. They make their theology conform to Scripture. When they do this, something happens. One of the Big Ideas of the Bible is revealed. This Big Idea is that:

### God delivers those who belong to Him

### Old Testament Examples of God Delivering His People

- We see it in the story of the Passover when God delivers His people, the Hebrews, from the Pharaoh's Egypt (Exodus 12). God instructed Moses to declare to Pharaoh the anointed words, "Let **my** people go!"
- We see it in the story of God delivering David and the armies of Israel from Goliath and the Philistine army (1 Samuel 17).
- We see it in the story of His servant Job being delivered from his pride and his prosperity restored two-fold (Job).
- We see it in the story of His servant Daniel being delivered from the hungry lions in Babylon (Daniel 6).

### New Testament Examples of God Delivering His People

- We see it in Jesus follower, Mary Magdalene, who witnessed His Crucifixion, burial, and resurrection and who was previously delivered from seven demons (Luke 8:2).
- We see it in the story of Zacchaeus, a son of Abraham, who was delivered from greed, corruption, and Hell (Luke 19).

- We see it in the stories of resurrection stories of Lazarus, Tabitha, Eutychus, and others who were delivered from physical death by being raised from the dead.
- We even see it in the Resurrection of Jesus, who is not only One of God's people, but God's only Son, God incarnate, and God Himself!

Pastors from the developing regions see that God consistently delivers those who belong to Him. As such, these pastors rarely take issue with the fact that Christians, the ones who belong to God under the New Covenant, need to be delivered from demons too. What does this look like in day-to-day practice? They just obey the Great Commission, part of which commands every believer to be occupied with the role of casting out devils:

*And these signs will follow those who believe: In My name they will **cast out demons**; they will speak with new tongues.*
Mark 16:17 (NKJV)

Additionally, pastors in developing countries see the divine order in Scripture. They do not read a passage of Scripture and assume that God just spoke in random, coincidental order. For example, they read a passage like the following and see a God-ordained, sequential order:

*"The Spirit of the Lord God is upon Me, Because the Lord has anointed Me To **preach** good tidings to the poor; He has sent Me to **heal the brokenhearted**, To proclaim **liberty to the captives**, And the opening of the prison to those who are bound.*
Isaiah 61:1 (NKJV)

And they read its parallel verse in Luke's Gospel:

*The Spirit of the Lord is upon Me, Because He has anointed Me To **preach** the gospel to the poor; He has sent Me to **heal the brokenhearted**, To proclaim **liberty to the captives** And recovery of sight to the blind, To set at **liberty those who are oppressed**.*
Luke 4:18 (NKJV)

## The Children's Bread

What is this divine order that they see? First, the Gospel is **preached**. People hear this preaching, believe, and then are born again. They become believers filled with the Holy Spirit.

Next, broken hearts are **healed**. This is the healing of the soul, which is the heart, will, thoughts, emotions, and the mind. For us, it consists mainly of healing the traumatized parts of the mind that resulted from abuse, rejection, and other deep hurts. Jesus can heal these. In Session Deliverance, this healing of the soul is referred to as *inner healing*. Of course, this healing can refer to physical healing as well.

And lastly, the captives are set at **liberty**. This liberty that Isaiah and Luke refer to is *spiritual liberty*. It is setting people free from the power of sin, and then by extension, the demons that got in through this sin. This is deliverance.

So, God's divine pattern becomes clear to the humble pastors and teachers:

Salvation→Healing→Deliverance

Does this mean that salvation is a mandatory prerequisite in order to receive deliverance from demons? No, absolutely not. We already saw in the definition of Evangelistic Deliverance that God can and does deliver unsaved people in order to demonstrate His sovereign power and to confirm His word (Mark 16:20). He shows His power in order for men to be confident in the truth of His word. This reassuring confidence attracts men to Himself.

Returning to the divine order: Humble pastors in developing countries see God's order in the Passover. They see that the Passover is a story of *deliverance.*

Who received deliverance during the Passover? The Hebrews did. Who were the Hebrews? They were (and are) God's children. They were those who believed on Him for salvation. The Hebrews were His holy possession, and God redeemed them. The Hebrews belonged to God, and God delivered them. Moses wrote:

**6** *For you are a people **holy** to the LORD your God. The LORD your God has chosen you out of all the peoples on the face of the earth to be his people, his treasured **possession**. **7** The LORD did not set his affection on you and choose you because you were more numerous than other peoples, for you were the fewest of all peoples. **8** But it was because the LORD loved you and kept the oath he swore to your ancestors that he brought you out with a mighty hand and **redeemed** you from the land of slavery, from the power of Pharaoh king of Egypt.* Deuteronomy 7:6-8 (NIV)

And who were God's holy people delivered from? Pharaoh. Who was Pharaoh? He was a type of Satan. Where were the Hebrews delivered from? Egypt. What does Egypt represent? The ways, evils, and sin of our Godless world. These evils would include the demons as well.

Humble and frequently Spirit-filled, pastors of the developing world see that God delivers *His Holy People*—those who already believe in Him, those who are sanctified by Him and belong to Him—from Satan and the ways of this world.

The humble pastors see the pattern continue into the New Testament as well. Jesus taught what will set us free:

*And **you** shall know the truth, and **the truth shall make you free**.* John 8:32 (NKJV)

Who is the "you" in this verse? The "you" refers to Jesus's disciples. We know this because it says so in the previous verse:

*Then Jesus said to those Jews who believed Him, "If you abide in My word, **you** are My disciples indeed."* John 8:31 (NKJV)

Therefore, and this is key, those who are set free are the disciples of Jesus. It doesn't say that those who get delivered *become* the disciples. It says that the ones who are already His disciples are the ones who will get set free.

Some might say that we 21$^{st}$ century Christians are not the disciples referred to in John 8:31. However, this is not true! All of us who abide in His word are His disciples, even today. The book

## The Children's Bread

of John wasn't written to be read by the original Twelve or even the Seventy-Two. The Gospel of John was written for *us* to read!

Humble, Spirit-filled, and God-fearing pastors see this quickly. They see that we modern Christians are Jesus's disciples and that we are the ones who will know the truth and that this truth will set *us* free. They see that we disciples of Jesus are the ones who are set free from the yoke of sin and that, as His disciples, we have been given authority to break the heavy yoke of sinful devils.

Intellectually proud pastors will miss this. Intellectually proud pastors assume they are immune from having demons by virtue of their salvation. Intellectually proud pastors profess theologies that scoff at the notion that Christians can have demons.

So, when it comes to driving out demons, what do the ministers of the Gospel do in these less academically sophisticated regions? They don't intellectualize it. They don't debate it. They don't attempt to separate the sheep from the goats. They don't accuse people who manifest demons of not being saved. They don't construct theological proofs to "prove" that real Christians can't have demons. Instead, they just start casting out demons—out of anyone who needs it!

In his book *They Shall Expel Demons* (1998), Derek Prince told a humorous but revealing story about casting demons out of anyone who needs it:

> A Christian young man told me that Brother Jones, a well-known evangelist, had prayed for him and that he had been delivered from a demon of nicotine.
> "I thought Brother Jones doesn't believe a Christian can have a demon," I replied.
> "You're right," the young man answered. "But when Brother Jones prayed for me, he didn't know I was already a Christian."
> That left me pondering.
> *In that case,* I said to myself, *it would seem that unbelievers have an "unfair" advantage over Christians, because they can receive prayer for deliverance from a demon. But once they become Christians, they are no longer eligible!* (pages 142-143)

## Deliverance from the Fires of Hell

Incidentally, the attitude of God's heart that He delivers those who belong to Him applies to salvation as well. Salvation is essentially our deliverance from the Hell that our sins merit.

God gives the grace of salvation to those who belong to Him. What is meant by this? This means that God saves those who He has *chosen* to be saved. He delivers the people who belong to Him from the eternal torment of Hell. He saves those who are *predestined* to be saved:

> **4** *Just as* **He chose us** *in Him before the foundation of the world, that we should be holy and without blame before Him in love,*
> **5** *having* **predestined** *us to adoption as sons by Jesus Christ to Himself, according to the good pleasure of His will.*
> Ephesians 1:4-5 (NKJV)

Yes, of course, we have the free will to accept or reject this offer of deliverance from Hell. However, those who are being saved (those who are born again) are those who have belonged to Him since the beginning and always have. We were chosen before the foundation of the world to receive His Salvation. *God delivers those who belong to* Him.

When the angel came to Joseph in a dream to reassure him that he should take pregnant Mary as his wife, the angel said:

> *And she will bring forth a Son, and you shall call His name JESUS, for He will save* **His people** *from their sins.*
> Matthew 1:21 (NKJV)

Who did Jesus come to save? He came to save **His** people. Jesus came to deliver *His* people from the Hell that the wages of their sins merit. God saves His people. God delivers those who belong to Him.

*The Children's Bread*

## *Big Deliverance and Little Deliverance*

We can rightly say then that there are two kinds of deliverance. There is Big Deliverance, and there is Little Deliverance. Big Deliverance is deliverance from the fires of Hell, which is salvation in Jesus Christ. And Little Deliverance is deliverance from demons, which is obtaining spiritual freedom through the driving out of demons in the Name of Jesus Christ. In both of these types of deliverance, *God delivers those who belong to Him.*

In addition, each type of deliverance has *repentance* as its foundation. In order to be born again, one must repent (Luke 13:3). And in technical Session Deliverance, the PRM repents of sin as part of the process of breaking and removing legal rights. Therefore, repentance is the foundation of both Big Deliverance and Little Deliverance.

In fact, in order to be saved, man must make the technical step of repenting of sin in his heart. Man must make the decision to turn from his sin. Of course, it is God who gives man this repentance, just like it is God who gives man the necessary faith. However, it is fair to say that salvation is technical deliverance from Hell since it requires man to *respond* to the Gospel message. Man must accept and receive repentance from God first before God delivers him from eternal condemnation:

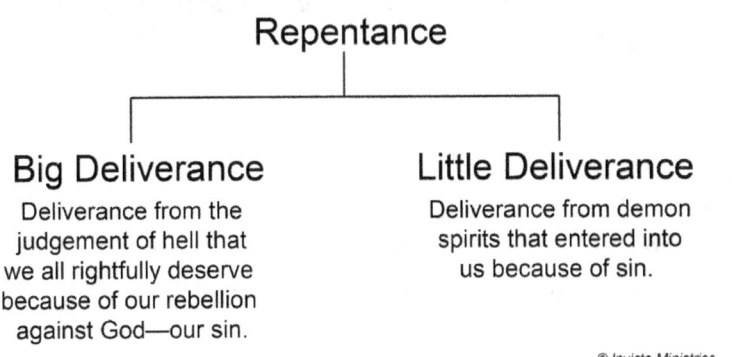

© *Invicta Ministries*

## Back at Home in North America

Now back to where I'm from. In North America, the level of intellectual and theological arrogance among believers is staggering. As a result, some Christians look down on others who have different interpretations of Scripture than them.

Ministries of deliverance are especially targeted by these kinds of individuals. We are told that we are false teachers because we are saying that Christians can have a need for deliverance. One thing these individuals have in common:

*They are NDMC's, and they have intellectualized that a Christian cannot have a demon. They do not engage in Session Deliverance and most likely do not engage in any kind of deliverance at all. They never try and confront demons in their own congregants. And lo and behold, no one ever manifests demons in their churches. As a result, they are "positive" that Christians can't have demons.*

They are NDMC's, and while they themselves have rarely, if ever, cast out a demon in their lifetime, they are convinced of the spiritual "fact" that Christians can't have demons. Perhaps they have arrived at this conclusion because if they had arrived at the opposite view, the possibility would open that *they* might have demons. And since this would be unconscionable, they teach the "fact" that it is *theologically impossible* for Christians to have indwelling demons.

## Pharisaic Reasoning

The NDMC's reason that they cannot have demons because of who they are—Christians. In the Bible, there is a story of another proud group who claimed that they could not be in bondage by virtue of *who they were*. This group was the Pharisees. I liken the NDMC's who teach that Christians can't have demons to the proud Pharisees.

After Jesus taught that it is the truth that sets us free, the intellectually and spiritually sophisticated Pharisees responded by saying that *they* could never have been in bondage in the first place:

> *They answered Him, "We are Abraham's descendants, and **have never been in bondage to anyone**. How can you say, 'You will be made free'?"* John 8:33 (NKJV)

This is precisely the thinking of the typical NDMC. The NDMC says, "We are Christians and have *never* had any demons. How can you say that we might need deliverance?"

Do you see the obvious parallel here? When the NDMC's insist that a Christian can't have a demon, they are expressing an attitude of spiritual arrogance. In other words, they don't believe they are susceptible to something simply due to their self-created, prideful identity. This is classic Pharisaic reasoning.

However, just like the Pharisees were wrong, the NDMC's who say that Christians can't have demons are wrong too. Christians can have demons, and that is OK. God has ordained deliverance for those who belong to Him. And as we will see later in Chapter 10, deliverance from demons is the *Children's Bread*. Deliverance is the nourishing food that He has for us, children of God, those who belong to Him. Thank You, Jesus, that God's heart is and always will be that:

**God delivers those who belong to Him**

## The Big Debate

The debate of whether a Christian can have a demon is a debate for the NDMC's. When one reads the testimonies of the deliverance ministers at the beginning of this book, it becomes obvious that the ones who actually work in the ministry of deliverance are not too interested in this debate. For example, Ezequiel Ferreira from Brazil testified that he would prefer to just do his work delivering evangelical Christians than engage in this debate. The debate belongs to those who do not do deliverance. The debate belongs to the NDMC's. On the other hand, individuals who actually sit with others to conduct deliverance have no need to debate this issue.

It is only the NDMC's who insist that it is theologically impossible for a Christian to have a demon. It is also the NDMC's who do not do Session Deliverance and, most likely, do no deliverance at all. Only the NDMC's maintain the erroneous, prideful, and ultimately Satanic concept that Christians can't have demons. By maintaining this concept, the NDMC's ensure that no one gets delivered—neither the nonbelievers nor the Christians.

Meanwhile, those of us who actually work in the ministry of deliverance, and specifically, in Session Deliverance, have been painstakingly documenting the casting out of demons from *Christians* now for decades. On average, I sit with about seven believers in Jesus Christ every week doing full (two-three hours long) Deliverance Encounter sessions. Most of these sessions average upwards of three hours and are meticulously documented in my session notes. Some Deliverance Encounters are even video recorded and placed on our ministry's YouTube channel in order to serve as public testimonies to the power of the Name of Jesus.

Of course, this casting out of demons from Christians is nothing new. By no means did it just begin in the last decades. Deliverance of Christians from demons has been taking place since the first century.

Secular historians like Elizabeth Ann Leeper know that in the ancient Christian church, exorcism was part of the new convert's preparation for water baptism. Deliverance prayer spoken over the one to be baptized became known as a "minor exorcism." This pre-baptismal exorcistic prayer lives on today in different denominations. Remember that people first believe and *then* are baptized (Mark 16:16, etc.). This means that the early church knew that newly born-again Christians could have demons, and they wanted to exorcize these demons before baptizing them.

My ministry, Invicta Ministries, conducts water baptisms twice per year here in South Florida. I can attest to the fact that, on occasion, some individuals about to be baptized have manifested demons while wading out to be immersed. Demons hate baptism due to the intense presence of the Holy Spirit during this act of obedience. As a result, some demons will be agitated to the point of manifestation. These demons will need to be cast out before the precious individual can undergo baptism. We have been baptizing since December of 2016 and have seen these in-water manifestations multiple times. And keep in mind, we only baptize believers.

It is just now in the 20$^{th}$ and 21$^{st}$ centuries that the debate of whether a born-again Christian can have demons has become such a cumbersome issue. I know that Satan has a vested interest in ensuring that Christians continue to believe that they are immune to having indwelling demons. I have no doubt that the entire debate of whether a Christian can have a demon was a scheme hatched in the very pits of Hell.

Some of the most effective, powerful, and anointed deliverance ministers of the 20$^{th}$ and 21$^{st}$ centuries are all in agreement: A Christian can have a demon. The names of some of these modern-era deliverance ministers include the likes of Derek Prince, Lester Sumrall, Frank, and Ida Mae Hammond, Bob Larson, Edra Hays, Paul Cooprider, Jay Bartlett, and perhaps even *you*.

For these servants of God and thousands of other deliverance ministers who have come after them, including me, there really is no debate. Once again, the debate belongs only to the NDMC's. It is the NDMC's who say that Christians can't have demons. It is the NDMC's who insist on denying Christian believers the deliverance that they need.

The NDMC's are the ones who refuse to come to our public deliverance meetings to witness for themselves how the hand of God moves to set Christian believers free. They are the ones who refuse to listen to the testimonies of Christians who have gone through the process of deliverance.

Instead of actually doing deliverance, the NDMC's just keep formulating their theological proofs to "prove" that Christians can't have demons. They keep telling hurting Christians that their problems are not demonic but instead are related to deficits in their Christian walks. They tell the spiritually hurting Christians that all they need to do is read their Bible more, go to church more, and stop trying to blame everything on the devil. They tell hurting Christians that the only way that the devil could possibly attack them is from the outside. They tell hurting Christians that real spiritual warfare just means changing their thinking patterns. Sometimes, they even tell hurting Christians that they don't have demons but instead that God is punishing them for something.

No NDMC ever sits with Christians one-on-one to minister deliverance. And the majority of NDMC's don't take the time to cast out demons from *nonbelievers* either. It is rare to see NDMC's do any deliverance at all. Very few NDMC's do Evangelistic Deliverance like Reinhard Bonnke and his successor Daniel Kolenda of Christ for all Nations.

This means that most NDMC's God-given authority to drive out devils (Luke 9:1, Matthew 10:1, etc.) goes unutilized. Basically, they do nothing and then judge the others who do do it.

How many pastors can you think of that do *zero* deliverance? I imagine that you can think of many. How many pastors can you think of that do at least some deliverance, like Evangelistic Deliverance? Very few. How many pastors can you think of that routinely sit with Christians to cast out their demons? Even fewer still.

Because of the general lack of available deliverance for Christians, multitudes of born-again believers do not get the deliverance that they need. The members of the Church do not find relief. This is because their church leaders do not accept that their flock's issues may have demonic roots. As a result, indwelling demons go unchallenged and unconfronted. The consequence? These Christians have to keep living with their demons, these unseen evil spiritual forces, which insidiously work to hinder their faith, health, peace, joy, and ability to execute their own God-ordained ministries powerfully. By the grace of God, some of them find ministries like mine and come to receive the help they need.

I often wonder how much torment, strife, failure, pain, and sickness the average Christian lives with that he doesn't really have to. Demonically-induced infirmity alone is bad enough. I have cast out many demons that were on the inside of Christians who had assignments to put diseases such as endometriosis, back pain, heart attacks, auto-immune issues, sexual dysfunction, pain, and many other horrible maladies on their born-again victims.

The following are two cases of physical healing that took place after deliverance sessions with our ministry:

## Case #1: Samantha's Neck Injury

There is a Christian woman that I have seen in session over Skype named Samantha. This woman had a car accident in western New York involving a deer on a country road. She re-agitated a pre-existing neck injury and allegedly did additional damage. After undergoing an MRI, her doctor diagnosed the previous scar tissue as well as an additional injury. He said that she now had a collapsed vertebra in the third cervical. The doctor informed Samantha that this injury would require serious surgery and four to six months in traction, *and* additional surgeries afterward.

When Samantha called me to tell me all this, I *knew* it was spiritual. I clearly discerned it. Shortly afterward, we had a Skype Deliverance Encounter. During this session, a spirit of Satan was cast out of her. At the end of her session, Samantha informed me that, "I now have the full range of motion in my neck without any pain!"

Samantha went back to her doctor, who performed another MRI. Miraculously, there was no more scar tissue, nor was any vertebra collapsed or herniated. The doctor then demanded of Samantha, "I need to know what you did." Samantha responded by telling the doctor that she had received deliverance prayer. The doctor then said, "I'd like to call you insane, but I can't deny what I am seeing here."

Demons were causing Samantha's "injuries." Once the demons were cast out, the problem was gone.

### Case #2: Sebastian's Sexual Dysfunction

I once had a Deliverance Encounter with Sebastian, who was in his late 20's. He was married, but demons were attacking him with sexual dysfunction. He was unable to carry out the sexual act with his wife. During his session, one of the demons that was cast out was Jezebel. While this demon was manifesting, it confessed that it had been attacking Sebastian in the area of his reproductive organs.

Soon after our first session, I met with Sebastian for a second Deliverance Encounter. He was elated and high-fived me. With a huge smile, he informed me that after our first session, he was able to make love to his wife like normal. Sebastian's demons were putting on the dysfunction. Once they were cast out, he could return to normal sexual function.

After seeing many healing stories in my ministry like the two cases above, I have often thought to myself, *What a rip-off! This person has been living with this demon for years, and he or she has spent so much money on doctors, therapy, and other "solutions," when the real solution was so simple:* COME OUT IN THE NAME OF JESUS!

## Demons Can Be on the Inside or on the Outside

When I say demons "on the inside," I am referring to unclean spirits that have been permitted by God to enter their victim and lodge themselves in the *mind* (the soul) and in the *body*.

I am not referring to, nor do I use, impossible-to-define terms such as obsession, vexation, or possession (Chapter 8 discusses the p-word) as these terms are unhelpful, confusing, and perhaps even harmful. In my ministry, I will not try to qualify an individual's demonization using these terms.

Instead, I teach my deliverance ministry students something far simpler: Demons can be in one of two places—and one of two places only. Demons can be on the *inside* of a person, in the mind, or the body. Or the demon can be on the *outside* of a person. There is no other possibility.

What *can* vary from case to case is the strength and specific functions of the demons and the complexity of the legal rights that these demons enforce. Not all demons were created equal, and not all legal rights carry the same spiritual weight.

Some demons are low-level pushovers who, when discovered, will actually beg the deliverance minister to cast them out. In contrast, other demons have massive levels of strength that they use to resist every effort to expel them. There is certainly a hierarchy of demonic power.

Regardless of a demon's strength, however, a demon needs some legality in order to resist being cast out. Demons need God's permission to be inside of their victims. My ministry teaches the total sovereignty of God. Nothing happens without God's approval in the matter. Satan can do nothing without God's permission.

Some demons are permitted to stay because of one simple undealt-with sin, while other demons enforce a litany of unbroken multi-generational curses, ungodly soul-ties, and ungodly strongholds. Undealt-with inner healing issues also permit multitudes of demons to hide and not be expelled. Still, other demons have no legal rights at all since these were previously broken. They remain in their victims only because they have never been properly challenged and cast out in the Name of Jesus.

However, regardless of a demon's strength and existing legal rights, a demon can either be on the inside of its victim or on the outside of its intended victim. There is no third possibility. The following two diagrams illustrate where demons can be in relation to their victim:

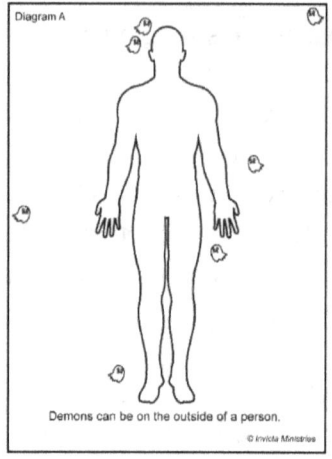
Demons can be on the outside of a person.

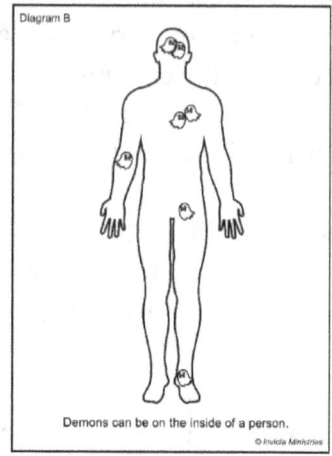
Demons can be on the inside of a person.

Diagram A shows how demons can be on the *outside* of the person roaming, flying, tempting, monitoring, touching, making noises, whispering in the ear, harassing, attacking, violating sexually, moving objects, vibrating objects, appearing as shadows, lights, objects, or living things, inhabiting geographic places, and being attached to physical (i.e., cursed) objects.

Diagram B shows how demons can infect the *inside* of a person. Demons that are on the inside can be in their victim's mind, affecting thinking, emotions, or perceptions. Or, demons can be somewhere inside of the victim's physical bodily organs—in specific locations like the neck, the spine, the stomach, the knee, the heart, the ovary, etc. Not only can demons dwell in specific organs of the body, but the victim can often feel these demons move within her body, especially in response to strong prayer.

## *Point of Entry and Legal Right*

Point of entry is the *initial* legal right that a demon utilizes to get in. It is almost always the result of some sin. When I minister during Session Deliverance, I may ask the demon, "How did you get in?" When I do this, I am asking for its point of entry. In most cases, the aphorism is true, "a demon needs a sin to get in."

## *The Children's Bread*

Once a demon has succeeded in invading the soul and or the body of its victim, new sins can then provide additional legal rights that fortify and strengthen the demon's original position.

The sin itself is not the legal right. The legal right is the permission that God gives the demon because of the sin. A legal right is also the spiritual license that a demon possesses to remain "legally" inside of its victim. "Legally" means that the demon has God's permission to be there. As long as God's permission to the demon still stands, the demon will not be cast out. When I am in session, I will often interrogate the demon by asking the forceful question, "Does God permit you to remain any longer?"

A demon with legal right will not be cast out unless God overrides this legal right (which He sometimes does during Sovereign Deliverance). When God overrides His own legal right, He is actually rescinding it. When understanding the concept of legal right, we must always remember that God is sovereign, and He permits or doesn't permit the demons to remain according to own His good pleasure.

God may give the demon legal right when there is undealt-with sin, which is sin that hasn't been cleansed by the Blood of Jesus. (There are other kinds of legal rights as well, and these are taught in our online school, Invicta University). Even though God hates the demon, His own law "protects" the demon from being cast out since the individual with the demon has undealt-with sin against Him. This undealt-with sin separates the individual from God. God cannot work freely in an individual with whom He is separated. As a result, God does not usually move to forcefully expel the demon. However, all this can change in the twinkling of an eye. When the individual repents, confesses, renounces, and forsakes the sins that give the demons legal right, the individual now moves back into communion with God. At this point, the sin has been dealt with. It is now covered by the Blood. God can now move freely. In most cases, He will then move to expel the demon.

New sins can provide for additional legal rights. These additional legal rights embolden the demons to carry out their assignments more overtly. They also allow the demons to more effectively resist the efforts of the deliverance minister to torment them and cast them out. These additional legal rights empower the demons to resist the workings of the Holy Spirit. The Bible tells us that the Holy Spirit can be resisted (Acts 7:51).

For example, the original point of entry for demons might have been sexual molestation (demons can enter children when they are abused). Then, when the individual later engages in fornication, pornography, and other sexual perversions, additional legal rights are accumulated by the demons. These new sins allow additional demons to enter too.

In Session Deliverance, the more legal rights a demon has, the more work that must be done in order to cast the demon out. The deliverance minister knows that these legal rights will have to be broken and removed before he issues the forceful command of expulsion.

When I ask a demon the question, "What legal right do you have to be there?" And the demon answers, "We have many legal rights to be here, so we're not leaving!" I know that I may have a long process on my hands. If I hear this and I discern it to be the truth, I know that there will be some lengthy groundwork to be done before the demon is "ready" to be cast out.

I think of this groundwork like the prep work that a painter does to the surface before he begins applying the paint. Just like in painting, the prep work in deliverance ministry is often more time-consuming and difficult than the final stage of applying the paint—the expelling of the demons.

Outwardly, this groundwork is done by the deliverance minister as he conducts Deliverance Counseling and as he leads the PRM through well-placed RAM prayer that targets specific legal rights. This RAM prayer includes breaking curses, forgiving trespassers, breaking ungodly soul-ties, and many others.

Inwardly, this groundwork involves the PRM having Godly sorrow, receiving repentance from the Lord, having a contrite heart, and desiring to come out of agreement with the demons. In other words, it involves the PRM *submitting* to the Lordship of Jesus and *resisting* the devil. This submitting and resisting will be discussed in detail in Chapter 16.

All indwelling demons have, or have had at one time, some legal right to be there. Recall that the crux of Technical Deliverance is first to break, eliminate, cancel, and remove demonic legal rights. And second, to cast out the demons that previously held on to, and enforced, these legal rights.

## *Abortion Clinic Analogy*

Think of a demon's legal right as a civil law that permits an abortion clinic to operate in a city (demons indwelling a person). The people voted for politicians who enacted this law (the sin that gave rise to this legal right). As long as this law is on the books (no repentance, renouncing, etc.), the abortion clinic can stay. The abortion clinic (the demons) can tell the pro-lifers (the deliverance minister), "The law protects us, and we have a right to be here, and you can't make us leave." No matter how much the pro-lifers who protest outside yelling, "Get out of our town!" (telling demons to go when they have legal right to be there), the abortion clinic stays. The local government will even protect the clinic—even though the mayor of the city (God) is actually against abortion. The mayor cannot do anything because the people invited the abortion clinic (the free will of man to sin) to be in their city. However, if the people would vote the pro-abortion politicians out of office and vote in new politicians (repent and renounce sin) who are against abortion, the law that enabled the abortion clinic to exist could be struck down (break the curse). At which point, the abortion clinic would have to go—even if they resist at first! Before leaving, surely the abortion clinic would say, "How can you make us go? We have been here fifteen years doing abortions. This city wanted us to be here. You can't do this. We will put up a fight! However, when the sheriff (the Holy Spirit) comes to evict them, they have no choice but to go."

*Mark Chase*

How many times has the deliverance minister heard a demon say something like the following: "We have been here for a long time! You can't do this! We're not leaving!"?

## *No Right, Never Challenged Demons*

Many times, the deliverance minister will encounter demons that no longer have any legal rights to indwell their victim. This occurs when the legal rights have already been removed (through repentance, being born again, forsaking sin, curse-breaking, etc.), but no one has ever confronted and cast out these demons. I call these "No Right, Never Challenged" (NRNC) demons in my ministry.

Every deliverance minister has stories of confronting demons with the question, "Why are you in this woman?" And then hearing the demon reply, "Because no one ever told me to go!" This is the classic response of the NRNC demon.

I posit that the presence of NRNC demons in Christians is somewhat common in the church today. Many Christians have actually eliminated the legal rights of their demons by their repentance, their confession of Christ, their forsaking of sin, etc., but since their NDMC church does not practice any sort of deliverance, not even Power Encounter Deliverance, their demons go unchallenged. The demons remain NRNC's. The demons remain in their Christian victims, and their NDMC churches keep neglecting the problem.

While demons remain on the inside of a person, they can continue to torment and attack their victim from *within*. Whether demons have legal right to indwell or not, there is a multiplicity of ways that indwelling demons can torment their victims.

Some demons torment by putting physical infirmity and pain on their victim. We have seen demons putting everything from arthritis to obesity to depression to HIV on people. Other demons attack by putting voices in their victims' heads, telling them to commit acts of violence, sexual perversion, idolatry, or to speak blasphemy. Some demons torment by making their victim feel fear, anger, paranoia, rejection, worthlessness, or hopelessly condemned before God. Some demons accuse their victims of having committed the "unpardonable sin" of blasphemy of the Holy Spirit. Demonic torment can take the form of attacks on one's thinking, learning, decision-making processes, and even the victim's faith in God. There are just so many ways that demons are known to attack their victims.

Regardless of the type of attack, the original point of entry, or the accumulated legal rights, demonization in Christians is handled effectively through Session Deliverance by its fundamental technical principle: break and remove the legal rights and then cast out the demons in the Name of Jesus.

## *Two Battlefronts Is Too Much for Many*

A person with demons on the inside must now fight on two simultaneous battlefronts: The battle against the flesh *and* the battle against the indwelling demons.

The first battlefront is the struggle that every man and woman descended from Adam must deal with. This is the battle of overcoming and crucifying the "flesh." The flesh is our human sinful desires and nature. Demons on the outside tempt individuals to cave to their sinful desires. The Apostle Paul talked about his own difficulty in overcoming the sinful nature:

*I don't really understand myself, for I want to do what is right, but I don't do it. Instead, I do what I hate.*
Romans 7:15 (NLT)

The second battlefront is the attacks launched by indwelling demons. These demons put all kinds of torment, weakness, unsound thinking (mental illness), ungodly emotions, hindrances, pain, and sicknesses on their victims. Indwelling demons will relentlessly attack in these areas until they are forcefully expelled in the Name of Jesus.

Victims of demonization must fight on both fronts. They

fight the battle of crucifying the flesh as all Christians must do, *and* they now need to fight to overcome the incessant and destructive assignments of the indwelling demons.

Since Christians can indeed have demons, countless members of the Church are embroiled in both battles simultaneously. These Christians war against the flesh, as every believer must do, and they also have to war against indwelling demons. I have ministered to thousands of Christians that must cope daily with managing these two simultaneous battlefronts.

The flesh, the first battlefront, can be overcome by self-control, being filled with the Spirit, being in the word, having accountability, worshiping, attending church, fasting, being interceded for by other Christians, etc.

However, when a Christian has demons *in addition* to the challenges of the flesh, it can be overwhelming. I have seen Christians whose fleshly nature desires to indulge in the sin of pornography. And then, in addition to this fleshly lust, they also have demons called Sexual Perversion, Lust, Masturbation, or Jezebel, which further stoke their sin fires within.

The sad truth is that many who live with these two concurrent battlefronts never win the war. They end up backsliding to the point where they become so ashamed that they never again call on the Name of God to help them. It is only by the intervention of the Holy Spirit that people such as these can overcome these situations.

In fact, without the grace of God, *no one* can win this war. Thankfully, God intervenes by leading many of these Christians with demons to deliverance ministries like ours where they can get the spiritual help they need.

## *The Forceful Command and Projecting Holy Spirit Power*

Once demons have embedded themselves on the inside of their victim, they will not come out, for the most part, unless they are forcefully commanded to come out. In the deliverance ministry, we call this the *forceful command*. The forceful command is issued in both Sovereign Deliverance and Technical Deliverance.

An example of the forceful command is given to us by the Apostle Paul when he delivered the psychic girl from the Python spirit. From the story of the Fortune-Telling Slave Girl:

> *And this she did for many days. But Paul, greatly annoyed, turned and said to the spirit,* ***"I command you in the name of Jesus Christ to come out of her."*** *And he came out that very hour.*
> Acts 16:18 (NKJV)

The forceful command is an order given in the Name and authority of Jesus Christ and by the power of His Spirit. Forceful commands have legally binding power. However, this is only the case when it is executed by a *Christian* (Acts 19:13-16).

The forceful command is a type of *projection of Holy Spirit power*. When a Christian believer commands with authority, "Out in the name of Jesus!" she is *projecting Holy Spirit power*. She is executing the will of God by serving as a vessel to project the power of the Holy Spirit. God uses her by moving through her to do His will. This projecting of power is real and can be felt:

> ***But Jesus said,*** *"Somebody touched Me,*
> *for I* ***perceived*** *power going out from Me."* Luke 8:46 (NKJV)

When a Christian projects this power, she is utilizing the authority that has been given to her as a disciple of Jesus (Matthew 10:1, etc.). When she issues this command, she is literally acting as a member of the body of Christ (1 Corinthians 12:27). It is as if Jesus Himself were doing it. As such, the Holy Spirit is in agreement with what she is doing. At her words, the Holy Spirit takes action and moves to expel the demon. In this way, she is *projecting* the power of the Holy Spirit.

There are other ways to project Holy Spirit power besides the forceful command. For example, a deliverance minister could lay hands on the PRM or place a Bible or physical cross on the

PRM's forehead. I call these kinds of projections "applying spiritual pressure." Other forms of projecting Holy Spirit power include rebuking the demon and applying anointing oil on the PRM during a demonic manifestation.

The deliverance minister could project Holy Spirit power by calling down (spiritual, not literal) Holy Fire, similar to how Elijah did (1 Kings 18:38). The disciples knew that Holy Fire was still an option even in the New Testament (Luke 9:54).

The deliverance minister could take his physical Bible and "pierce" the demon, wielding it as a literal Sword of the Spirit (Ephesians 6:17). God gives great authority to those who operate under His authority and in His Name. This includes the authority to direct the power of God's Spirit—when the deliverance minister's will and purpose align with God's. Demons tremble when they encounter Christians who understand the authority and power that they have been entrusted with. Projections of Holy Spirit power alone can be enough to dislodge and evict demons. The most commonly employed projection of power is the forceful command. For example, "Go in the Name of Jesus Christ of Nazareth!"

NDMC's are rarely interested in walking in this type of authority and power. They are usually far more concerned with proving that all of this projecting of power ended after the last disciple died. This, of course, is the Satanic lie of cessationism which says that the Gifts of the Holy Spirit (1 Corinthians 12) are no longer distributed to believers today. Most cessationists agree that God still does miracles. However, they don't believe that God uses *individual believers* to work His miracles.

## *Disputable Matters of Faith*

As Christians, we are called not to dispute or quarrel with one another regarding issues that are not absolutely clear in Scripture. I like the term "disputable matters of faith."

A disputable matter of faith is a spiritual issue that we ought not to defend too vigorously. It is a theological point that could have different interpretations—even by Spirit-filled people—and therefore, we need to tread lightly so as to not cause other believers, and nonbelievers for that matter, to stumble. I like how the NIV translates Paul's words:

> *Accept the one whose faith is weak, without quarreling over **disputable matters**.*   Romans 14:1 (NIV)

Here, Paul exhorts us not to argue about issues that are questionable. The NKJV calls these issues "doubtful matters." In other words, we are not supposed to dispute with other Christians, especially weaker Christians, about matters that are disputable or doubtful. Why? Because these issues do not have clear-cut Biblical answers, and by disputing them, we can cause others to stumble. In other words, we could be right in our theology yet still hurt others.

For example, we should not argue with our brothers and sisters in Christ about whether Holy Communion needs to be wine or grape juice. Or the timing of the Rapture—is it pre-, mid-, or post-tribulation? Or even if there is such a thing as the Rapture, to begin with. We should not dispute over the "correct" formula for baptism as this would also be a disputable matter of faith.

Disputable matters of faith do not have a unanimously clear Biblical answer, and therefore, we shouldn't be so dogmatic about them. Each of us certainly has our own revelation, and we need to have faith in that revelation and live by it. However, we shouldn't force our revelations on others if it is a revelation regarding a disputable matter.

On the other hand, there are Biblical matters that are clearly non-disputable. These are the non-negotiables. They are the first-order Biblical concepts that we will defend, even if it causes others to stumble. Some of these non-disputable matters of faith would include the following:

- That men's hearts are deceitful and full of every kind of sin. In other words, men are evil (Luke 11:13)
- That all men everywhere must repent in order to be saved
- That Jesus was sinless

- That Jesus was more than just a Prophet—He was and is God incarnate
- That Jesus was and is the prophesied Hebrew Messiah
- That Jesus was crucified, gave up His Spirit, buried, and then rose from the dead three days and three nights later
- That Jesus is the only way to salvation and that there is no other way to God (John 14:6)
- That there are literal demon spirits
- That there is a literal place called Hell

Regarding these non-disputable matters, we should be willing to hold our ground and speak boldly, with love and gentleness, of course, even with nonbelievers or weaker Christians. If someone tells me that he is questioning whether Jesus is God in the flesh, I believe that I can be dogmatic and not waiver. Even if by doing so, I cause this individual to become frustrated and get angry at me. I will stand firm and gently and lovingly declare the truth.

So, what about the issue at hand in this book: The question of whether a born-again Christian can have a demon? Is this a "disputable matter of faith?" Or is this issue one of those non-negotiables where we stand our ground no matter what? In my heart, I know the answer to this question. I see it clearly repeated in Scripture:

### *God delivers those who belong to Him*

I see that under the New Covenant (Jeremiah 31:31 and 1 Corinthians 11:25), it is the Christians (Jews or gentiles who have made Yeshua or Jesus Lord) who belong to God. Therefore, it is the Christians who God delivers. And if the Christians are the ones who are to be delivered, then it can be inferred that the Christians *need* to be delivered. Christians need to be delivered first from sin (Big Deliverance) and second from the demons that got in from this sin (Little Deliverance). Therefore, Christians can have demons, and they need to be delivered from these demons.

For me, the issue of whether Christians can have a demon is not a disputable matter. However, I know that most Christians, namely the NDMC's, simply don't have the revelation or empirical experience to properly deal with this issue. They are simply not prepared to process this concept.

Why is this? First, because they do not allow the Holy Spirit to speak to them on these matters. They have hardened their hearts to the matter. Second, they don't scour the Bible for evidence with an open mind. And third, they do not take the time to actually work in the ministry of deliverance so that God can show them who will come to them requesting deliverance.

They do not regularly sit with people to cast out their demons. They do not go to places where they can witness deliverance taking place in public settings. (And there are weekly deliverance meetings and seminars that take place in various cities in the USA every week, so there is little excuse.)

And perhaps there is a darker reason why the NDMC would say that Christians can't have demons. Maybe these individuals just don't want to consider the possibility that *they* could have demons themselves. If the NDMC ever conceded that a Christian could have a demon, that would open up the possibility that *they* themselves might have demons. I think that for the average NDMC, this is unconscionable. Remember from the definitions in Chapter 1 that the NDMC correlates having a demon with being unsaved. Therefore, the NDMC believes that anyone with demons is not and cannot be born again.

## Demons Are Assigned to Keep Christians Believing That They Can't Be Demonized

There is a demonic, spiritual side to believing that a Christian can't have demons. While an NDMC is not capable of discerning this and would most certainly deny it at all costs, I am aware of demons that are assigned to attack their victims in the area of mind control, confusion, mind binding, doubt, legalism, denomination, religion, and even unbelief.

In my paradigm, when I see an individual who staunchly maintains that Christians can't have demons, I know that this person is under demonic attack himself. He most assuredly has demons that are assigned to keep him believing the falsehood that a Christian can't have a demon. For example, I know that the Jezebel spirit is highly active in the suppression of the ministry of deliverance—especially deliverance for Christians. Other possible culprits might be demons of Religion, Legalism, or Denomination.

Why would the enemy be interested in making Christians believe that they couldn't possibly have demons? The answer is simple: self-preservation. By propagating the belief that Christians can't be demonized, there is a far lesser chance that these demons will be exposed. No demon wants to be detected, exposed, and then cast out. By remaining undetected in their victims, unclean spirits are able to finish their assignments—which are always to steal, kill and destroy (John 10:10).

## Unbelief in the Presence of Demons Is Powerful Legal Right

Satan knows that unbelief in his presence gives him full and continuous legal right to remain. When an individual says that he can't have any demons because it is theologically impossible (or for some other reason), his demons are now perfectly safe from *ever* being cast out. I often teach that unbelief in the demons' indwelling presence is the second strongest legal right possible. The first strongest legal right, by the way, is when someone *wants* his demons. These are the cases of the *familiar spirits,* and this concept is discussed further in Chapter 4. Unbelief that Christians can have demons is an example of a *Satanic thinking pattern* (STP). See Chapter 5 for more on STP's.

Once a husband and a wife came to my public deliverance meeting. When I confronted demons in the husband, there was no demonic reaction. But when I did the same with the wife, a demon manifested easily. Her demon began to speak through her and taunt me. I asked her demon if it "had" the husband too (by this, I was asking if a demon by the same name was indwelling the husband).

## The Children's Bread

To which, the demon responded that it did indeed have the husband. Utilizing the forceful command, I then commanded the demons to leave the wife. The wife had clear demonic expulsion, as was evidenced by coughing and spitting up.

After the wife's deliverance, she told me something that clearly explained why the husband didn't manifest as she did. She said that her husband doesn't really believe in demons, and he certainly doesn't believe that *he* could have any demons.

I made a teachable moment out of this and explained that the husband's unbelief that demons exist and his belief that *he* couldn't have any demons give his demons perfect legal right to hide in his mind. His demons have the second-strongest legal right possible. His demons will never have to manifest until he renounces these lies.

In Session Deliverance, declaring the truth and renouncing lies is something that the PRM does during RAM prayer. But before the PRM is ready to do this RAM prayer, he will need to be convicted of these lies and repent of them. In Session Deliverance, the deliverance minister leads the PRM in this process by conducting good Deliverance Counseling.

The legal right of unbelief gives demons immunity from deliverance prayer. Only a sovereign act of God could override this, which, by the way, can and does happen when an individual is delivered via Sovereign Deliverance. Remember that God can choose to deliver *anyone*, even when legal right exists, according to His sovereign good pleasure.

However, I would say that it is far less common for God to deliver someone who doesn't consciously believe that he needs to be delivered than for God to deliver someone who presses in and clamors for God's healing because he knows he needs it.

Therefore, it is to Satan's supreme advantage to keep the NDMC's from realizing that a Christian—either they themselves or any other Christian—could possibly have a demon on the inside. It is absolutely to the benefit of the enemy to keep Christians in ignorance regarding this matter.

Satan knows that God's people perish for lack of knowledge (Hosea 4:6). As a result, demons are assigned to attack NDMC's by seducing them into and keeping them bound up in this anti-deliverance lie. As such, believing that a Christian cannot have demons is literally a doctrine of demons:

> *Now the Spirit expressly says that in latter times some will depart from the faith, giving heed to deceiving spirits and **doctrines of demons.*** 1 Timothy 4:1 (NKJV)

Am I saying that every NDMC has demons? No. However, I have no doubt that many do. I know that demons have very good reasons to want to influence NDMC's in order to keep them believing this. I also know that demons profit when the NDMC's declare their theological "proofs" that Christians can't have demons.

Demons are laughing in victory when the NDMC pastor assures his flock that Christians can't have demons. Demons also celebrate when the NDMC debates this issue and ridicules the ministries of deliverance.

And I have no doubt that many NDMC's are in spiritual bondage without even knowing it—just like the intellectually superior Pharisees were in bondage and yet believed wholeheartedly that they could never be so (John 8:33).

And why wouldn't many NDMC's have demons? Other Christians do. I have sat with respected pastors, pastor's wives, worship leaders, and other church leaders in private session who have manifested demons. Does this mean they were not really born again? No. Does it mean that they didn't have the Holy Spirit? Absolutely not. Does it mean that God doesn't use them to do mighty works for the Kingdom? Of course not. God can use any servant who is willing to be used by Him—even if this servant has a physical or spiritual sickness. Look at Paul. The Apostle had a messenger, or angel, of Satan. However, that didn't stop God from using Paul mightily!

Lester Sumrall, an evangelist who also conducted

deliverance, told a story of a first-hand account of seeing a Christian with a demon. He had been invited to preach at a full Gospel church. After service, a woman approached the altar to receive prayer. There, she began to manifest a demon. The demon spoke through her in a masculine voice and proceeded to claim legal right on the grounds that she was watching and enjoying pornography. Sumrall confronted the woman about it, and she admitted it. She also repented of it. He then cast out her demon. The shock came when he learned who this woman was. This woman turned out to be the Sunday school teacher of the church! (YouTube Video: "Demons and Deliverance Part 15 of 21")

Every Christian has had his or her road-to-Damascus encounter with Jesus. This includes you and me and every NDMC. Every Christian did evil before knowing the Lord. This evil has now been dealt with. It is now covered by the Blood of Jesus and is forgiven by God. However, a lot of this sin had the potential to serve as points of entry for demons. And just because the person (you, me, or the NDMC) is now born-again, that doesn't mean that every demon suddenly and instantly flew out at conversion. What does this mean? It means that a lot of Christians, including many NDMC's, have what I call *holdover demons* from their previous lives of sin. When a born-again Christian has demons, these demons are mostly spiritual holdovers that got in years ago. Now, these demons need to be forcefully expelled from their victims (who happen to be born-again Christians now). See Chapter 5 for more on holdover demons.

The fact is that there is not one verse in the Bible that indicates that at conversion, every single demon is expelled from the new believer. In fact, in the Bible, we see conversion and deliverance as two separate events. There are stories where people believe on Jesus unto salvation, and there are separate stories where people are delivered from demons.

*Mark Chase*
## *Unbelief Does Not Change Reality*

Regardless of an NDMC's beliefs on the matter, *Christians can still have demons*. Why? Because unbelief does not change reality. Below are five examples to illustrate this concept:

• Just because one doesn't believe in gravity doesn't mean that this law of physics is suddenly nullified due to disbelief. If a person who didn't believe in gravity were to jump off a tall building, the reality of this law of physics would become completely apparent.

• Just because an atheist does not believe in God does not mean that the atheist will not have to face Him on Judgment Day.

• Just because an intelligent and educated college professor says that it is morally right to terminate the life of an unborn baby in the name of "women's reproductive rights" doesn't make him correct.

• Just because a popular politician says that Biblical views on marriage are "on the wrong side of history" does not make her correct either.

And in the same way:

• Just because a well-respected Bible teacher does not believe that Christians can have demons (he says so on his apologetics website) doesn't make him right. He may be right on many other Biblical issues, but he is wrong on the issue of Christians having demons.

Why? Because unbelief does not change reality. I propose that if these smart and educated NDMC teachers would just get on with actually *doing deliverance* like it says to do in the Great Commission in Mark 16:17, they would quickly see the error in their reasoning. Anyone who begins to deliver people on a regular basis will quickly see that it is the *Christians* who will come to receive deliverance. Anyone who begins to conduct deliverance will quickly realize that Christians can have demons. They might even realize that *they themselves* need deliverance!

## *When the Issue Can No Longer Remain A Disputable Matter of Faith*

Many times, I am willing to let the question of whether a Christian can have a demon just be classified as one of Paul's disputable matters. After all, even though I know that it is God's heart to deliver those who belong to Him, and I know that I cast out demons from Christians on a daily basis in my ministry, I know that there is no one verse in the Bible that EXPLICITLY states that a Christian can or can't have a demon.

So, I am patient, and I allow the issue to slide. I focus on the big picture—that even though the NDMC's do not believe in deliverance for Christians, they still worship the same God that I do. I know they love Jesus and are doing good works for the Kingdom. They are evangelizing and helping the poor and the widows. They are preaching Christ crucified and that He is the only way to salvation.

However, I can only be patient up to a certain point. This certain point comes when I see *Christians who are suffering from spiritual sickness (i.e., they have demons) and are being deprived of the only medicine that can cure them—the deliverance of Jesus.* This is when my patience runs out. It is at this point when I can no longer see this issue as a disputable matter of faith.

It is as if spiritually suffering Christians have the antidote right in their medicine cabinet, but they are being told by their doctor that it is impossible for them to need this medicine and even that it is wrong for them to take this medicine in the first place. So, they never take the medicine. They never get healed of their spiritual sickness.

I become impatient when Christians come to me desperately seeking healing from a problem that their church or their pastor won't even acknowledge that they have. I become impatient with this issue when I read in the Bible that God gives Christians authority over the enemy, but the Christians are not being trained to walk in this authority. As Pastor Edra Hays says in her testimony, Christians are being *disempowered* by the false belief that Christians can't have demons. It causes us not to walk in our authority over demons that Scripture is clear about:

> *Behold, I give you the **authority to trample on serpents and scorpions**, and over all the power of the enemy, and nothing shall by any means hurt you.* Luke 10:19 (NKJV)

Why aren't suffering Christians being trained to walk in the authority of Jesus Christ and subsequently get free from the devil's snare? Because they are receiving the wrong teaching. Their pastor, their denomination, their favorite YouTube channel, their well-intentioned but misguided friend, some apologetics website, etc., is telling them that they can't have demons by virtue of the fact that they are Christian. As a consequence, they continue to experience demonic suffering, hindrances, and torment. They never get the correct treatment for their spiritual sickness.

The following example comes from an excellent but NDMC, Christian apologetics website. This site teaches that a Christian could not possibly have a demon on the inside:

*...Surely the Holy Spirit would not allow a demon to possess the same person He is indwelling. It is unthinkable that God would allow one of His children, whom He purchased with the blood of Christ (1 Peter 1:18-19) and made into a new creation (2 Corinthians 5:17), to be possessed and controlled by a demon. Yes, as believers, we wage war with Satan and his demons, but not from within ourselves...Demonic influence and oppression are realities for Christians, no doubt, but it is simply not biblical to say that a Christian can be possessed by a demon or demonized...* (www.gotquestions.org in their article, "Can a Christian be demon possessed?")

Note the use of the word "possessed" in this article. This problematic and un-Scriptural word will be discussed in detail in Chapter 8. I believe that it is time that we in the ministry of deliverance take a stand on this issue and publicly defend the truth: First, that born-again Christians can, in fact, have demons. Second, that the only solution for this is to be obedient to the Great Commission and to cast them out in the Name and authority of Jesus Christ.

## *Christians Contact Us Who Have Demons*

My ministry receives calls from Christians, including pastors and other church leaders who are seeking help in their struggle against the demonic. Right now, as I sit at my desk editing this section, a pastor from Ohio has just emailed our ministry requesting deliverance. Last week, I had a Skype Deliverance Encounter session with a Baptist pastor from Long Island, New York.

These church leaders who call us hope that we can help them with issues that they have not been able to overcome alone. They call us hoping that we can give them the relief that their denomination isn't allowed to give. Or worse yet, they hope that we can give them relief from a problem that their denomination won't even acknowledge as being real. The pastor from New York that I mentioned above knew that his denomination would not agree with him seeking deliverance from demons. However, he was fed up with the torment. During his session, a Jezebel spirit manifested.

Christians who call us report the presence of idiopathic sicknesses. These are sicknesses that arise spontaneously and have no known cause or origin. People report destructive relationship cycles that include adultery, pornography, divorce, strife, rage, fear, control, and manipulation, etc. They tell us about nocturnal sexual harassment and violation at night when they are alone in their bed. They report tormenting voices that tell them to kill themselves, commit some evil, or that they have committed the unpardonable sin of blasphemy of the Holy Spirit.

Regardless of the specific issues that Christians call us about, a common theme among those who contact our ministry is the following: They have not been able to get relief or healing from other sources. They have gone to their local church or pastor, who either dismissed their case or didn't have the knowledge of how to deal with their issues. They have tried the medical route, the pharmaceutical route, the New Age route, and even the witchcraft route. But their problems persist. This is when they finally pick up the phone and call a deliverance ministry such as ours.

## *NDMC Churches Can Do Little to Help Christians Who are Suffering from Demonization*

Next, I will share three examples of the NDMC church failing to administer Jesus as a cure for the spiritual sickness of demonization of Christians. Remember that an NDMC church does not do any Session Deliverance (sitting with folks for deliverance appointments), and they most likely do no deliverance ministry whatsoever. NDMC churches believe that it is theologically impossible for Christians to have indwelling demons.

### *Example #1*

The following is an actual email that was received by my own ministry:

---

j*********@gmail.com
Wed 1/30/2019 8:45 PM

Good evening Pastors,
Blessings to you both. My name is J****. After many months of heavy internal and external turmoil, The Holy Spirit gifted me with the answer of what would help my suffering. I needed deliverance, which I had no idea what that meant, because unfortunately, most churches believe that once you receive Jesus in your heart, there is no room for "anything dark." By the grace of God, I found your videos on YouTube. Please send me the questionnaire whenever you can. I look forward to hearing from you.

Thank you,
J****

(C) 305-***-****

## The Children's Bread

### Example #2

Another woman from Ontario, Canada, contacted our ministry requesting deliverance ministry. This woman explained to us that she had attended her church for fifteen years. At a certain point, she went to her pastor asking for help.

She told him about her nightmares, torment, and rage. However, instead of receiving some kind of deliverance prayer, her pastor denied that there could be anything spiritual about her problem. He then asked her, "Why do you think you are so important that Satan would attack *you*?"

He went on to say that she shouldn't look for a demon under every rock and then questioned the possibility that she could even be a target of evil spirits.

Of course, the Bible makes it clear that *we* are the targets of the demons. When Paul tells *us* to put on the full armor of God in Ephesians 6, he is not addressing the pagans. He is writing to the Church—to your church and my church. He says that *we* wrestle against demons:

*For **we** do not wrestle against flesh and blood, but against principalities, against powers, against the rulers of the darkness of this age, against spiritual hosts of wickedness in the heavenly places.* Ephesians 6:12 (NKJV)

Many Christians, like the woman from Ontario above, come to my ministry after being turned away by their own pastors. Sometimes it is a simple matter of lack of knowledge since their NDMC church doesn't have a clue about what to do.

Other times it is worse. This is when people are turned away by their church because their pastor has a theological prejudice against the casting out of demons, and especially the casting out of demons out of the members of his own congregation.

## Mark Chase

### Example #3

My wife and I once watched a program on Christian TV in which a woman who leads a large international ministry made the emotional decision to "come out" with her severe anxiety that she lived with. And for the record, I think it is great when church leaders are humble enough to expose their weaknesses and inner struggles. It crushes the stereotype that Christian leaders are somehow immune to spiritual and emotional darkness.

My wife and I were excited because this coming out by this ministry leader would be the perfect segue to teach how Jesus alone can make the darkness of anxiety, panic, and fear flee from our lives. And make no mistake about it, there are *demons* of Anxiety, Panic, Fear, and others who attack in these areas. I know because I have cast them out on many, many occasions.

This woman's revelation about how she wrestles with these issues could have been the perfect opportunity to explain how, that by the Blood of Jesus, we can overcome these and other mental illnesses. By the Blood of Jesus, we go from crippling anxiety, panic, and fear to sound mind. This church leader could have invoked powerful Scripture to encourage her viewers:

*For God has not given us a **spirit of fear**, but of power and of love and of a **sound mind**.* 2 Timothy 1:7 (NKJV)

And:

*...casting all your care upon Him, for He cares for you.* 1 Peter 5:7 (NKJV)

And:

*He restores my soul...* Psalm 23:3 (NKJV)

And again:

## The Children's Bread

*The Spirit of the Lord is upon me, because he has anointed me to proclaim good news to the poor. He has sent me to proclaim liberty to the captives and recovering of sight to the blind, to set at liberty those who are oppressed.* Luke 4:18 (ESV)

However, my wife and I were surprised when instead of preaching the victory of Christ over fear and anxiety, she then brought a mental health clinician onto the set and essentially told the viewers, "If you are suffering from anxiety like me, then you need to get proper medical help. There are medications that can help with this. You need to seek the clinical help of someone like this…"

Instead of "call on Jesus to deliver you," it became, "don't be ashamed about your mental health issue; there is secular help available for your problem."

I remember being disappointed by this woman's message to her audience. Why did I feel this way? I will tell you why. As I just mentioned, I have met and cast out *demons* by the names of Anxiety, Panic, Fear, PTSD, Parkinson's, Bipolar, Schizophrenia, Depression, and demons of pretty much every other mental illness that is listed in the *Diagnostic and Statistical Manual of Mental Disorders, 5$^{th}$ Edition (DSM-V)*. I am well aware that the primary target of the enemy *is* the minds of the believers. The enemy wants to give mental illness and unsound thinking to God's people.

This NDMC ministry leader and the Christians who viewed this program live needed to hear about the victory of Jesus over Fear. They needed to hear that we cast our anxieties on Him. They needed to hear that anxiety and mental illness had been defeated at the Cross. And they really needed to hear that Jesus Himself gave us power and authority to command Fear and Anxiety to go.

When the viewers were told—by an important female spiritual role model—to go first to the outside secular world to get medical help for a condition that very likely has a spiritual root, people were given the wrong advice, in my opinion.

In an analogous situation, Paul tells us that we are not to take our legal matters that we have between brothers to the secular courts:

## Mark Chase

*Dare any of you, having a matter against another,
go to law before the unrighteous, and not before the saints?*
1 Corinthians 6:1 (NKJV)

Therefore, if we are not to take our legal problems to the outside world, why are we taking our spiritual matters there? If we shouldn't be sending two disputing brothers to the secular courts, then we certainly shouldn't be sending our brothers and sisters to secular healers to deal with our spiritual sicknesses.

And I can assure you that most mental health issues *are* spiritual. Once again, name the mental condition, and most likely, either myself or another deliverance minister has seen a demon by that name. Strong deliverance and healing prayer in our churches should be the first line of defense against these issues. Going to the secular clinicians should be secondary in importance and practice.

I want to make one thing perfectly clear right now. Neither my ministry nor I am against secular clinicians, therapists, psychologists, or psychiatrists. We are not anti-doctor or anti-medicine. I myself visit the doctor. In my ministry, I have even had cases where secular mental health medicine was an important component of a person's overall spiritual healing.

What I teach, however, is this: When the problem is spiritual, no doctor and no secular therapy can *heal* it. *When a problem is spiritual, only Jesus can heal it.* A broken heart cannot be miraculously bound up by research-based therapy models, nor can demons be cast out by a pill, therapy, or surgery. And I repeat for emphasis: When it comes to mental health issues as well as physical infirmities, nine times out of ten, there is a spiritual, read, demonic root to it.

With regards to doctors and healing, there is, once again, a divine order. This order is:

Seek the spiritual healing of Jesus → Seek the healing of the physicians

How do we know this divine order? We see it in Scripture in the tragic end of King Asa:

## The Children's Bread

**12** *And in the thirty-ninth year of his reign, Asa became diseased in his feet, and his malady was severe; yet in his disease* **he did not seek the Lord, but the physicians.** **13** *So Asa rested with his fathers; he died in the forty-first year of his reign.*
2 Chronicles 16:12-13 (NKJV)

King Asa did not seek the Lord for his healing; he only went to the doctors. He did not adhere to the divine order—and he died. For the sake of the born-again believers out there that suffer from pain, idiopathic sickness (when sickness is idiopathic, its origin is likely demonic), chronic sickness, chronic fatigue, dysfunction, infertility, brain fog, confusion, and mental illness, I urge Christian leaders not to repeat Asa's mistake.

Therefore, what I teach is first to seek the healing and deliverance of Jesus and *then* let God use the doctors.

## Curses Over Congregations

As a deliverance minister, my mind is trained to always be aware of authority relationships. One aspect of this awareness is how those in authority can bless or curse those who are under their authority.

In my ministry, we call this type of authority *spiritual authority to act*. Regarding cursing: Husbands can curse their wives by not treating them as the weaker vessel. Teachers can curse their students by telling them they cannot learn. Parents can curse their children by provoking them to wrath. Leaders are responsible for those under them and will give an account to God regarding their treatment of them:

*Obey those who rule over you, and be submissive, for they watch out for your souls,* ***as those who must give account****. Let them do so with joy and not with grief, for that would be unprofitable for you.*
Hebrews 13:17 (NKJV)

For those of us who are leaders in the Church, there is another curse. It is one that can land on entire congregations. Brace yourself. *A curse can land on an entire congregation when the leader of the congregation teaches his congregants the lie that since they are Christians, they cannot have demons.*

As soon as the pastor in authority makes this declaration and the flock internalizes this *Satanic thinking pattern* (which is a lie) as truth, demons, at least theoretically, have legal right over the entire church and its congregation. In Chapter 5, you will learn more about the dangers of espousing Satanic thinking patterns. The Satanic thinking pattern that Christians can't have demons is also a sin. It is a sin since God reveals over and over again in His word that:

### *God delivers those who belong to Him*

When men choose to disbelieve this overriding Biblical concept, demons can gain legal right and remain undetected until this lie is renounced.

Similar curses fall on entire congregations when the pastor openly affirms other Satanic thinking patterns. For example, if the pastor defines marriage in a way that is different from how God does. Or that smoking marihuana is pleasing to God. Or that murdering unborn babies is acceptable to God in some specific cases (situational ethics).

The above examples would constitute other situations in which curses could land on entire congregations just because the authority declared a lie over his followers. Leaders have spiritual authority to act over those under them. They can bless them and curse them and even speak for them spiritually. Parents can confess the sins of their children, husbands can repent on behalf of their wives, etc.

As a result, the leaders are spiritually responsible for those under them, and they will give an account for their leadership—did they bless and protect those under them? Or did they curse them and expose them to the enemy?

*The Children's Bread*

# Two Assertions

I will now make two assertions that I believe can help us to understand the answer to the question, *can a Christian have a demon?* I believe that the validity of both of my assertions can be tested by simple survey. Therefore, I urge you to test the veracity of these assertions yourself by asking people that you know, both NDMC's and those who work in deliverance alike.

## Assertion #1

**Only the NDMC's believe that Christians can't have demons.**

The first assertion that I will make in this book is the following: I posit that the only ones who insist that Christians can't have demons are precisely the same individuals who do not actively work in the ministry of deliverance. Who are these individuals? They are the NDMC's.

As I defined earlier, the NDMC's are those Christians who do not regularly sit with people to conduct Session Deliverance. In addition, the majority of NDMC's do not do any kind of deliverance at all.

It is easy for you to test this statement. Whenever you encounter someone who insists that a Christian can't have a demon, *respectfully* and *humbly* ask him one simple question:

*Sir/Pastor/Reverend/Dr., how many people do you sit with every week in order to cast out their demons?*

His answer will be predictable. He will almost definitely respond that he *doesn't sit with people on a routine or regular basis to do any kind of deliverance at all.* If he is the pastor of a church, he might reply that *his members do not and cannot have demons, and therefore such deliverance is not needed within his church.*

This is deeply ironic. The very people who never sit with the spiritually hurting, hindered, and tormented on a regular basis are the very ones that have the harshest words for deliverance ministries like ours. They don't do Session Deliverance, and they most likely do no deliverance at all, yet they teach with "authority" that Christians can't have demons.

While we deliverance ministers are sitting with Christians day in and day out ministering the healing and deliverance of Christ, we receive the attacks of the NDMC's that declare that what we are doing is theologically impossible. They don't seem to consider the suffering of the Christians who are hurting from demonization—some of whom sit in their own sanctuaries every Sunday.

Instead, many NDMC's prefer to defend their theology. They prefer to say that, "If someone has demons, then that means that they were never really born again, to begin with." Once again, that same reputable Christian apologetics website:

*Seeing someone whom we thought to be a Christian exhibiting the behavior of being demonized should cause us to question the genuineness of his/her faith. It should not cause us to alter our viewpoint on whether a Christian can be demon possessed/demonized. Perhaps the person truly is a Christian but is severely demon oppressed and/or suffering from severe psychological problems.* (www.gotquestions.org in their article, "Can a Christian be demon possessed?)

Sadly, these NDMC's never bother to speak to the people that we minister to. They never talk to them about their hurts. They never bother to come to our public deliverance meetings and seminars to see for themselves how born-again believers celebrate after being delivered by praising Jesus, crying tears of relief, and sometimes speaking in tongues. They don't want to hear the testimonies of how they came to faith in Jesus or what it was like to receive the deliverance of Jesus. And most serious of all, they never avail themselves to conduct any sort of deliverance ministry themselves. Of course, if they did, they would quickly realize that it would be mostly *Christians* who would come to them to receive deliverance.

Instead, the NDMC's launch their viewpoints behind the walls of their theological castles, spiritual opinions, prejudice, and sophisticated academic doctrines. More on doctrine in Chapter 9.

The NDMC's tell Christians that they do not need deliverance because no demon can be inside them. And if a Christian does receive deliverance (demonic expulsion can be dramatic and undeniable), they will simply brush it off by saying that this person who was delivered was never really born again anyway.

They will say that those "Christians" who received deliverance were just fake Christians, Christian posers, seekers, false converts, or at best, backslidden Christians who had fallen from grace and had lost their salvation. Or, as the apologetics site above stated, maybe they really were born again, but they have psychological problems or suffer from demonic "oppression" only.

## *The NDMC "Solution" Given To Christians with Demons*

What solution does the NDMC give to Christians who are being attacked by demons from the inside? First, they will tell this person that they can't possibly have indwelling demons. Then, the NDMC will explain that their problems are not demonic but instead stem from deficits in their Christian walks. In other words, that they need to attend church more, pray more, read their Bibles more, or give up some sin that prevents them from truly being saved.

However, I would make the following point: Did Jesus or a disciple ever tell a demoniac, "You just need to go to synagogue more"? Or, "You just need to read the scroll of Isaiah again; then you'll feel better"? No, they didn't. What did they do? They used their divine authority and cast the demons out of the demoniacs!

Finally, the NDMC will likely rebuke them for trying to blame everything on the devil. They will surely quote C.S. Lewis and accuse them of giving the devil too much attention. The NDMC will then go on to explain that it is their sinful fleshly nature that is to blame and that they just need to exercise more self-control and attend church more.

## The Real Solution

Legal rights must be broken and removed. Then, demons must be dealt with in one way and in one way only: They must be commanded to go in the Name of Jesus!

And if they resist, they must be confronted by the Holy Fire of God. They must be bound and loosed. They must be cut off from their functions. They must be crushed, burned, smitten, and tormented by the Name and authority of Jesus Christ of Nazareth and by the power of His Spirit. Sometimes, even holy angels must be called on to assist in weakening the demons further. This is *angelic assistance*.

Then the forceful command must be issued anew, and power must be projected. Demons must be resisted since this is God's will. All this, even if the person with the demons is a born-again Christian.

## Armchair Quarterbacks

I will make an analogy here. The NDMC's who say that Christians can't have demons are like the armchair quarterbacks. An armchair quarterback is a fan of American football who, despite never having played the game, believes he has the authority to judge the performance and game decisions of the real athletes on the field. They sit on their sofas, drink beer, eat potato chips and correct the professional players when they make a mistake by yelling at the television.

This is how the objections feel. The NDMC's, the ones who do not practice Session Deliverance, and most likely no deliverance at all, are exactly the ones who feel that they have been God-ordained to condemn the ministry of deliverance as being something that born-again believers do not need.

In other words, the NDMC's are like the armchair quarterbacks who speak about that which they have no experience and really do not understand either. They have never really asked the Holy Spirit to show them the truth. They don't allow themselves to see the overarching Biblical concept that:

### *God delivers those who belong to Him*

They do not allow God's word to show them this truth. They never interview those Christians who get delivered in order to hear their testimonies. They do not understand the concept of how demons enter through point of entry (the initial legal right) and then stay until they are cast out in the Name of Jesus. They make the un-Biblical assumption that, at conversion, all demons suddenly disappear. They skip over the commandment (Mark 16:17) to cast out demons, yet they criticize those who are trying to be obedient. They just speak based on their opinions that stem from a lack of willingness to understand. Perhaps Jude's verse could pertain to this situation:

*Yet these people* **slander whatever they do not understand**, *and the very things they do understand by instinct--as irrational animals do--will destroy them.* Jude 1:10 (NIV)

### *Assertion #2*

### All deliverance ministers know that Christians can have demons.

I will make another assertion. I propose that there is not one single deliverance minister anywhere on *planet Earth* who will affirm that a Christian cannot have a demon. No one who regularly and routinely engages in Session Deliverance holds that a Christian cannot be demonized.

I am grateful to the seven deliverance ministers at the beginning of this book who have offered to testify about this issue and allow their testimonies to be published. I suggest that you go back and reread what these mature and veteran demon casters have to say about the question of whether a Christian can have a demon.

I make this second assertion not out of pride or bravado but out of concern. Specifically, it is out of concern for the suffering Christians who are out there seeking, but not finding, healing for spiritual sickness. Some of them may even be members of your church or denomination. Many of them are suffering deeply as a result of the demons that got in when they were abused, molested, abandoned, or rejected in childhood. Others are downright tormented by fear, anxiety, fits of rage, demonic voices, seeing shadows, being held down, experiencing sleep paralysis, seeing demons, experiencing frequent night terrors, and many other hideous signs of demonization. Additionally, many of these suffering Christians are dealing with chronic sicknesses that have a spiritual root. When they are seen by the doctor, no explanation for their sickness can be given. Other suffering Christians have severe marriage issues that can't seem to be overcome, like strife, control and manipulation, adultery, pornography, and even infertility, impotence, and pain during sex. It is a fact that demons attack even the reproductive organs of their victims—I have found Jezebel to be notorious for attacking the sexual and reproductive organs.

Many of these Christians painfully cry out, "If God loves me, why does He let me suffer like this?" Of course, what they haven't been taught at their NDMC church is that God has already given them the authority to break out of these things. Their problem is that their leaders did not teach them about their authority over demons. Their church leaders do not exercise or do not know about their own authority over demons. Most likely, this happens since their denomination affirms that Christians can't have any spiritual sickness to begin with.

It is for the healing of these kinds of Christians that I make this second assertion. I want to highlight the problem so it can be addressed. I want these spiritually suffering Christians to get the help that they need—the healing and deliverance that only God can give. Jesus gave His disciples (remember, that means us—see John 8:31) the authority to set people free from demons. This is the

Christian's authority over demon spirits. Exercising this authority is what many hurting Christians of today need:

*And when He had called His twelve disciples to Him, He gave them **power over unclean spirits**, to cast them out, and to **heal all kinds of sickness** and all kinds of disease.* Matthew 10:1 (NKJV)

I believe that my two assertions will stand the test of scrutiny and time. If you are aware of an exception to one of these assertions—in other words, you locate a legitimate deliverance minister with an open, active, transparent, and documented ministry, who believes that Christians cannot have demons, then I would like to know about it. In Chapter 17, I issue this and five other challenging questions that are directed toward the NDMC church.

## The Majority of People Who Seek Help Are Christians

The fact of the matter is that anyone who begins working in the ministry of deliverance will quickly find out that the majority of individuals who will come to them for deliverance will be *fellow Christians*—which is why we recommend that every NDMC *just start doing deliverance.*

This is exactly what Pablo Bottari realized. He saw that 90-95 percent of those who are delivered are believers. Sure, there will be the occasional Hindu, Buddhist, Catholic, seeker, pagan, or "spiritual person," but the majority will be Christians. This is so since non-Christians have been blinded by the enemy. Their blindness will cause them to stumble in the darkness, unable to find the true solution to their spiritual sickness. It is only by the grace of God that the spiritually blind find help. This type of help comes in the form of Sovereign Deliverance. In Sovereign Deliverance, God finds the demonized, not the other way around.

And thank You, Jesus, many of these spiritually blind do end up finding deliverance ministries like ours. Some who receive deliverance at our ministry are not born again. These precious individuals receive deliverance through Power Encounter Deliverance. Through their deliverance, they personally witness the power of the living God and hopefully end up repenting of their sins and trusting in Jesus.

Will every Christian who calls a deliverance ministry be truly born again? Certainly not. Not everyone who claims to be born again really is. However, the majority who will come and receive deliverance will be.

Many will even be pastors and worship leaders. Many will have large ministries themselves and serve the Lord every day. Many will show the clear fruits of being carriers of the indwelling Holy Spirit, such as possessing one or more of the Gifts of the Holy Spirit (1 Corinthians 12) and even have undeniably authentic testimonies of conversion. I have had Deliverance Encounter sessions with Christians who have known the Lord longer than I have been alive.

I once had a session with a precious Christian woman named Kathryn, who was born in 1919. After the prayer portion of her session, she spoke in tongues and said, "I feel so cleansed from the inside out, a new person."

Kathryn was 100 years old during her Deliverance Encounter session!

*The Children's Bread*

## *We Bless Those Who Come Against The Ministry of Deliverance*

I want to reiterate something very important. I am not cursing the NDMC's, no matter what their reason is for not delivering other Christians. I will not curse the NDMC even if he curses me. In fact, I speak blessing over the NDMC's and their ministries. I consider anyone who is born again in Christ to be my brother or sister in the faith. And I teach my students to do the same. In no way would I break fellowship with an NDMC simply because of their views on whether a Christian can have a demon or their lack of involvement in the ministry of deliverance. I also encourage my students not to avoid fellowship and worship with the NDMC's simply because they are NDMC's.

Just because God has not given an individual the revelation that His people need to be delivered doesn't mean that he is not born again. I already said that engaging in deliverance does not make us born again. We are born again because we have repented of our sins and have confessed with our mouths that Jesus is Lord. The fact that God has called us to the ministry of deliverance does not make us better than others who haven't been called to this ministry. Every deliverance minister must resist spiritual pride.

In this book, I have been convicted of making two points. First, that Christians can indeed have indwelling demons and subsequently need deliverance from these demons. And second, the only ones opposed to Christians receiving this deliverance are those who do not practice the ministry of deliverance to begin with.

So, I bless those who resist my own deliverance ministry and those who resist ministries like mine. I continually ask that the Holy Spirit fill and be present in my own ministry. I pray that I am convicted of the truth always. And for me, this truth has been setting the captives free, even if it means that the person who I am setting free is a *Christian.*

I also pray that those Christians who are under the authority of an NDMC (in their churches, ministries, Facebook Groups, and the YouTube channels they subscribe to), and maybe even under a curse as a result of their leader's bad doctrine, receive the deliverance that they really need. I pray, "Lord Jesus, open up a way for Your people to be healed and delivered!"

But that doesn't mean that I won't publicly proclaim my own revelation on the matter. It doesn't mean that I won't offer my gentle instruction on the topic in the hopes that the NDMC will be convicted of the issue and begin to offer the remedy of Jesus to fellow Christians who deal with spiritual sickness. And having demons is a spiritual sickness that needs to be *healed*:

*Some people brought to Jesus a man who was blind and could not talk because he had a demon in him. Jesus **healed** the man, and then he was able to talk and see.*
Matthew 12:22 (Contemporary English Version)

Finally, it is not about us; it is about Jesus. It is about magnifying the Name of Jesus and especially about bringing His Gospel message to the world. If the NDMC ministries preach that the Gospel of Jesus is the only way, I am with them to the end, and I bless them in the Name of Jesus.

## Correlation with the Gifts of the Holy Spirit

The revelation that I have received is that born-again Christians can have demons on the inside. And the fact that they have these demons doesn't make them unsaved either. I believe that this revelation is backed up and even demonstrated by Scripture which I examine in Part 3 of this book.

The fact that Christians can have demons is a revelation that has been confirmed by the ministry that God has placed me in. It is also a revelation that has been received by a multitude of other deliverance ministers and countless lay practitioners within the ministry of deliverance.

The following is a fascinating observation that I have made: I have found that most Christians who actively seek the presence of the Holy Spirit rarely take issue with the notion that Christians can have demons. It is uncommon for Christians who covet the Gifts of the Holy Spirit (1 Corinthians 12) to believe that Christians cannot be demonized. Christians who purpose to imitate Christ's miracles in their own ministries will rarely oppose the ministry of deliverance for fellow believers.

On the other hand, Christians who do not actively walk in the Gifts of the Holy Spirit or affirm that the Gifts have ceased will usually be against the ministry of deliverance for Christians. I believe there is a real correlation here; however, my opponents will say that this is simply coincidental. I urge you, the reader, to consider and pray about this. See what the Holy Spirit shows you.

## Deliverance Is Not Just for Christians Either

I want there to be no misunderstandings as to my message. I am by no means saying that deliverance is *only* for Christians either. God certainly expels demons from the unsaved as a sign to demonstrate His power and to confirm His word. This occurs during the execution of sovereign Power Encounter Deliverance. The psychic girl in Acts 16 is an excellent Biblical example of a pagan receiving deliverance from a demon via sovereign Power Encounter Deliverance (verse 18). Hebrews 2:3-4 mentions this kind of confirmation.

God certainly delivers the unsaved as a confirming sign; however, the point that I do wish to make in this book is that deliverance is not *just* for the pagans and the atheists. It is not *just* for the sinners, the "bad" people, the lost, the Satanists, the rapists, and the murderers. It is not *just* for the Catholics. It is not *just* for those who serve other gods. It is not *just* for those who do not attend your church or who are outside of your denomination.

Instead, deliverance is *also* for the born-again, the saved, those possessing the imputed righteousness of Christ, the Holy Spirit-filled, the Holy Spirit-led, the Baptists, the Presbyterians, the Methodists, the Messianic believers, the Pentecostals, the

Charismatics, the Christians of all denominations and non-denominations. And lastly, deliverance is for the followers of Jesus just like you and me.

I began conducting Session Deliverance in 2012. Since that time, God has clearly revealed the answer to me regarding the question of whether a Christian can have a demon. I have also learned many other things about the ministry of deliverance and the Christians who come to receive this ministry. The pages in this book tell some of what I have learned.

# Chapter 3

# Lies of the Devil

I have a teaching entitled, "The Top Lies of Satan and His Demons about Deliverance." It is an important lesson because it shows how Satan systematically deceives people regarding his schemes and strategies. Each of Satan's lies has a backup lie. This means that if a person overcomes and unbelieves the first lie, Satan then presents him with the next successive lie. In other words, if the person succeeds in not believing Lie #1, then Satan gives that person Lie #2. If the person figures out that Lie #2 is a deception, Satan will give him Lie #3, and so on.

Satan's goal is to keep his victims in a constant state of spiritual vulnerability. A person is spiritually vulnerable to demons when there is some open sin that is not being dealt with. Believing Satan's lies, which are all Satanic thinking patterns, gives legal ground to demons in a person's life. Believing, embracing, proclaiming, and defending Satan's lies as truth is a form of open, undealt-with sin.

Remember that sin that is "not dealt with" is sin that has not yet been cleansed by the Blood of Jesus. This cleansing of sin takes place when a Christian repents of it, renounces it, and asks God to forgive him for it. Once a sin has been cleansed by the Blood of Jesus, the legal right is canceled. Satan can no longer legally use the sin as a legal right. Satan may bluff, but he really can't use it. Here are the first three of the Top Ten Lies of Satan and his Demons:

| Lie #1 | There is no devil. The devil doesn't exist. And for that matter, demon spirits don't exist either. |
|---|---|
| Lie #2 | There is a devil and demons, but they are not real "spirits." They are just symbols of evil, mental illness, the flesh, etc. |
| Lie #3 | There are demons that are real spirits, but certainly, these demons could never be inside of a *Christian.* |

There are multitudes of Christians here in North America, and perhaps where you live as well, that are completely ensnared by Lie #3. They believe Lie #3. They teach Lie #3 in their ministries. Satan has them trapped and doesn't even need to proceed to Lie #4. One of the primary goals of this book is to expose, crush, demolish, and pull down the stronghold of Lie #3.

If you are interested in learning more about Satan's lies, you will find the complete teaching in Level One of our online deliverance school, Invicta University.

## *When a Christian Believes That Christians Can't Have Demons, He Is Giving Legal Right For Demons to Be Inside of **Him***

When a Christian believes Lie #3, he is giving full consent for demons to enter into his mind and body and or to remain there. By accepting this false belief, he is giving demons legal right to stay inside of him. It is ironic that when an individual doesn't believe that a Christian can have a demon by virtue of being a Christian, he is giving legal right to the very demons that he thinks he can't have!

Satan accuses this Christian before God (Revelation 12:10), saying, "Your son doesn't believe Your word that You deliver those who belong to You. He doesn't believe Your word that those who belong to You need to be delivered. Therefore, I want access to him. And, once I am inside, I want to remain protected and concealed." In most cases, God grants Satan this legal right. This is because God lets Satan touch His people when they rebel against Him—this includes when they don't believe His word.

Recall the reasoning of the Pharisees. They were rebelling against God when they proclaimed that they had never been in bondage to anyone (John 8:33). Jesus came to correct them on this point, but most Pharisees didn't want to hear it. They preferred their self-righteous religion over spiritual freedom.

For this reason, we ask people on their pre-session survey, the *Personal Spiritual Profile* (PSP), the following question: Do you believe that Christians can have demons? If this question is answered NO, then I know that this issue must be addressed during Deliverance Counseling before any demons are confronted during that person's Deliverance Encounter session.

If this issue is not addressed, demons might not have to manifest. They can effectively say, "I don't have to manifest and expose myself because she doesn't believe that I could even be here." Again, the Satanic thinking pattern of unbelief becomes legal right. Belief in Lie #3 becomes a powerful cover for demons to lay low and resist ever being exposed, much less cast out.

As long as Satan holds this legal right, he knows that he has the high ground. He is safe to remain on the inside of a person and carry out his assignment, which is always to steal, kill and destroy in that person's life. Stealing family relationships, time, finances, and peace. Killing ministries, marriages, and physical health. Destroying men's and women's blessings and destinies.

I once had a Deliverance Encounter session with a man who had demons named Lack, Poverty, and Locusts. The demon said, "We eat all that is meant for him. We take it before he gets it. We want him broken and poor and hopeless." Yes, it is true. Demons steal, kill, and destroy even in the area of finances.

Unbelief is powerful legal right for demons. I have observed in my own ministry that in most cases, God does not override His own legal system and force demons to go when they have a right to be there. Of course, God is God, and He can and does do this in cases of Power Encounter Deliverance such as

Evangelistic Deliverance. God is always sovereign, and He delivers men according to His good pleasure—even when the demon possesses some legal right.

Remember that faith is critical in one's healing. If the person does not believe she has a problem, how can she have faith that God will move to heal this problem? If a person doesn't believe that she could have demons, she probably won't be delivered from her demons.

The concept of the necessity of admitting that there is a problem first is true in Big Deliverance too. If a man cannot admit that he has sinned against a holy God, then he cannot really repent. And without repentance, he cannot be born again:

*I tell you, no; but unless you repent you will all likewise perish.*
Luke 13:3 (NKJV)

## Six Cases of Christians Who Are Stuck on Lie #3

### Case #1: Juan the Born-Again Ex-Witch

Juan is a mature, born-again Christian in his 60's. He is originally from Cuba. He used to practice *Santería* witchcraft when he was in his 20's, but he has long since renounced that and now earnestly follows Jesus. He is gifted in the prophetic and, as a native Spanish speaker, has traveled extensively in Latin America doing the work of the Lord.

However, it bothers Juan that he frequently experiences night terrors that involve hideous demons persecuting him. He also sees shadows and other visual manifestations of demons that frighten him during waking hours. He began to suspect that demons must be following him around and harassing him. As a result, Juan decided to come to Invicta Ministries' public meeting on a Friday night.

Juan knows that he is under spiritual attack. But there is a problem. He doesn't think that he could have demons—on the inside. He thinks his problem is that, because of his anointing,

## The Children's Bread

demons target him, follow him, and attack him *from the outside*. Since he refuses to consider the possibility that he might have demons on the inside, his demons have a strong legal right to stay put.

When I began to pray for Juan at the meeting, I told him, "Juan, you are obviously a man of God who travels and does missionary work. This would make you an ideal target for the enemy. Satan wants to stop your work. He is tormenting you with these demonic visions. But, I do not think the demons are only on the *outside* of you. I believe that you have indwelling demons that need to be forcefully expelled. It is very likely that your demons got in when you used to practice *Santería* witchcraft."

When Juan heard this, he immediately retorted, "Pastor, I have the Holy Ghost. There is no way that I could have demons. Can you just pray so that these things stop following me around?" I then explained to Juan how a lack of belief could give the demons the legal right to remain and, therefore, resist being cast out. However, Juan didn't want to hear it.

Knowing that there was a possibility that God might sovereignly deliver Juan through Power Encounter, I prayed for Juan, commanding every demon to go in the Name of Jesus. I even commanded any demons that were on the outside of him, following him around and harassing him, to go away and never come back again.

Juan began to feel nauseated, and he thought that he was going to throw up. He felt a twisting in his stomach. But nothing came out of his mouth. What had happened here? Juan's demons were tormented by the Holy Spirit, which I was projecting via the forceful command. However, in the end, they were able to legally resist being cast out because of Juan's false belief that he couldn't have indwelling demons.

In this case, God, according to His good pleasure, *did not* sovereignly override Juan's demons' legal rights and make them go. As a result, Juan went home with his demons that night. The next morning while he was brushing his teeth, he was terrified when he saw what looked like a demon face looking back at him in his bathroom mirror.

## Case #2: The Rise and Fall of Pastor Rob

Pastor Rob was an anointed and hugely popular pastor of an NDMC mega-church that he himself had founded. Before giving his life to Jesus and long before becoming a pastor, Rob worked in the adult entertainment and secular music industries. Sex, drugs, and rock and roll were his lifestyle before knowing the Lord.

Years later, at the peak of his ministry career, he would minister to over 15,000 at weekend services as well as impact hundreds of thousands during the nationally syndicated radio broadcasts of his teachings. Pastor Rob had it all: powerful testimony of conversion, strong giftings, successful ministry, beautiful family and marriage, charisma that attracted everyone, and the honor and respect of multitudes of followers.

However, this all suddenly ended when he was forced to admit to committing serious "moral failures" both inside and outside of his church. These moral failures consisted primarily of pornography addiction and adulterous sexual relationships. Some of which involved women who worked in his own church office. As a result, Pastor Rob was forced to step down from the leadership of the church by his Board of Directors. In disgrace, he was forced to leave the same church that he himself had founded years ago.

For the NDMC's who witnessed the fall of Pastor Rob, the moral of the story was obvious. Pastor Rob simply failed to crucify his flesh. He fell to the "works of the flesh" (Galatians 5:19). He didn't exercise self-control and fell into sin. The only question on their minds was, "Could Pastor Rob be restored?"

However, for those of us who work in the ministry of deliverance, something far more nefarious was discerned. Those of us who sit with people in session to set people free from demons knew immediately that this was no simple case of the flesh. We knew that this was the fruit of undetected and unconfronted *demonization*.

## The Children's Bread

Specifically, that Pastor Rob had never been delivered from the holdover demons that he had picked up earlier on in his life. Pastor Rob's previous lifestyle of sin provided for a plethora of opportunities for demonic points of entry. These undealt-with demons then waited patiently for an opportune time and eventually succeeded in stealing his ministry, killing his marriage, and destroying his life.

Even though Pastor Rob had renounced his previous lifestyle and experienced a radical and Spirit-filled conversion, he still had demons that had gotten in years ago. All of his demons did not come out of him at his conversion to Christ (as the NDMC's would assume would happen). And since his NDMC denomination doesn't practice deliverance or even consider that Christians can have demons, Pastor Rob never got the spiritual help that he needed. Pastor Rob never went through a process of deliverance. And to make matters worse, Pastor Rob no doubt got new demons from the new pornography and adultery as well.

Near his end, Pastor Rob could not keep his sexual sins secret anymore. His sexual perversions came into the public eye. The local news channels were even showing up at his church. Eventually, his own Board was forced to exercise discipline and release him from all ministerial duties. Pastor Rob's fall devastated the church and severely traumatized multitudinous followers who had, without realizing it, idolized Pastor Rob. It was so serious that his church needed to staff counselors, who no doubt were also NDMC's, to provide therapy to hurt, and probably in some cases, demonized, church members.

Even though he had become a gifted and powerful communicator, pastor, and teacher, his indwelling holdover demons (as well as new demons) relentlessly attacked him in the sexual area until he fell. His final battle as a pastor took place on two battlefronts—one on the battlefront of his flesh and another on the front of the demonic. In the end, it was just too much for Pastor Rob, and he fell.

Pastor Rob's fall was not a random event. Satan had crafted this plan from the beginning. First, Pastor Rob's demons would cause strife in his marriage. This would make pornography highly attractive for him. Second, the females in Pastor Rob's life, who also had demons, would be exploited to tempt Pastor Rob into physical adultery. This Satanic scheme worked. Pastor Rob relapsed into pornography addiction, and he fell into multiple adulterous affairs. Since Pastor Rob had been such a high-level asset in God's Kingdom, there was much celebration in Hell over all this. It was a sad day for Christianity.

Why did all this happen? Two things came together to form the perfect spiritual storm. First of all, before Rob became Pastor Rob, he picked up tons of demons from all his sexual sin, drugs, and other rebellious indulgences. Second, he began his ministry without ever getting deliverance. In other words, Pastor Rob began his ministry full of demons. This was able to happen since the NDMC denomination to which he belonged doesn't believe in deliverance for Christians. Actually, his denomination doesn't offer deliverance for non-Christians either. As a result, it never occurred to anyone, including Pastor Rob himself, that he needed to do anything more than repent of sin and become born again. It didn't occur to anyone that demons would have to be exorcised from his mind before giving him so much authority.

So, Pastor Rob was a ticking spiritual time bomb. It was not if, but when, he would fall into a trap that his own demons would lead him to.

And to add insult to spiritual injury, after Pastor Rob fell from grace and lost everything, *still,* no one in his church considered that indwelling demons were the culprit. Still, no one considered that other members of the church might need deliverance too. Still, no one considered beginning a deliverance ministry within the church.

Satan ensured that even after the fall of Pastor Rob, the church would remain steadfastly NDMC. Satan made sure that the ministry of deliverance would never be welcome on the church's campus. Satan was keen on making sure that this church would never pose a direct threat to his kingdom.

In the final analysis, the NDMC's chalked up Pastor Rob's fall as a sad "moral failure" that happened as a result of the lack of self-control over his fleshly desires.

# The Children's Bread

## Case #3: People Who Manifest Demons in Church Are an Embarrassment and Need to Be Hidden Away

Reverend Mike O'Dwyer has served as Head Pastor to his reformed congregation for over thirty-five years. He is an NDMC since he does not sit with members of his church for any kind of Session Deliverance. He doesn't cast out demons from non-members either. Deliverance is not a part of Reverend Mike's ministry at all. He is aware of the demonic, though, since he once personally witnessed a demonic manifestation right in the church.

It happened thirty-six years ago, while he was still a seminary student serving as an intern at the church of his mentor, Reverend John. While Reverend John was reading the Words of Institution in preparation to serve Holy Communion, a church member suddenly began to growl and call out in a guttural voice, "He belongs to me! You can't have him!"

Reverend John abruptly stopped at, "…and when He had given thanks, He broke…" He instructed two deacons to quickly remove this interrupter and take him to an isolated room and hold him there until service was over.

Reverend Mike never forgot about this event. It also scared quite a few people who were there that Sunday. After service, Reverend John called a meeting with his church elders. Young Mike was there. Reverend John explained that the member who growled and called out during service did indeed have a demonic spirit. However, this type of intrusion of the devil is not to be tolerated. He went on to say if that kind of foolishness ever happens again during a service, that the member in question must be removed immediately "to avoid embarrassing the Name and honor of Jesus Christ in His holy sanctuary."

Reverend John continued. He said that if someone does manifest a demon as this church member did, then he is not really a true member of the church. He will need to be reinstructed in the denomination's catechism, and a new confession of Christ will have to be made.

These words really impacted young seminary student Mike. Now, three decades later, at his own church, Reverend O'Dwyer holds to his mentor's philosophy. He periodically instructs his Leadership Team that if anyone begins to "act demonic" during church service, they are to be removed immediately and taken somewhere where they can "cool down." Reverend Mike explains to his team that these kinds of devilish displays can severely affect church attendance and even giving, so they are not to be allowed.

### Case #4: Michelle's Pastor Doesn't Understand

Michelle is born again. She also has demons. Michelle's spiritual torment encompasses many issues. She deals with debilitating depression, voices urging suicide, and many times feels a suffocating weight on her chest. She has been diagnosed with fibromyalgia, chronic fatigue syndrome, fibroids, and irritable bowel syndrome. Her marriage also suffers due to her husband's passivity. He never leads in the marriage and leaves all the spiritual decisions up to Michelle.

She does the right thing by going to her spiritual leader, Pastor Gary, for help. However, due to her NDMC pastor's theological prejudice and inexperience in the area of deliverance, Michelle does not find the relief that she desperately needs.

"Surely, Pastor Gary will know what to do," Michelle says to herself. Michelle had an appointment with Pastor Gary, and she explained her symptoms to him. However, upon hearing her story, Pastor Gary declared to her with confidence, "Michelle, it's all in your mind."

Pastor Gary went on to explain that all of her spiritual issues were already settled at the Cross and that now, Michelle just needed to do her part: read her Bible more, attend Tuesday night Bible study, and most importantly, make an appointment with a good therapist. He recommended the one that his wife goes to for her depression. Pastor Gary even suggested to Michelle that she specifically ask for a prescription for Wellbutrin, the anti-depressant that his wife takes. Pastor Gary indicated that this mediation has "worked wonders" for his wife.

Michelle then told Pastor Gary about some deliverance videos that she had been watching on a certain YouTube channel. "Pastor, I found this deliverance ministry on YouTube, and I saw this man cast demons out of this Christian woman. She even had a demon called Depression…" Pastor Gary interrupted her with a chuckle and told her that it is very important that she only listen to teachings that align with "sound doctrine."

He then reminded Michelle that their denomination had been around for more than a hundred years, and they have never had to do any "exorcism rituals" or any other unbiblical practices. "Besides," he concluded, "it is impossible for a Christian to have a demon. The Bible says that we are new creations in Christ. That clearly means that Christians can't have any demons."

### *Case #5: Gavin's Dad Didn't Give Good Advice*

Gavin has been a Christian for about eight years now. He enjoys spending his free time listening to worship music videos on YouTube. One day, as he was scrolling through pages of praise and worship songs, something caught his eye. It wasn't a music video. It was a video entitled "Jezebel Cast Out."

He didn't fully understand what it was at the time, but something compelled him to watch it. He clicked on it and began to see something that he had never seen before. There was a man holding a Bible praying over a woman. He was praying in a way that Gavin had never heard before. The man in the video was saying, "In the Name of Jesus, I command Jezebel to come out of her! Leave in the Name of Jesus and never come back again!" The woman in the video then began to cough and spit into a trash can.

While Gavin watched, he himself began to feel queasy. He felt something inexplicable, and certainly not pleasant, begin to rise up inside of him. He felt heat all over his body. It became difficult for him to visually focus on the video. Then he felt the need to spit up just like the woman in the video. Gavin didn't understand what was happening, and he barely succeeded in tapping the stop button.

"What was that?" Gavin asked out loud as he was regaining his composure. He decided to call his dad to get his opinion on what had just happened. Gavin thought, *my dad has been a church deacon for over twenty years. Maybe he can explain what just happened.*

Over the phone, Gavin's father explained, "It sounds like you were seeing someone who was claiming to be an "exorcist." To be honest, I don't know if that really exists anymore. I think that stuff like that only happened during Bible times. Really, Gavin, you need to be careful what you watch on YouTube. There are a lot of strange people with strange new doctrines out there. Everything that you see on YouTube isn't necessarily Biblical."

Then Gavin asked his dad why he became nauseous while watching the video. His dad replied, "Who knows? Maybe you ate something that didn't sit well with you. Whatever it was, son, it had nothing to do with that video. That much I can guarantee you."

### *Case #6: A Pastor from Oklahoma Was Ill-Prepared To Deal with the Demonic*

Once, a Christian man from the state of Oklahoma contacted our ministry. He told us a sad story that could have happened in any NDMC church in North America today.

This man told us how he once manifested demons during a church-sanctioned cell group meeting. He felt his arms and legs burning, and this sensation was moving towards his core. He fell prostrate to the floor and realized that he could not move—some spiritual force was paralyzing him. The other cell group members prayed for him, but nothing seemed to help. In a panic, the man's wife then called the church's pastor and urgently pleaded with him to pray for her husband, who was still lying immobile on the floor.

After the pastor listened to the wife's plea, he asked to speak with her husband. They pressed the phone to the man's head, and the pastor told him, "You need to get up off the floor and stop messing around. People might get the wrong idea about all this."

*The Children's Bread*

This Christian man from Oklahoma had demons inside of him. And these demons were able to torment him to the point of making him temporarily lose physical control over his body. Thankfully, this man did finally receive deliverance from demons later on from a different deliverance ministry.

No doubt, his pastor was unprepared for waging any kind of spiritual war and incredulous that a member of his congregation could possibly have demons. Ultimately, this pastor was an NDMC who was bound up in Lie #3.

## God Delivers Those Who Belong to Him

That a Christian can or can't have a demon can neither be proven nor disproven by one single *explicit* verse in Scripture. There is not one verse that says, "A Christian can't have a demon." Nor does any verse exist that says, "A Christian can have a demon."

However, when NDMC's attack our ministry and demand, "Show me one verse in the Bible that says that Christians can have demons!" I respond with, "I already know the answer to this question about whether Christians can have demons. I cast demons out of Christians on a daily basis. Some of them might even attend your church. Therefore, the burden of proof is on you. Please show me one verse in the Bible that says that Christians *can't* have demons." Of course, the NDMC cannot provide such a verse since no such verse exists. Invariably, the NDMC will simply quote a verse that relates to one of the arguments that are listed and refuted in this book.

When we look at the whole of the Bible, we see the repeating and grand spiritual truth:

**God delivers those who belong to Him**

Mark Chase

## Old Testament Examples of God Delivering His People

- We see it in the story of Adam and Eve how, after the Fall, God delivered them from the shame of their nakedness by giving them skins of animals (Genesis 3).
- We see it in the story of Noah's Ark. While God judged the entire world that had become corrupt and full of violence, He delivered His servant Noah and his family from the Flood. (Genesis 7)
- We see it in the story of Gideon and how he and his 300 men were delivered from the Midianite army of 135,000 men (Judges 7).
- We see in the story of His prophet Jonah how God delivered him from certain death after he was in the belly of a great fish for three days and three nights (Jonah 2).

## New Testament Examples of God Delivering His People

- We see in the story of the *Flight to Egypt* how God delivered Joseph, Mary, and the Baby Jesus from the murderous intentions of King Herod by taking them safely to Egypt to take refuge until the king's death (Matthew 2).
- We see how the Prodigal Son was delivered from his horrible decision to demand his inheritance early and subsequent bankruptcy. In this story, the Prodigal Son's father undeniably represents God Himself. (Luke 15).
- We see how Jesus delivered the couple who was married at Cana from the shame of running out of wine during the middle of the wedding feast (John 2).
- We see how Jesus delivered His disciples from the storm and certain death of drowning while crossing the Sea of Galilee (Mark 4).

If we are willing to take Scripture at face value while at the same time shedding our theological prejudices and personal preferences, we will see that Scripture clearly points to the fact that

God's people—from the Israelites enslaved in Egypt to the modern Christians of today—are the ones who God delivers. And by extension, we see that God's people, therefore, have a *need* to be delivered.

## *Overcome the Lies*

We overcome the lies of Satan and his demons by standing on the truth of Jesus. Lies must be demolished by truths. The Bible speaks truth, and the Holy Spirit will confirm this truth if we humbly seek Him. But if we arrogantly reject the truth and embrace the lies, the Satanic thinking patterns of Satan, we give Satan clear legal ground in our lives—even if we are Christians.

Now let's look at the most common Scriptures and NDMC theological arguments that are used to prove the "fact" that Christians can't have demons.

*Mark Chase*

*Part 2*

*The NDMC Arguments That Are Used to "Prove" That a Christian Can't Have a Demon*

*Mark Chase*

# Chapter 4

# Objection #1:

# *Light and Darkness Cannot Dwell in the Same Vessel*

(Light-Can't-Dwell-with-Darkness Argument)

Your name is Brian, and you are a Christian. Six years ago, you decided to leave your old idolatrous lifestyle behind. You made a decision to stop fornicating, to stop smoking weed, to stop lying on your taxes, and to *never* go back to those Asian massage parlors. You realized that all of this was evil sin, and it separated you from God.

It all started a few months earlier when a friend invited you to his church led by Pastor Vic. One Sunday, Pastor Vic's message of the Gospel hit you like a ton of bricks. You realized that God's wrath abided on you and that if you didn't repent, you were deservingly on a highway to Hell. You even realized that your sin and rebellion against God justified the punishment of Hell itself.

You were so convicted that you tearfully made your way to the altar that morning and repeated the prayer that the pastor spoke. You cried out from the core of your broken being, "Lord, I admit I have sinned against You and only against You have I sinned…I repent of my sins…I make Jesus Lord of my life…all my sin is now nailed to the Cross…Lord, write my name in the Book of Life…Fill me with Your Spirit…In the Name of Jesus, amen." You felt an indescribable joy. For the first time, you felt the Spirit of God touch you. In that very instant, you knew that you had just been transformed. You were born again!

After this prayer, Pastor Vic congratulated those who had the courage to come to the altar. He said that there was rejoicing in the presence of angels in Heaven that very morning.

He also declared triumphantly (and truthfully) that you were now a new creation in Christ Jesus and that the old had gone and the new had come. He ended by saying that now you have been given a wonderful Helper called the Holy Spirit who will teach you and equip you to live the Christian life.

From that point on, you began your new life as a born-again believer in Jesus. Your life now had meaning, and you were grateful that God had stepped in and brought you back from the brink. If He hadn't, you could have spent eternity in Hell. *Thank You, Jesus!* You often say to yourself.

From day one, there was a noticeable difference in the way you treated people. You were gentler and kinder. You actually began to put others' needs before your own. It wasn't long before you began to evangelize on the street. Your old friends were amazed (and some were disgusted) that *you* had decided to follow Jesus.

You were given the honor of becoming an usher in the church. And soon after, at a seminar with a visiting pastor, you received the Baptism of the Holy Spirit and began to speak in tongues.

As if all this weren't enough, some months later, you met a wonderful Christian woman named Jennifer and began dating. A year later, the two of you got married. Your life was really turning out for the better.

Now, two years into your marriage, however, you began to

notice a problem in your life. On the outside, everything was going great: you and Jennifer are expecting your first child together, you are going to church two, sometimes three nights a week, you are serving in the church, and even beginning to lead a Bible study at home. You even got promoted in your job, which meant that you were finally able to buy your own house to start your family.

However, on the inside, where no one else could see, you feel tormented. For a reason you are unable to explain, you had begun watching pornography again, albeit secretly. Jennifer doesn't know yet because she never checks your phone. And a nagging and accusing voice in your head keeps saying, "You didn't really change when you became a Christian…You're still the same loser that you used to be…and God hasn't really even forgiven you…You're just a pretender…"

One day while driving home, an urge so strong that it could not be overcome made you pull into the parking lot of a massage place. "I'm just going to get a back massage for my stress," you assure your conscience. My wife doesn't need to know. Afterward, as you are leaving, you can hardly believe that the massage girl just performed a sexual act on you. You had been unfaithful to your faithful wife, Jennifer.

"This is getting out of hand," you think to yourself. I will go speak to Pastor Vic. He said I could come to him anytime. He will understand. He will be able to help me.

In your meeting with the pastor, you tell him that you feel like some irresistible attraction takes hold of you and pulls you to do and think certain things, especially in the sexual area. You mention how you were exposed to your uncle's pornography when you were eight years old. You even open up (for the first time in your life) about being molested by a female babysitter when you were ten. You go on to tell Pastor Vic about the voices. You also mention the nightmares that you just started having.

Then you muster the courage and ask, "Pastor Vic, is it possible that there are *demonic spirits* inside of me making me do things?" With a look of genuine concern and a loving smile, Pastor

Vic declared with authority, "Brian, you can't possibly have demons. You see, you are a Christian now. And it is impossible for Christians to have any demons. The fact that you have the Holy Spirit is proof. You're just going through some tough times and need some good marriage counseling. I believe that God can heal your marriage even with the adultery." Then, Pastor Vic quoted the famous, but non-existent, Bible verse:

*Light and darkness cannot dwell in the same vessel.*

"You see, Brian, it is therefore impossible for a demon to dwell alongside the Holy Spirit. I have seen you speak in tongues. That is evidence of the presence of the Holy Spirit inside you. You, therefore, cannot and do not have any demons inside of you making you do anything."

Then Pastor Vic lovingly reaffirmed his solution for your crisis, "You just have a lot of stress in your life. My wife and I will be praying for you. I am also going to ask our elders to pray for you. In addition, I am also going to refer you to a good Christian counselor to start some marriage counseling for you and Jennifer. She will help you to start processing some of your sexual and emotional issues. I'm really sorry about what that babysitter did. By God's grace, Jennifer will forgive you. I also suggest that you pray more and read your Bible more. I will see you next Sunday."

Unintentionally and certainly not maliciously, Pastor Vic misquoted Scripture and subsequently caused Brian some serious confusion. So, what did the Apostle Paul really say about light and darkness? Here is the real passage of Scripture:

**14** *Do not be unequally yoked together with unbelievers. For what fellowship has righteousness with lawlessness?* **15** *And **what communion has light with darkness?** And what accord has Christ with Belial? Or what part has a believer with an unbeliever?*
2 Corinthians 6:14-15 (NKJV)

What does this passage mean? And does it teach us that a Christian can't have a demon?

## The Children's Bread

## *This Passage Is About Binding Relationships*

This important Pauline passage refers to the kind of *legally binding human relationships* that we are to have as followers of Christ. It refers to the people we are to be "yoked" together with. *The yoke is a Biblical metaphor of a binding relationship or partnership.* It signifies that two walk together as one in some sort of binding relationship such as a marriage or business partnership.

Specifically, Paul focuses on the *faith* of the two parties. Are they both believers? Or, is only one a believer? Paul clearly implies that it is physically *possible* that a believer can be yoked together with an unbeliever. However, Paul warns us not to do it:

*Do not be unequally yoked together with unbelievers.*

This is key. While it is possible to be unequally yoked together, we shouldn't do it. And if we do do it, the outcome will not be good:

*There will be no fellowship, no communion and no accord with that person.*

What is a yoke? According to the Merriam-Webster dictionary, a yoke is "a wooden bar or frame by which two draft animals such as oxen are joined at the heads or necks for *working together*."

A yoke connects two oxen so that they can work together and pull in the same direction together. A yoke *binds* the two oxen together. But what if the two oxen are unequal? What if one ox is weak and lazy and the other is strong and ready to plow? This yoke will now become a burden to both oxen since both oxen are not in agreement on how to work.

For the lazy and weak ox, it will be a burden because the other ox will try to make him work. And for the strong and ready ox, it will be a burden because he can't carry out the job that he wants to do since the other ox doesn't want to work. It is a lose-lose situation.

However, is it physically possible for a lazy ox and a hard-working ox to be yoked together? Yes. Will the pair be able to work together productively? No, they will not. Do they belong together? No, they are unequally yoked. For a yoke to work properly, both oxen must be equal in their desire and ability to work. Both oxen must be in agreement on how they will work.

The same is true in a binding relationship between two people or parties. For the pair to be equally yoked, both must be relatively equal in desire, purpose, and ability. Two unequal people in a relationship will not be able to properly connect with each other, they will not be productive, and in the Christian spiritual sense, they won't be able to have *fellowship, communion,* or *accord* with one another. *Accord* means *agreement.*

Paul never says that it is *impossible* for two unequal things (oxen, people, etc.) to be yoked together. He just said that if they are unequally yoked, they won't be able to have fellowship, communion, or accord. And as the dictionary says, they wouldn't be able to "work together." Therefore, this is the essential meaning of 2 Corinthians 6:14-15:

*It is perfectly possible for two unequal things to be yoked together. The problem is that if two unequal things are yoked together, they will not be able to function together properly, and they won't be able to have fellowship or communion. As a result, the Christian is called not to do it. And if a Christian does violate this rule and yokes himself unequally with another, the result will be that the two won't be able to work together properly. And spiritually, there will not be communion, fellowship, or accord between both parties.*

So, Paul calls us to be in binding relationships with other people only when both are equal. By "equal," Paul means that both are *in agreement about who Jesus is in our lives*. He did not say that it is impossible for us to be yoked to someone with whom we are not equal. In fact, he implies that it is quite possible. However, he warns us not to do it.

Do you know of a relationship that is unequally yoked? In other words, a relationship where the two parties have different views regarding Jesus? Perhaps you know of a marriage where a believing spouse is married to—yoked together with—an unbelieving spouse. Perhaps, you yourself might be unequally yoked with someone in a marriage or some other legally binding relationship. If you are, you need good Spirit-led guidance, healing, and deliverance to overcome this situation.

In my ministry, I have seen too many of these unequally yoked marriages where one spouse desires to pull the plow towards the Cross, and the other wants to pull the plow towards the world. In these cases, both spouses disagree about who Jesus is. Not only is it supremely discouraging for the believing spouse, but it can also turn a marriage into a "living hell."

I have sat in session with many believing wives who tearfully ask me how they are to be obedient to their unbelieving husbands when they do not support her faith in Jesus, when they ridicule her desire to go to church, or when they do not allow her to pursue her process of healing and deliverance.

I have to say that it is painful for me as a deliverance minister to sit and hear about the plights of these unequally yoked women. However, the reality is that many of these wives entered into their covenantal marriage relationships without ever taking Paul's Biblical exhortation in 2 Corinthians 6:14 into consideration. And, most didn't consult the Holy Spirit on the matter either.

As an aside, I want to make it clear that it is not always the wife who is more advanced spiritually. While fewer in number, I have also sat with husbands who desire to seek Jesus who are married to wives that care nothing about knowing the Lord or the deliverance of Jesus.

In order to save us from these unequally yoked relationships, Paul, therefore, tells us to be in relationships where both partners can act in one accord. Relationships where we will both pull in the same direction. Relationships where both agree on the primacy of Jesus. These are equally yoked relationships.

If we love Jesus, we are to yoke ourselves up with other people who love Jesus so that we can pull the plow together in the same direction—towards the Cross of Christ. We are not to be yoked with nonbelievers. We are not to yoke up with, or bind ourselves with, someone who is not equal with us—in other words, with someone who is not a born-again believer like ourselves.

This passage isn't just about marriage covenants. It can refer to any kind of legally binding relationship. We are not to bind ourselves to business or ministry partners who do not share our faith in Christ. We ought not to enter into binding contracts with people who could later oppose us due to our faith.

## Applying This Passage to Deliverance

Paul was specifically referring to *human* relationships in 2 Corinthians 6:14. However, the underlying principle of this verse can apply to other kinds of legally binding relationships as well. This principle is that if we are yoked together with someone or something that disagrees with our views about Jesus, then there can't be communion, fellowship, or accord between the two.

When we transfer this passage over to the realm of *deliverance*, we see that being "yoked together" means the same thing as "having a demon." When a person has a demon on the inside, he is yoked together with his demon. The demon is yoked up to the victim's body or mind. The yoke of demonization is a legally binding yoke between a person and an unclean spirit.

Demonization is a legally binding relationship between the victim and his indwelling demons. It is a contract of sorts. Why is this? The victim entered into this contract through some sin. The sin gave legal right. The legal right permitted the demons to enter and be yoked to the victim. The yoke now represents this legally binding contract between the victim and his demons.

People who have demons are bound by contract to their demons due to the demons' legal right. For this reason, people can't just "get rid" of their demons just because they don't want their demons anymore. In order to get rid of one's demons, the yoke must be broken. The legally binding contract of sin (legal right) must be nullified. This is done by repentance and by the power and authority of the Name of Jesus. The deliverance minister assists the PRM in the process of voiding these demonic contracts during Session Deliverance—namely through effective Deliverance Counseling and focused RAM prayer.

Similarly, marriages and business contracts can't just be discarded and ignored. Certain legal proceedings must take place in order to annul these agreements.

## Unequal and Equal Yokes with Demons

When a person has a demon, he is now *connected* to his demon. By virtue of the fact that the demon is on the *inside* of him, this person and the demon are now "yoked together." Wherever he goes, the demon goes, and wherever the demon is, he is.

Remember, however, that there are two possible kinds of yokes: There is the *unequal yoke* that Paul specifically mentions, and by inference, we also know that there is the opposite kind of yoke, the *equal yoke*. Equally yoked means that both parties are in *agreement*. Unequally yoked means that both are in *disagreement*.

If the person who has the demon is a nonbeliever, then he is automatically *equally yoked* with his demon. This is always the case since, by definition, all nonbelievers are *in agreement* with Satan.

On the other hand, if the person who has the demon is a *Christian*, then the opposite *should be* occurring: He should not be in agreement with his demon. This means that a Christian with a demon should always be *unequally yoked* to his demon. The Christian should be naturally *resisting* his demon. The Holy Spirit helps him to do this. Even though he walks together with his demon (it is in him) by way of a legally binding contract (some legal right), a Christian and a demon should never be in agreement.

The Christian probably entered into this contract with the demon long before he was ever born again. Since then, he has changed his views and beliefs. He has renounced Satan. He has switched sides. Now, as a Christian, he has the *authority in Jesus Christ* to void this contract, or yoke, with the demon. This voiding is the breaking and removing of legal rights. This is what the deliverance minister guides the PRM in doing during technical Session Deliverance, first by way of good Deliverance Counseling and second through well-placed RAM prayer.

## A Christian With Demons Should Have No Fellowship with His Demons

Even though a Christian is spiritually yoked to his demons (they are inside of him), there cannot be, or at least, there should never be, any communion between this Christian and his demons.

Therefore, even though a Christian who has a demon technically walks with his demons (they go everywhere he goes) and is yoked together with them (they are inside of him), there is no fellowship, communion, or accord (agreement) between him and his demons. God says that there cannot be fellowship between light and darkness. Since the Christian is the *light of the world* (Matthew 5:14) and the demons are members of the *domain of darkness* (Colossians 1:13), there is no fellowship or communion between a born-again Christian and any indwelling demons.

Yet, this born-again Christian *can* be yoked together with demons. Just as it is possible for a believing wife to be yoked together with an unbelieving husband or a lazy ox with a hardworking ox, a Christian can be yoked together with demon spirits. This is because the Christian and the demons are both inside of the same human body, or "house." The "house" is a Biblical metaphor for the human body (2 Corinthians 5:1).

## Changing Geography Does Not Set You Free from Demons

Have you ever met someone who tried to escape from their problems by moving to a new city? If you do, then you know it didn't work. A person cannot get rid of her problems by changing her geographic location. Problems are gotten rid of by submitting them to the healing and deliverance of Christ.

Therefore, if someone who has a demon rents a U-Haul and relocates to a new city, he will not get rid of his demon. His demon will still be right there in him when he arrives at the new city. The same old problems will quickly begin anew.

Escaping to a new location does not expel demons. This is precisely why people who try to solve their spiritual problems by moving to a different geographical area never get free from their problems. The same concept goes for people who try to get free from their problems by changing their names. It doesn't work.

Their problems will follow them (literally) wherever they go. This is because their indwelling demons go with them wherever they go. Their problem is demonization, not geography. Changes in geography do not deliver a person; only repentance and the authority of the Blood of Jesus can do this.

When a person, Christian or not, has a demon on the inside, he and the demon are locked together in a sick union. If he is a Christian, it is a sick, unequal yoke. And this sick union will go on until his death or until the demon is cast out of this Christian.

Having a demon on the inside means that the victim is yoked together with that demon. And we should not desire this yoke one bit. We should desire to remove this heavy yoke and put on the yoke of Jesus in its place (Matthew 11:29).

Just as it is possible for a born-again Christian woman to be yoked together in marriage with a nonbelieving mocker of the Gospel, it is also quite possible for a born-again Christian to be yoked together with a demon. In both cases, the two are not in agreement. In both cases, the result will be the same: a legally binding, unequal yoke.

In the cases of yokes with other *people*, we are always to seek to be equally yoked. This is the essence of Paul's teaching in 2 Corinthians 6:14. In cases of *demonization*, we should want the opposite—we should want to be unequally yoked—which means that we are not walking in agreement with any demon, inside of us or not.

Ultimately, we don't want *any* yokes at all with demons. We want *all* the demons expelled. This is the goal of the process of deliverance. However, until they are all expelled, we need to make sure that we are not in agreement with them regarding their murderous, idolatrous, and destructive plans for our lives.

## *Paul Did Not Say That Christians Can't Have Demons*

I hope that it is clear now that in 2 Corinthians 6:14, Paul did not say that it is impossible for "light to dwell with darkness," as Pastor Vic misquoted. Light can dwell with darkness, albeit without communion, fellowship, or accord.

What Paul did say was that if light and darkness *do* dwell together, then there will not and cannot be any agreement between the two. Light and darkness can never be in agreement. As a result, Paul exhorts us not to be *unequally yoked* with other people. And likewise, we should never want to be *equally yoked* with demon spirits. With the evil and unclean demons, we must never be in agreement!

*The Children's Bread*

## Demons Are Like Rats

Here is an analogy: There could be rats in the house (the physical abode) of an individual. However, that doesn't mean that the one who resides in this house is in agreement with his rodent problem!

## Familiar Spirits

While it may seem counterintuitive, some individuals actually *want* their demons. An individual may want their demon because their demon gives them something of value. This could be talent, fame, wealth, some spiritual ability, the power to manipulate men, the ability to get sex, etc.

The classic New Testament example of a familiar spirit is the passage about the *Fortune Telling Slave Girl* of Acts 16. This girl had a Python spirit "by which she predicted the future" (verse 16). In other words, her indwelling demon gave her the ability to do her psychic work.

In cases where a person *wants* his or her indwelling demon, the demon has now become a *familiar spirit.* The individual becomes *familiar* with his or her demon (not to mention completely equally yoked with it). As a result, a familiar, give and take relationship forms between the person and the indwelling demon. Contrary to popular understanding, a familiar spirit is not a demon that is "in the family."

In cases of demonization by familiar spirits, the individual is automatically *equally yoked* with his demon. The individual is in complete agreement with whatever the demon is offering him or her. In these cases, there *is* fellowship, there *is* communion, and there *is* accord between the individual and the demon.

Until the person receives proper Deliverance Counseling and learns the truth that the demon doesn't really care about the person but instead wants to *kill* the person, he will generally have no desire to renounce and break this sick and Satanic equal yoke.

Amazingly, some PRM's will actually decide to back out of the deliverance process once they find out that they will lose a certain spiritual gift or ability after their familiar spirit is cast out. For some individuals, the power that a demon gives them is worth more than their eternity. They would prefer to spend an eternity in Hell rather than renounce their familiar spirit and trust in Jesus instead. This is the eternal tragedy of many with familiar spirits. In Scripture, those with familiar spirits are known as *yiddeonim*. Therefore, it is the eternal tragedy of the *yiddeonim*.

The greatly misunderstood concept of familiar spirits is taught in-depth in the curriculum of our online school of deliverance, Invicta University.

## *God and Satan Can Be Together, but They Won't Be in Accord*

And what about Christ having no accord with Belial (2 Corinthians 6:15)? This, of course, is true. God and Satan *can* be together—but they will never be in accord or in agreement. And God can never be yoked to Satan, a demon, or any evil. Instead, our God is a yoke breaker!

However, we know from Scripture that Satan goes *before* God day and night accusing the brethren (Revelation 12:10). Yet God and Satan are not in accord. Jesus stood face to face with Satan himself in the wilderness (Matthew 4). But, by no means were Jesus and Satan in accord. And Jesus walked together with Judas Iscariot during His ministry. But He and the Betrayer were not in accord either. Jesus went and preached to the spirits in prison. Was He in accord with them?

Similarly, Jesus ate with sinners (Matthew 9:11). He walked with them. I personally imagine Jesus sitting with prostitutes, adulterers, drug dealers, murderers, and the like. He ministered to them. He was telling them the way to salvation. However, that doesn't mean that He was in fellowship, communion, or accord with those sinners—at least not until they repented. He was there with them to give them the Good News, not to affirm or tolerate their sinful lifestyles.

Fellowship, communion, and accord with God do not occur

until man admits he was wrong and comes into agreement with God. This happens when he repents of his sin and confesses Jesus as Lord. The sinners are not yet His friends until they are born again. Only when the sinner is born again is he now in communion with the God who gave him salvation. Once man is born again, he is yoked together with God in a special, salvific way. This is a wonderful yoking! Jesus beckons us to be yoked to Him by His Spirit right now:

> ***Take My yoke upon you*** *and learn from Me, for I am gentle and lowly in heart, and you will find rest for your souls.*
> Matthew 11:29 (NKJV)

Amazingly, there is yet another wonderful yoking that we Christians will one day experience. This yoking will take place after the Wedding Feast of the Lamb (Revelation 19:7), when the marriage between Jesus and His Church is consummated. And when this happens, not only will we be yoked with Jesus, but we will be fully and completely *equally* yoked to Him. Although we can't fully comprehend what this means, it should be a wonderful source of hope for all of us!

## *The Tripartite Nature Explains How Christian Demonization Is Possible*

In this chapter, we saw that good and evil can be together but that they cannot be in communion, fellowship, or accord. We saw that the *Light-Can't-Dwell-with-Darkness Argument* does not demonstrate that Christians can't have demons.

In the next chapter, we will examine the critical and foundational concept of the *tripartite nature of man*. When man's tripartite nature is understood, it becomes perfectly clear how it is theologically possible for a born-again Christian to simultaneously have the indwelling Holy Spirit *and* a demon spirit inside of him or her.

Even though the Holy Spirit and a demon spirit can be inside the same Christian body or bodily "house," they are not side by side. In the following chapter, we will see that, *even though the demons are in the same house as the Holy Spirit, they are actually in different "rooms" of that house.*

The tripartite understanding is foundational to the ministry of deliverance and is the key to understanding how the ministry of deliverance can be needed by the born-again Christian. It shows us where the demons are in relation to the indwelling Holy Spirit. It explains exactly what is regenerated at the new birth in Jesus Christ. And it helps us understand the discipline of inner healing.

Both the individual who is earnestly seeking the answer to the question of whether a Christian can have a demon and the student of deliverance ministry alike will appreciate the concept of the tripartite nature of man. It is a wonderful and *Biblical* revelation. The ministry of deliverance and inner healing makes sense once this foundation is laid. The importance of the tripartite concept simply cannot be overstated.

# Chapter 5

# *Understanding Man's Tripartite Nature Resolves Objection #1*

In the previous chapter, we saw that opposites can be yoked together. The believing and unbelieving can be yoked together. The lazy and hard-working can be yoked together. Good and evil can be yoked together. An atheist can be sitting inside of a Spirit-filled church. We saw that opposites can reside together.

But, between the two opposites who are yoked together and who dwell together, there can be no *fellowship*. There can be no *communion*. And there can be no *accord*. Now, in this chapter, I will make the point that not only can there not be communion, fellowship, or accord between the Christian's indwelling Holy Spirit and his indwelling demons but that these two opposites reside in completely different and separate parts. They are both there, but they are not dwelling alongside one another.

I will show this by examining man's three-part nature. The subject of man's three parts is absolutely profound and represents a foundational concept within the ministry of deliverance. By comprehending it, both the deliverance minister and the PRM to whom he ministers will have a visual framework by which both can understand how and where demons operate in the mind of the believer.

This visual framework allows us to conceptualize how both the Holy Spirit and a demon spirit can simultaneously dwell inside of a born-again individual. Man's three-part nature also permits an understanding of the other critical area of our ministry, inner healing, which is primarily the healing of the fragmented soul.

It is correct to say that the comprehension of man's three-part nature is an absolute prerequisite that must be mastered before moving on to learning the *practice* of Session Deliverance.

## The Tripartite Nature

The tripartite nature is also known as the *triune*, or *trichotomous* nature of man. All three terms are synonymous. However, in my ministry, for clarity, we use the term *tripartite* almost exclusively. The tripartite model demonstrates how man is made up of three distinct and separate components, or regions.

In order to begin to understand man's tripartite nature, we need to go back to the beginning:

*So God [**Elohim**] **created man in His own image**; in the image of God He created him; male and female He created them.*
Genesis 1:27 (NKJV)

From this passage, we learn two essential things: First, that God is plural. *Elohim* is the Hebrew plural of *Eloah* which means God or god. Second, we learn that we are made *in the image* of this plural God, *Elohim*.

In the Old Testament, we see the Father. We see the Holy Spirit. And we see many glimpses types of the Son. And, in at least one OT verse, we see all three together when the Son is inferred:

*Come near to Me, hear this: I have not spoken in secret from the beginning; From the time that it was, I was there. And now the Lord **GOD** and His **Spirit** Have sent **Me**.* Isaiah 48:16 (NKJV)

In the New Testament, we receive confirmation and additional clarity regarding the plural nature of our God. We learn that Father is God. We learn that Son is God, and we learn that Holy Spirit is God. In the NT, we see clearly that our God is one God in three divine Persons: Father, Son, and Holy Spirit. This is the Godhead. And in the NT, we clearly and openly see the three Persons of God mentioned *together*. For example, God reveals His tripartite nature in Matthew's baptismal formula:

> *Go therefore and make disciples of all the nations, baptizing them in the name of the **Father** and of the **Son** and of the **Holy Spirit**.*
> Matthew 28:19 (NKJV)

And Paul closes his second letter to the Corinthians with a blessing that contains a similar description of the Godhead:

*The grace of the **Lord Jesus Christ**, and the love of **God**, and the communion of the **Holy Spirit** be with you all. Amen.*
2 Corinthians 13:14 (NKJV)

Our one God is three. While we cannot really understand it intellectually, we accept on faith that our God is three divine Persons in one God. He is three in one. In theology, this concept is referred to as God's "plural unity." In many churches, it is known as the Holy Trinity. God's tripartite nature can be diagrammed to aid us in our comprehension:

**The Godhead: God's Tripartite or Triune Nature**

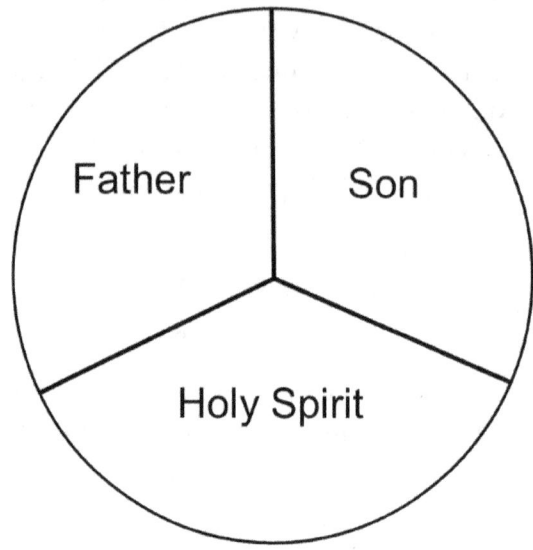

One God in Three Persons

Once again, Genesis 1:27 teaches us that our one God is plural AND that we are made in this plural image. Therefore, we humans bear, or carry, the image of God. We are the image-bearers of Elohim. We carry His image in ourselves. In a certain way, we *look like* God. We are made in His image. We have God's spiritual DNA in us. We are like Him. And as such, we are plural unities in a similar way to Him. Like God, we are also made up of *three parts*. We are tripartite too. Like the God who created us, we are also three-in-one. However, we are not FATHER-SON-HOLY SPIRIT. Instead, we are BODY-SOUL-SPIRIT.

I will emphasize this because it is foundational not only to the understanding of how a Christian can have a demon but also to the practicing of the ministry of deliverance and inner healing in general.

WE ARE THREE PARTS

WE ARE BODY, SOUL, AND SPIRIT

Understanding man's tripartite nature is critical in order to understand how a Christian with the indwelling Holy Spirit can have unclean demon spirits at the same time. Once we can grasp the concept of our tripartite nature, we can clearly understand how it is possible for a born-again Christian to have an indwelling demon. Everything begins to make perfect sense.

The most effective way to visually depict the tripartite nature of man is by using the *Larsonian tripartite model*. I named it this after my teacher Bob Larson, who uses this diagram extensively in his teaching ministry. I have found it to be the best vehicle to help students of deliverance and inner healing understand the concept of man's three parts. Here is the Larsonian tripartite model of man at conception:

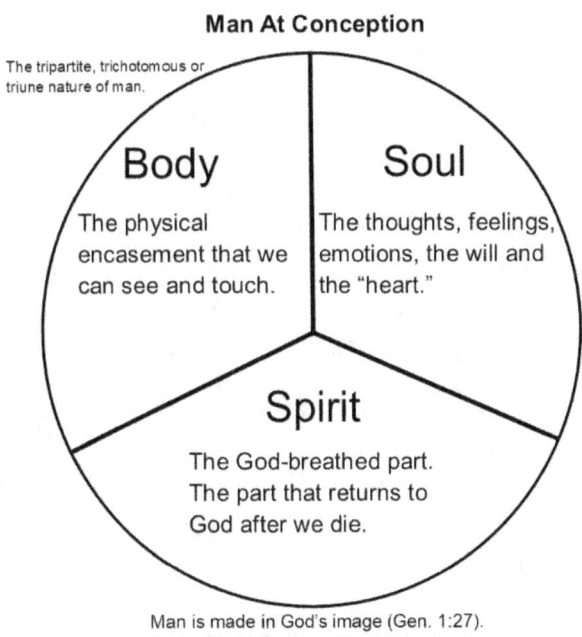

Man is made in God's image (Gen. 1:27).
God is three Persons. Man is three parts.

*Mark Chase*

# New Testament Scripture That Demonstrates Man's Tripartite Nature

In the original New Testament ancient Greek, the following words are used to denote "body," "soul," and "spirit":

| **English** | **Ancient Greek** | **Strong's Numbers** |
|---|---|---|
| body | *soma* and *sarx* (both can signify a physical body) | 4983 and 4561 |
| soul | *psuché* | 5590 |
| spirit | *pneuma* | 4151 |

Now, let's look at four New Testament Scriptures that clearly demonstrate the tripartite nature of man.

## *The Apostle Paul*

Paul shows us the tripartite nature in his closing instructions and blessing at the end of his first letter to the church at Thessalonica. It is the most straightforward verse in the Bible that demonstrates our three-part nature:

> *Now may the God of peace Himself sanctify you completely; and may your whole* **spirit** *[pneuma],* **soul** *[psuché], and* **body** *[soma] be preserved blameless at the coming of our Lord Jesus Christ.*
> 1 Thessalonians 5:23 (NKJV)

In this verse, we not only see our three parts listed clearly, but we also see a divine order teaching in this verse. We see a descending order of importance of our three parts. Our spirit is the most important, followed by the soul, and finally, our perishable body is of least importance.

## *The Writer of Hebrews*

The author of Hebrews demonstrates that the soul and the spirit can be *separated*. The fact that the soul and spirit can be separated implicitly shows that the soul and the spirit are *two distinct units.* In other words, that there is a distinct soul, and there is a separate and distinct spirit. Interestingly, the writer goes on to talk about joints and marrow, which are parts of the body. This would complete the tripartite nature of man:

*For the word of God is living and powerful, and sharper than any two-edged sword, piercing even to the division of **soul** [psuché] and **spirit** [pneuma], and of joints and marrow [parts of the **body**], and is a discerner of the thoughts and intents of the heart* [a synonym for **soul**].   Hebrews 4:12 (NKJV)

## Man's Bipartite Nature?

At this point, you might say that it is quite reasonable to say that man, like God, is three in one. However, most modern Christian Bible scholars do not agree with the tripartite description of man. In fact, most American theological seminaries and study Bibles teach that man is *two* parts instead. They teach that man is bipartite, or dichotomous. Here is how they would describe man's nature in graphic form:

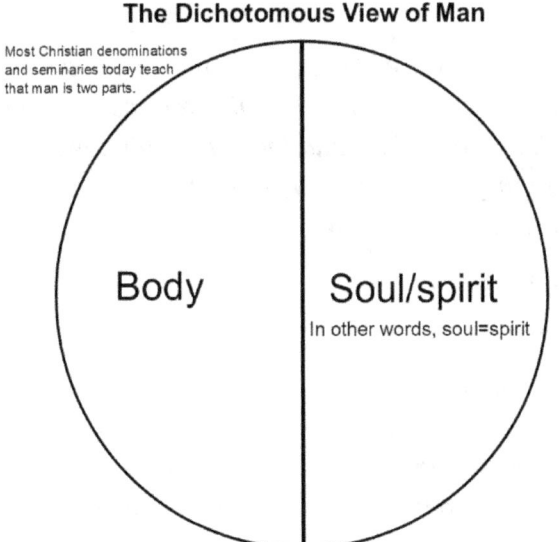

Most of the early church saw man as tripartite. Later, in the Reformation, John Calvin taught that man is two parts. This has had a profound effect on modern theology.

Most modern teachers, pastors, and theologians teach that man is two parts: body *and* soul-spirit. In other words, they teach that soul and spirit are synonymous. The result of the bipartite view on the ministry of deliverance has been profound—in a very negative way.

The bipartite belief has been so damaging to the ministry of deliverance for the following reason: When the bipartite belief is upheld, it is far more difficult to see how one can have the Holy Spirit and a demon spirit at the same time. A demon dwelling in the body is conceivable, but a demon dwelling in the same part or region as the Holy Spirit? That is unacceptable.

Deliverance ministers like myself do not accept that a demon could reside alongside the indwelling Holy Spirit either. In fact, I know of no deliverance minister that believes that a demon can dwell in the regenerated *spirit* of a believer. Deliverance ministers see instead that *the Holy Spirit dwells in man's spirit while the demons are in the body and the soul, which is the mind.*

Welsh evangelical speaker and "proto deliverance minister" Jessie Penn-Lewis wrote the classic *War on the Saints* (1912) more than 100 years ago. She understood, even back then, that believers can have demons:

*Multitudes of believers are "possessed" in various degrees but do not know it, as they attribute the "manifestations" to "natural" causes, or to "self" or "sin," and they put them down to these causes because they do not appear to bear the characteristics of demoniacal possession.* (page 81)

And Penn-Lewis knew that those demons were in the soul (mind) and body of the believers:

*But this truth about the working of evil spirits among believers, and the causes and symptoms of their power upon **mind** or **body**, has been so veiled in ignorance, that multitudes of children of God are held in bondage to their power without knowing it.* (pages 68-69)

*The Children's Bread*

Return to Genesis 1:27 once again. In this verse, Moses tells us that we are made in the image of God—the One True God Elohim, who is a plural unity. Take a moment to really internalize this truth. If God is three and we are made in His image, it would follow that we are three as well. The bipartite understanding simply doesn't line up with the truth that we are *created in His image*. Since God is three in one, we are also three in one.

## *Examples of the Bipartite Teaching*

*The Reformation Study Bible* (2005), which uses the English Standard Version (ESV) as its base text and is favored by many reformed denominations such as the Presbyterians, says that soul and spirit are synonymous. Regarding 1 Thessalonians 5:23, it teaches:

*Three words are used to emphasize the wholeness of the perfection. "Spirit" and "soul" are used as virtual synonyms in the Bible for the spiritual component of a person.* (page 1743)

The *Life Application Study Bible* (1984), which uses the New International Version (NIV) as its text, teaches on the same verse:

*The spirit, soul and body refer not so much to the distinct parts of a person as to the entire being of a person.* (page 2025)

John Calvin, perhaps the biggest influencer of the protestant reformers, said in his *Institutes of the Christian Religion* (1536) that man consists of a body and a soul, which is sometimes called a spirit. Calvin also said that when the word *spirit* is used by itself, it is equivalent to the soul:

*Moreover, there can be no question that* **man consists of a body and a soul***; meaning by soul, an immortal though created essence, which is his nobler part. Sometimes he is called a spirit. But though the two terms, while they are used together differ in their* *meaning, still,* **when spirit is used by itself it is equivalent to soul***...* (I:XV.2)

However, we should always be like the Bereans and look at the Scriptures for ourselves. And as we do so, we should ask God's Spirit to teach us in order that we may arrive at our own conclusions—hopefully at the truth.

## *The Secular Understanding of the Soul-Spirit*

The assumption of the synonymity of soul-spirit is so pervasive that even in the secular discussion of this issue, the soul is sometimes presumed to be equivalent to the spirit. Here is a quote from a recent article in the magazine *Psychology Today*:

*Natural science is missing the most obvious, relevant, meaningful feature of them all – the soul or spirit that we know must be there.* (Sherman, Jeremy. 2018. "Peace of Mind from a New Scientific Explanation of Our Souls." *Psychology Today*. https://www.psychologytoday.com/us/blog/ambigamy/201811/peace-mind-new-scientific-explanation-our-souls)

## *Mary, the Mother of Jesus*

Mary, the mother of Jesus, in her song called the Magnificat, which is also known as "The Song of Mary," describes her soul and spirit functioning independently:

> **46** *And Mary said: "My* **soul** *[psuché] magnifies the Lord,*
> **47** *and my* **spirit** *[pneuma] has rejoiced in God my Savior.*
> Luke 1:46-47 (NKJV)

Here, we see Mary's soul doing one thing—magnifying the Lord. And we see her spirit doing a completely different thing—rejoicing in her Savior. This is clear evidence that the soul and spirit are separate. We see Mary's soul and spirit functioning separately. Separation of function implies the separation of the units themselves.

As in the Hebrews verse, the fact that Mary doesn't

mention the body is inconsequential since no one argues against the fact that every human being possesses a physical body.

## *Jesus, Our Lord and Savior and God in the Flesh*

And did you know that even Jesus clearly delineates the three parts of man? I believe that by Him doing this, we have the ultimate confirmation of the tripartite nature of man.

Jesus, like His mother, also differentiates between soul and spirit by stating functional differentiation. In other words, He shows that His soul and Spirit are carrying out different operations. However, unlike His mother Mary, Jesus also mentions the body, completing the tripartite framework.

As Jesus agonized in the Garden of Gethsemane, the Gospel writer recorded that Jesus's soul was *sorrowful* while His Spirit was *willing*. Once again, differentiation of function implies differentiation of the units themselves. Jesus spoke these words on the night before His Crucifixion:

> **38** *Then He said to them, "My soul [psuché] is exceedingly sorrowful, even to death. Stay here and watch with Me."* **39** *He went a little farther and fell on His face, and prayed, saying, "O My Father, if it is possible, let this cup pass from Me; nevertheless, not as I will, but as You will."* **40** *Then He came to the disciples and found them asleep, and said to Peter, "What? Could you not watch with Me one hour?* **41** *Watch and pray, lest you enter into temptation. The spirit [pneuma] indeed is willing, but the flesh [sarx] is weak."* Matthew 26:38-41 (NKJV)

Jesus, therefore, clearly differentiates between soul and spirit. And although Matthew uses the word *sarx* instead of Paul's *soma* for body, it needs to be understood that both ancient Greek words *soma* and *sarx* can signify the physical part of the human body. For example, in a separate passage, we see how *sarx* can also signify the physical body:

> *See my hands and my feet, that it is I myself. Touch me, and see.*
> *For a spirit does not have flesh* [**sarx**] *and bones*
> *as you see that I have.* Luke 24:39 (ESV)

On the night before going to the Cross to be crucified, Jesus demonstrates the tripartite nature of His *human* side. Jesus is unique, of course, since not only did the man Jesus have the three parts of body, soul, and spirit, He also was and is one of the three Persons of the divine Godhead. Jesus *is* God the Son.

There are additional Scriptures in both Testaments of the Bible that reinforce the concept of the tripartite nature of man. These additional passages of Scripture are taught in our advanced levels of deliverance ministry training. However, the four Scriptures shown above are completely adequate to firmly demonstrate the critically important concept of the tripartite nature of man.

## *Demons Can Enter a Nonbeliever Through Sin*

Now, let's look diagrammatically at an unsaved, unregenerate, nonbeliever. Through rebellion, which is sin against God, demons can gain access to the inside of a person (the body or mind). Recall the points of entry and the legal rights that were discussed earlier.

When there is sin, God may give permission to demons to enter into a human victim—into the physical body and or into the mind, which is the soul. After which point, the victim is now demonized or has a demon or demons on the inside.

Most everyone agrees that nonbelievers can be demonized. Even those who are in opposition to the ministry of Session Deliverance and ignorant to the fact that Christians can have demons (the NDMC's) would rarely deny that a non-Christian could have demons.

Here is what an unsaved person with demons would look like using the Larsonian tripartite model:

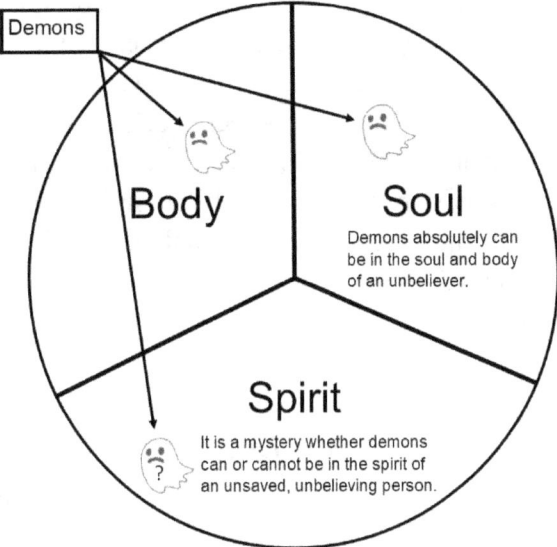

Demons can occupy the body, soul and *perhaps* the spirit of a **nonbeliever**.

## *Demons in the Spirit of a Nonbeliever?*

There is no debate that demon spirits can be in the body and soul of an unsaved person. However, it is a mystery whether demons can be in the *spirit* of a nonbeliever.

There are two opinions within the ministry of deliverance. Some deliverance ministers think that demons can be in the spirit man of an unbeliever. Others say that demons cannot be in the spirit of an unsaved person since the spirit always belongs to God and that man's spirit is His property which returns to Him when the person dies (Ecclesiastes 12:7). They say, therefore, that no demon can ever be in man's spirit—saved or unsaved.

I personally believe that demons *cannot* be in the spirit of an unsaved person. I believe that the human spirit is God's territory which He does not share. However, I will not be dogmatic about this since the Bible offers few clues on this issue.

Mark Chase
## The Spiritual Rebirth

Now, let's look at what happens when this unsaved individual is born again. The Bible says that when man repents and trusts in Jesus as Savior, his spirit is regenerated. We learn in John's Gospel that the Holy Spirit gives birth to the believer's new spirit. The Holy Spirit comes and dwells in his spirit. He receives the nature of God. He is now born of the Spirit. Although the precise nature of the spiritual rebirth cannot be intellectualized, we know that the Holy Spirit gives birth to the believer's new spirit:

> *Flesh gives birth to flesh, but the* ***Spirit gives birth to spirit****.*
> John 3:6 (NIV)

## Holdover Demons

When a born-again Christian has demons, it is most likely that these demons got in *before* he was ever born again. Since the Bible doesn't teach that every demon flies out at salvation, and we know that most Christians never get deliverance after they get saved, the demons remain. I call these unconfronted, unchallenged, undealt-with, and uncast-out demons, *holdover demons*.

A Christian's demons are most likely, but not always, holdovers from his previous life of sin. His demons most likely got in when he used to fornicate, watch pornography, practice New Age, play fantasy and violent video games, love the world, smoke weed, hurt people, steal, and blaspheme.

Recall the story of Pastor Rob in Chapter 3. His story clearly demonstrates the concept of holdover demons. Missionary Ezequiel Ferreira also said in his testimony at the beginning of this book that he delivers evangelical Christians from demons who used to practice sins like the ones listed above.

It is also common for a Christian's demons to have gotten in even *before* adulthood. I frequently see holdover demons that got in during childhood when the PRM was abused, rejected, abandoned, or molested. Every deliverance minister knows the sad truth that when children are abused, they can become demonized.

And the root of holdover demons can go back even further than childhood. Deliverance ministries like mine encounter holdover demons that got in while the PRM was still in the *womb*. This can happen when the PRM's mother or father considered aborting, the mother was physically abused when she was pregnant, or the mother or father did witchcraft, prostitution, or other evil while the PRM was in his or her mother's womb. Sins during pregnancy can provide points of entry for demons to enter into a *zygote*, *embryo*, or *fetus*.

All these holdover demons that were there before the Christian's born-again experience will now need to be forcefully cast out in the Name of Jesus. This is why Session Deliverance exists—to help these Christians!

## *Post-Conversion Demonization: New Demons Can Get in After a Person Is Born Again*

When Christians have demons, the great majority of these (if not all) got in before they were ever born again. These are the holdover demons.

However, it is also *possible* for new demons to enter into a Christian *after* having been born again. I realize that this will be a shock for many to hear. However, it makes complete sense once one understands the concept of legal right and undealt-with sin. The phenomenon of new demons getting into the mind and body of an already born-again individual is what I refer to as *post-conversion demonization.*

While post-conversion demonization is definitely possible, I do believe that it is less common than demonization that occurs *before* salvation. I also believe that it is more difficult for demons to gain legal entry into a born-again individual than into an unsaved person. This is especially the case when the born-again Christian strives to submit to God and resist the devil.

I teach that being a Christian is not some sort of automatic guaranteed immunity from all future demonization. Having the indwelling Holy Spirit is not an amulet that wards off all demons. Instead, demons are warded off by submitting to God and resisting the devil (James 4:7). See Chapter 16 for more on this important deliverance verse.

Even the born-again Christian must forsake sin in order to avoid becoming infected with new demonic entrants. Even the Christian must fill his house with things of the Lord. Think about a Christian who gives in to temptation and smokes weed. Or that couple at church who say that pornography isn't bad as long as both agree to watch it together. If a Christian's sins are not dealt with properly through timely repentance and confession, chinks are created in his armor. Chinks in the armor can let in demons.

There are a variety of sins, most of them very subtle, that demons can attempt to utilize in order to gain access into Christians. This concept is taught further in the Lectures of Invicta University. For the sake of brevity, I will discuss only four of them here in this book:

- Overt sin

- Passivity

- Ignorance

- Satanic Thinking Patterns

## Overt Sin

Christians can get new demons by doing the obvious: Adultery, pornography, bitterness, unforgiveness, rage, fear, drugs, etc. Remember that Christians are capable of falling and committing these sins, and a Christian doesn't necessarily lose his salvation just because he does fall into one of these sins.

## Passivity

When Christians are passive and refuse to walk in the authority that God has given them, demons can gain entry. For example, when husbands are not willing to be the spiritual authority in their marriages is a common manifestation of passivity in Christians. Another example of passivity is when Christians do not utilize their authority in Jesus Christ to preach the Gospel boldly to others. This is evangelism.

There is another area of passivity that relates specifically to the topic of this book. This is when Christians refuse to walk in their God-ordained authority to trample on snakes and scorpions. In other words, they do not utilize their *authority over demons* to drive out unclean spirits from their human victims. When Christians are passive in this area, the enemy actually gains legal ground in that Christian's life. Passivity in any of these or other areas *can* create a vulnerability for post-conversion demonization.

## *Ignorance*

Another pathway to post-conversion demonization is ignorance. This occurs when Christians indulge in something that is sinful out of ignorance of God's laws or the devices and schemes of the enemy (2 Corinthians 2:11). For example, demons can gain access to a Christian if that Christian indulges in secular music and entertainment, practices yoga, gives approval to his children to celebrate Halloween, permits his children to enjoy the witchcraft and sexual perversion of Disney programs, etc.

I am referring here to sins that are committed out of ignorance. By "ignorance," I mean lack of knowledge. For example, when he sins because he is not cognizant of the spiritual backdrop of everything around him. Or because he is unaware of God's absolute moral law.

A state of ignorance happens when an individual does not seek the counsel of the Holy Spirit, when he does not seek the Truth in God's word, and when he follows the lead of the world instead of God. We are warned by the prophet Hosea that we perish for lack of knowledge (Hosea 4:6). This lack of knowledge is ignorance, and demons cause men to perish because of it.

## Mark Chase
## *Satanic Thinking Patterns*

I believe that much post-conversion demonization occurs due to the commission of a much more subtle sin than the above ones listed. A lot of post-conversion demonization happens as a result of the very subtle sin of believing, embracing, and defending *Satanic thinking patterns* (STP's).

An STP is a continuously held thought, belief, or attitude that stands contrary to either Biblical or revealed truth on some *critical* moral or theological issue. Having the wrong belief about the timing of the rapture is *not* an STP. Believing that God tolerates sin *is* an STP. Believing that Christians can't have demons or being passive when authority should be taken are STP's.

*When Christians believe, espouse, embrace, or defend an STP, demonic legal right can be generated. God can give demons legal right when one continuously holds a thought, belief, or attitude of the heart that stands contrary to either Biblical or revealed truth on some critical moral or theological issue.*

Believing, espousing, embracing, and defending STP's can give legal right to new demons to enter as well as provide legal ground to strengthen the existing demons' right to remain in an individual and to resist being cast out.

There are a myriad of examples of STP's. Some common ones that could permit post-conversion demonization include:

• Christians can't have demons
• There is no actual devil or demons
• If you don't bother the devil, he won't bother you—in other words, fear of the devil
• In the Bible, demons are not actual spirits; they are just prescientific descriptions of mental illness
• Jesus isn't God
• God accepts my lifestyle; God made me who I am
• I have not transgressed all of God's moral law; in fact, I am a "good" person
• Tolerating Jezebel (for example, a passive husband)

*The Children's Bread*

STP's are lies and, as such, can only be dismantled and removed by the embracing and acceptance of *truth*. STP's are sin and need to be repented of. The STP's themselves are not what needs to be cast out, as Pastor Rick believes in Chapter 8. Instead, it is the demons that need to be cast out. The believing and embracing of STP's can give legal right to these demons. For those who want to go deeper, STP's are taught on in more detail in our online school, Invicta University.

## *The Demonization of the Backslidden Believer*

While it is possible for Christians to get new demons from obvious overt sins, spiritual passivity, ignorance, and from embracing STP's, I believe that the majority of post-conversion demonization occurs during the backslidden state.

Being backslidden means that the one who was born again has given up the forsaking sin and has returned to the conscious and willful enjoyment of sin. The one who is backslidden is completely aware that what he is doing violates the commandments that he used to keep as a practicing follower of Jesus.

When an individual decides to stop forsaking sin and returns to *willful* sin, he has effectively renounced Jesus as Lord. Jesus said that if we keep His commandments, we will abide in His love:

*If you keep My commandments, you will abide in My love, just as I have kept My Father's commandments and abide in His love.*
John 15:10 (NKJV)

And likewise, we can infer that if we do not keep His commandments, we will not abide in His love. When an individual is not abiding in His love, I believe that this individual has renounced Jesus as Lord. As a result, I do not believe that he or she is born again anymore. Remember, I am speaking about continuous *willful, purposeful* sin, not the normal sin that all

Christians fall into every day—which we also confess daily.

Am I saying that a Christian can *lose* his or her salvation? No, I am not. Please put down your stones! However, God will not force a person to remain obedient. God gives even His children the right to choose whether to walk in holiness or turn back to rebellion. The Father did not force the Prodigal Son to remain. The Father permitted him to leave.

I say that one cannot lose his salvation; however, one can *renounce* his salvation. Religious Christians will resist what I am saying here. Spiritual Christians will know it to be true.

John Calvin said that the saints persevere. In other words, "once saved, always saved." However, I see the Bible teach something else. I see the Bible teach that believers can *choose* to reject Jesus—even after their salvation. There are clear references to those who have once known the truth but have decided to become disobedient. Paul says that some believers will turn and reject Jesus:

> *Now the Spirit expressly says that in latter times* ***some will depart from the faith****, giving heed to deceiving spirits and doctrines of demons.* 1 Timothy 4:1 (NKJV)

The writer of Hebrews said:

> **4** *For it is impossible for those who were once enlightened, and have tasted the heavenly gift, and have become partakers of the Holy Spirit,* **5** *and have tasted the good word of God and the powers of the age to come,* **6** ***if they fall away****, to renew them again to repentance, since they crucify again for themselves the Son of God, and put Him to an open shame.* Hebrews 6:4-6 (NKJV)

By saying "*if* they fall away," the writer here clearly implies that it is possible for believers to fall away. The writer is not saying that it is impossible to fall away after having known the truth. Instead, he is saying that *if* they do fall away, it is impossible to renew them.

I believe that this kind of falling away after people have

"become partakers of the Holy Spirit" is tantamount to renouncing Jesus. And renouncing Jesus is equivalent to accepting Satan. The Bible teaches that one can serve only one master (Matthew 6:24).

The truth is that when a person commits willful sin after having known the truth, not even the Cross is sufficient:

> *For if we sin willfully after we have received the knowledge of the truth, there no longer remains a sacrifice for sins.*
> Hebrews 10:26 (NKJV)

If there no longer remains a sacrifice for sins, then that means that there is sin that is not atoned for. Unatoned-for sin is sin that has not been cleansed by the Blood of Jesus. And sin that has not yet been cleansed by the Blood of Jesus is sin that has not been "dealt with," as we deliverance ministers say. Sin that has not been dealt with can be used by demons as point of entry and legal right.

In Session Deliverance, a deliverance minister leads the PRM in actively "dealing" with his sin through effective Deliverance Counseling and then through the utilization of specific RAM prayer to break curses, sever ungodly relationship ties, pull down ungodly strongholds, etc.

## *Holdover Demons Diagrammatically*

The next diagram represents the newly born-again believer. Note that the demons that were there *before* conversion are *still* there—in the soul and body. These demons didn't all just fly out of him the moment he got saved. Remember:

> *There is not one verse in the Bible that indicates that all demons fly out of a person at the moment of conversion.*

The truth that demons do not all leave when a person is born again is a critical point to understand when we consider the question, "Can a Christian have a demon?" In order to help the NDMC understand this, it is profitable to ask the NDMC to provide even one verse that indicates that demons instantly disappear at the moment of conversion. The NDMC will quickly realize that there is no such verse. The doctrine that Christians cannot have demons is a man-made doctrine, not a Biblical one.

After an individual is born again, the holdover demons are still there. These holdover demons did not all fly out at conversion and will now need to be forcefully cast out in the Name of Jesus of this newly born-again individual:

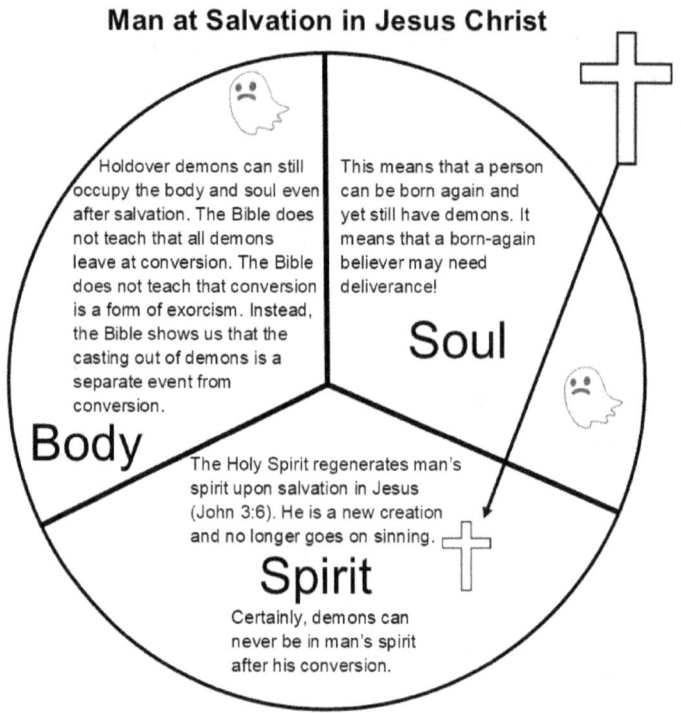

Now the Holy Spirit dwells in man's *spirit*. Demons, however, can still be in the body and the soul. This is the technical explanation of how a Christian can have a demon.

Through the tripartite model, we can see clearly and graphically how a Christian with the indwelling Holy Spirit can also have a demon. We see that the demons are in the body and soul while God's Spirit is in man's spirit.

Analogously, two people can be in the same house yet be in different *rooms* inside of that house. It all becomes so simple. The debate of whether a Christian can have a demon should be done and over based on the tripartite revelation alone.

## God's Omnipresence

And what about God's omnipresence (Jeremiah 23:24)? God is everywhere at all times. Therefore, why couldn't He be in the same bodily house as a demon? Can the NDMC decree that God cannot be in a certain place? Can the NDMC forbid God to be in a certain place?

## A Simple Six-Point Summary of How A Born-Again Christian Can Have a Demon

1. Before a person was born again, demons entered through sin.
2. When this person was born again, all of the demons that got in previously did not all instantaneously leave. The Bible does not teach that demons leave an individual the moment the individual is born again. The Bible never teaches that conversion is a form of exorcism.
3. When a person is born again, he receives the Holy Spirit. The Holy Spirit now resides in the born-again person's own spirit. However, the demons that were there before he was born again are *still* there in his soul (mind) and body.
4. A born-again Christian's demons are in different places than the indwelling Holy Spirit anyway. Therefore, if a Christian has demons, these demons do not dwell *alongside* the Holy Spirit. The demons and the Holy Spirit dwell in different "rooms" of the Christian's "house."
5. It is *possible* that a born-again Christian can get new demons by overt sin, passivity, ignorance, and by embracing Satanic thinking patterns.
6. Man's tripartite nature explains how a Spirit-filled, born-again believer can simultaneously have indwelling demons.

I believe that if the NDMC's would take the time to do four things, the debate of whether a Christian can have a demon could finally be put to rest. These four things are:

1. Understand the above six-point summary.
2. Realize that man is tripartite and not bipartite.
3. See the overriding pattern in God's word that:

    *God delivers those who belong to Him*

4. Just start *doing deliverance.* By doing this, the NDMC will quickly see that the majority of people who will come to him to receive deliverance will be fellow *Christians.*

## *A Common Misconception: If Someone Has A Demon, Then He Is Not Saved*

At the heart of the NDMC doctrine that Christians can't have demons is the misconception that *if someone has demons, then he can't possibly be saved.* In other words, the NDMC equates demonization with a lack of salvation. This is a Satanic thinking pattern held either consciously or unconsciously by every NDMC.

At my public meetings, I can spot this misconception through the comments of the meeting attendees. For example, before praying for an individual, I might ask an attendee if she thinks she has demons. If she responds with, "No, I am born again," I know that she embraces this NDMC misconception. And I know that she will have to demolish this misconception if she is to receive any deliverance from demons. This meeting attendee, like Pastor Vic in Chapter 4, are both stuck on Lie #3—that there are, in fact, demon spirits, but that a born-again Christian could not possibly have one.

The Satanic thinking pattern that demonization signifies an absence of salvation hinders Christians from getting the deliverance that they need. When the possibility of demonization is ruled out by virtue of salvation attained, the solution, which is deliverance ministry, is then ruled out too.

Men are saved because they repent and trust in Jesus. Men

are not saved because their demons have been cast out. Salvation and deliverance from demons are two separate events in the Bible.

## *There Is No Correlation Between Having Demons and Salvation*

Being born-again and having a demon are two completely separate characteristics. They are unrelated. The characteristic of being born-again and the characteristic of having a demon are as closely related as being born-again and having brown eyes. In other words, they are completely unconnected and have no bearing on each other. The characteristics of being born again and having indwelling demons are not correlated. In the same way, there is absolutely no correlation between salvation and eye color.

Once again, recall the story of Pastor Rob in Chapter 3. He was saved, he had the Holy Spirit, he had a powerful anointing on his life to do God's work—yet he had demons.

Having a demon doesn't necessarily mean a person is unsaved and on his way to Hell. In other words, having a demon is in no way God's seal of damnation. Having demons and salvation have absolutely nothing to do with each other.

Having a demon just means that in the past, there was sin that provided a point of entry for demons to get in. And now, these demons need to be dealt with by the Name and authority of Jesus.

Salvation, on the other hand, means something altogether different. Salvation means that a person has repented of his sin and has confessed with his mouth that Jesus is Lord (Acts 3:19, Romans 10:9, etc.).

The inverse is also true. Just because a person *does not* have demons doesn't mean that he *is* born again. Once again, the two characteristics are unrelated. Having or not having demons is not some sort of litmus test for salvation.

*Mark Chase*

## NDMC Doctrine Stops Christians From Receiving Deliverance

Christians with demons know that something is wrong. They experience the voices, the chronic sicknesses, seeing shadows, patterns of strife-filled relationships, alienation from family, confusion, unbreakable addictions, desire to manipulate, unmanageable lust, rage, fear, isolation, shame, guilt, etc.

But most of these Christians never consider making an appointment to see a deliverance minister. This is so since doing so would violate either theirs or their denomination's NDMC doctrine that a Christian can't have a demon. See Chapter 9 for more on doctrine.

## Fear and Misunderstanding Keep Christians from Receiving Deliverance

I believe that some Christians are hindered in receiving deliverance out of fear and misunderstanding. They do not seek deliverance ministry out of fear. They become fearful when they consider the possibility that by going to a deliverance ministry, a demon might be exposed in them. Since they embrace the Satanic thinking pattern that demonization correlates with lack of salvation, they fear that if a demon *did* manifest, then that would mean that they weren't saved. So, this Christian avoids seeing a deliverance minister and subsequently never gets the deliverance she needs.

This behavior pattern is similar to the person who avoids making an appointment with the dentist for fear that an infected root canal will be diagnosed. And just as a serious dental condition worsens without proper treatment, demonization and its accompanying Satanic fruit get worse over time in the absence of receiving the proper treatment—deliverance in the Name of Jesus.

*The Children's Bread*

## *Demonization is the Root Of Many Christians' Issues*

The fact that Christians can have demons explains why many born-again believers struggle with the inability to worship, pray, and read and understand the Bible. It also explains how born-again Christians can succumb to serious sexual sins such as adultery, prostitution, and pornography. Recall what Jessie Penn-Lewis said about how demonized Christians attribute their demonic manifestations to natural causes, self, and sin.

The spirit of a born-again, yet demonized, Christian has a will to worship and serve God. But the demons in the mind (coupled with the desires of the sinful flesh, of course) drive him or her to do evil.

This is how countless born-again Christians and even born-again Christian pastors, leaders, and household-name televangelists have fallen. This is what happened to Pastor Rob. How many other Christian leaders can you think of who made headlines when they fell? Do you think these leaders might have needed deliverance?

The fact that Christians can have demons gives us insight into how a Christian can commit sins like abuse, theft, rage, greed, lying, and violence. These demonized Christians have Jesus in their spirits, but the devil is in their minds. They can't overcome their problem since the NDMC church they attend teaches that they cannot have any spiritual problems to begin with.

As a result, one of three things happens: They are referred to secular practitioners for treatment, they are told that the solution to their problem is to just read their Bible more or to attend church more, or worse yet, they are written off as being unsaved.

*Mark Chase*

*Conclusion*

Understanding the tripartite nature of man allows us to comprehend how a Christian with the Holy Spirit can have an indwelling demon at the same time. The Larsonian tripartite model allows us to visually conceptualize how this is possible. Man's tripartite nature explains how demons can be in the born-again believer's soul and body while the Spirit of Jesus is in his spirit.

# Chapter 6

# Objection #2:

# The Body is the Temple

(Body-is-the-Temple Argument)

Another common objection the NDMC will use to argue that Christians can't have demons is the *Body-is-the-Temple Argument*.

### God's Temple

During the time of the Old Covenant, God's Spirit dwelled in the inner sanctums of the Tabernacle and, later, in the First and Second Temples. This inner part was known as the Holy of Holies. However, with the advent of the superior New Covenant, there was a shift in the dwelling place of God.

Beginning in the New Covenant, God's Spirit began to inhabit a different temple. This new temple is the body of every New Covenant believer. Paul reveals to us that the body of each born-again believer now becomes the temple of the Holy Spirit:

*Or do you not know that **your body is the temple** of the Holy Spirit who is in you, whom you have from God, and you are not your own?* 1 Cor. 6:19 (NKJV)

Therefore, God's Spirit no longer dwells within a man-made structure in Jerusalem. To punctuate this fact, God permitted the Romans to destroy the Second Temple in Jerusalem in AD 70. Today, some 2,000 years later, there is still no Jewish Temple on the Temple Mount. This is because, in the New Covenant, there is no longer a need for a physical Temple.

Because of this, God sovereignly allowed the Jewish Temple in Jerusalem to be destroyed. The destruction of the Temple wasn't a random event. God permitted it to be destroyed all according to His good pleasure. This destruction confirmed the words above that Paul had written some fifteen years earlier.

Ever since the Cross and the Outpouring at Pentecost, the Holy Spirit now resides inside of a new temple: the body of every born-again believer. Now each individual Christian believer becomes a living temple, filled with the Holy Spirit, whereby the believer offers himself up daily as a living sacrifice.

## *The Body-is-the-Temple Argument*

The Body-is-the-Temple Argument says that since our bodies are now the new temple to the Holy Spirit, then there can be no demons in the temple since God's Holy Spirit cannot dwell in the same temple as the demons. This is how the NDMC sees it.

However, understanding man's tripartite nature as well as understanding the three main parts of the Jewish Temple allow one to quickly overcome this NDMC objection.

We saw in the previous chapter that the Holy Spirit and the demon spirits can be in the same individual—in the same "house." However, they are actually located in different "rooms" of a person's bodily house. The Holy Spirit is in the born-again believer's spirit, and the demons are in the different rooms of the body and the mind, which is the soul.

*The Children's Bread*

Something parallel to this happened in the physical Jewish Temple. God dwelled in one specific area of the Temple—the Holy of Holies—while the people that were not ceremonially cleansed were only permitted to be in the other areas of the Temple.

The same occurs within our bodily Christian Temples. The Holy Spirit dwells in God's sovereign territory—in our spirits. There is no sin or uncleanness in our regenerated *spirits*; therefore, God can reside there. The unclean demons, on the other hand, can only dwell where they are permitted to by God—which is in our bodies and minds. Our minds and bodies, even though we are born again, can have uncleanness, sin, evil, and infirmity. Demon spirits can dwell within a Christian's body and mind.

## *The Tabernacle and the Temples*

The first dwelling place of God was the Tabernacle of Moses. The Tabernacle was a portable tent structure, and it was used until the First Temple was constructed by Solomon in Jerusalem in 959 BC. The First Temple was then destroyed in 586 BC. A new Temple was rebuilt in 515 BC. This rebuilt Temple was the Second Temple. This Second Temple was then destroyed in AD 70. Now, in present-day Jerusalem on the Temple Mount, there is no more Jewish Temple.

God purposefully allowed the destruction of the Second Temple as it was no longer needed in God's plan of salvation. The Old Covenant itself had been made obsolete (Hebrews 8:13) by the New Covenant, so there was no more need for a physical Temple where the rituals of the sacrificial system were carried out.

Jesus became the final blood sacrifice—the Passover Lamb of God. Eliminating the physical Temple was God's way of confirming what Paul reveals to us: That the body of each born-again believer is now His temple.

*Mark Chase*

## The Layout of God's Temple

The Tabernacle of Moses and both Temples in Israel had the same general layout and consisted of three primary parts:

1. The Outer Court (the Court of the Priests in the Temples)
2. The Holy Place (Hebrews 9:2)
3. The Holy of Holies (Hebrews 9:3)

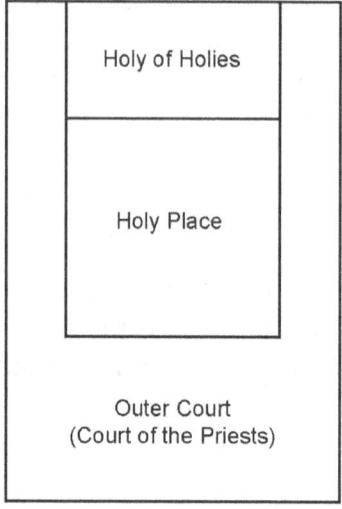

Simplified Diagram of the Tabernacle/Temple

During the Old Testament period, the forgiveness of sin for Israel was achieved when the High Priest ceremonially purified himself with the ashes of a sacrificed red heifer. Then, on only one day of the year, on Yom Kippur, the Day of Atonement, he would enter the Holy of Holies, where God dwelled and sprinkle sacrificial animal blood on the Mercy Seat, which was the lid of the Ark of the Covenant.

Not just anyone could enter the inner sanctum where God dwelled. Only the High Priest who had been purified by the ashes of a sacrificed red cow could enter the Holy of Holies, and he could only do this on the holiest day of the Jewish year, Yom Kippur.

## *The Temple in Israel is Emblematic of the Tripartite Nature of Man and God*

The Temple is a physical representation of both the tripartite nature of man and the tripartite nature of God. When representing man's three-part nature, the Holy of Holies refers to man's spirit. It is here that God's Spirit dwells when a man is born again. God's Holy Spirit dwells only in our spirits. It is our spirits that are reborn. It is our spirit that undergoes regeneration at the new birth in Jesus Christ. Next, the Holy Place signifies the soul. And finally, the Outer Court relates to our physical body. Our body is external to our soul and spirit.

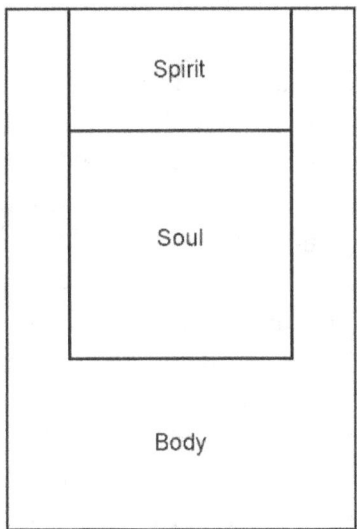

Man's Tripartite Nature in Relation to the Tabernacle/Temple

Therefore, what Paul said is true. We are the new temples of God. There is no more physical temple in Jerusalem. God allowed the Jewish Temple to be destroyed some 40 years after the Crucifixion. Now, each born-again believer is his own temple to the Most High God. Each born-again believer becomes the dwelling place of God's Holy Spirit. Each born-again believer now presents his body as a living sacrifice, holy, acceptable to God, which is his reasonable service (Romans 12:1).

## *God Dwelled in the Holy of Holies Not in the Entire Temple*

We see from the layout of the Jewish Temple that God did not dwell in the entire Temple. He dwelled only in the Holy of Holies. This part was sectioned off from the Holy Place by a veil. This is the veil that was torn in two when Jesus gave up His Spirit on the Cross (Matthew 27:51). The veil was in place to ensure that those outside of the Holy of Holies could not accidentally look in, see God, and die.

God did not dwell in the Holy Place, the Outer Court, or the other peripheral areas of the Temple. God dwelled in only one place—the Holy of Holies. However, one could correctly say that God dwelled "in the Temple." This is so even though He did not dwell in every part of the Temple.

In the same way, we can correctly say that God "dwells in every born-again Christian." This is so even though His Spirit only dwells in one place inside of us—in our regenerated spirits. God dwells in us but does not dwell in every part of us.

Likewise, we can also correctly say that a demon can also "dwell inside of a born-again Christian." This is so even though the demon can only dwell in one of two places. Demons can be in a Christian's mind-soul (his Holy Place) or in his body (his Outer Court). Demons cannot be where God is—in his regenerated spirit (his Holy of Holies). I don't believe that demons can be in the spirit of an unsaved person either. Man's spirit is always God's sovereign territory—a place that He does not share.

Therefore, it is correct to say that "a demon can dwell in a Christian." But this does not mean that the demon dwells in every part of the Christian. A demon can never dwell in the born-again man's regenerated spirit. A demon cannot dwell alongside the indwelling Holy Spirit in born-again man's Holy of Holies. This is how a Christian with the indwelling Holy Spirit can have a demon.

## *Conclusion*

The born-again Christian's body is the new temple of the Holy Spirit. This fact strengthens, not weakens, the case that a Christian can have a demon. It strengthens the case for the plausibility of the demonization of Christians since the Jewish Temple was divided up into three main sections, just as man is three parts. God dwells in one of these parts. Demons can dwell in the other two.

Man's born-again spirit is his Holy of Holies. God dwells there, and this part can never be defiled by unclean demonic spirits or even sin. In the same way, the Holy of Holies in the Jewish Temple could not be defiled by any man who was ceremonially unclean. Only one man could enter the Holy of Holies. This was the High Priest. And in order to enter this area, he needed to undergo a complex ritual of purification using the ashes of the red heifer.

However, man's Holy Place (his soul-mind) and his Outer Court (his body) *can* be defiled by indwelling demons. A born-again man's body and soul can also be defiled with sickness, sin, weakness, fear, lust, imperfection, temptation, evil desires, anger, and even mental illness.

Our regenerated spirits, however, are perfect and make us perfect before Him. This is good news since Jesus commands us to be perfect:

> ***Be perfect**, therefore, as your heavenly Father is perfect.*
> Matthew 5:48 (NIV)

Paul taught that the body of the born-again believer is the new temple of the Holy Spirit. This teaching does not preclude that demons can be somewhere "in the temple." It just means that demons cannot be in a Christian's Holy of Holies—the born-again regenerated human spirit. Christians can still have demons in the other parts of their bodily temples. Christians can have demons in their Holy Place, which is the soul. And, Christians can have demons in their Outer Court, which is the physical encasement, or body.

The Body-is-the-Temple Argument does not prove that a Christian can't have a demon. A Christian, whose body is the temple of the Holy Spirit, can indeed have demons inside the walls of his or her temple.

# Chapter 7

# Objection #3:

# *A New Creation in Christ Can't Have a Demon*

(New-Creation-in-Christ Argument)

*Therefore, if anyone is in Christ, **he is a new creation**; old things have passed away; behold, all things have become new.*
2 Corinthians 5:17 (NKJV)

Sometimes, an NDMC will see us casting demons out of Christians on our YouTube channel. Many of these NDMC's—Christians who do not sit with people to do Session Deliverance and most likely engage in no deliverance whatsoever—will sincerely wonder how this is theologically possible. They will ask, "If a Christian is a new creation, then how is it possible that he can have a demon?" Without even realizing it, these individuals hold to the NDMC position of the *New-Creation-in-Christ Argument*.

*Mark Chase*

The following is an example of one of these individuals posing this sincere question in one of the comment sections of our ministry YouTube channel:

ja▬commented: "I do not understand. If this man is a new believer in Jesus as his Lord and Savior, why does he have demons? Aren't we new creations in Christ and all things are new?

6 days ago

## *The Son of a Deliverance Minister*

I once had a conversation with the son of an anointed deliverance minister from the Caribbean. It is interesting because, while the father has a powerful ministry of healing and deliverance that serves people from his island nation, his son has become a staunchly anti-deliverance ministry NDMC. For this deliverance minister's son, it is not only theologically incorrect to say that a Christian can have a demon, but it is also blasphemous.

As I spoke to him, I realized that he had pretty much rejected the ministry of deliverance altogether and that he had a particular loathing for the "demonology" of his father. By using this word, he, of course, was insinuating that his dad had an unhealthy obsession with demons instead of Jesus. This, by the way, is a common attack of the NDMC against ministers of deliverance. NDMC's will accuse the deliverance minister of being more interested in Jesus's teachings on Satan, Jezebel, and Mammon than on the Gospel itself. The deliverance minister responds by pointing out that if Jesus felt the need to teach on demons, then this topic must be important and therefore worthy of study.

When I asked this deliverance minister's son to show me a verse that would prove that Christians can't have demons, he smiled in confidence, flipped through his Bible, and began to read:

*Therefore, if anyone is in Christ, the **new creation** has come: The old has gone, the new is here!* 2 Corinthians 5:17 (NIV)

But what does Paul mean in this verse? And does it really teach us that a Christian can't have a demon?

## Being Born Again Changes Us from the Inside

Think back to that beautiful moment when you were born again. You realized that you didn't want to go on sinning anymore. God's word touched you. You fell in love with Jesus. You realized just how sinful sin was, and you suddenly feared the Lord. You realized that you needed a Savior to deliver you from the Hell that you rightfully deserved. You did a one-eighty. You repented and turned away from sin. Just like Brian in Chapter 4, you cried out to God and confessed Jesus as Lord and believed in your heart that God raised Him from the dead. Instantly, everything changed.

At that very moment, the Spirit of God rushed into you and changed you. The Holy Spirit took up residence in your own spirit. In some mysterious and beautiful way, His Spirit gave birth to a new spirit in you (John 3:3). You began to walk in newness of life.

The Holy Spirit now dwelling in you began to influence, transform, equip, guide, and shape who you are, what you desire, and even what you think. The chief of these desires being to be more and more like Jesus. You didn't want anything to do with your old self. In fact, you became repulsed when you thought about what you used to say, do and believe. You began to die to yourself. As you began to grow in faith, you desired more and more to root out every area of sin in your life. Your fear of the Lord grew every day. You began to carry your own cross...

What happened here? I will tell you. When you did this, you became a "new creation." You became a living witness to Paul's verse. Life became new to you, and you became a new creature. Old things—old desires, old priorities, old thought patterns, and old behaviors—had passed away, and all things had become new. You were born again in Jesus Christ!

However, can we or should we interpret Paul's "new creation" verse to mean that there can be no more demons inside of a born-again believer? Did Paul teach that all the demons that were there before being born again suddenly flew out? Let's answer these questions through the lens of our tripartite nature.

## Did God Give You a New Body at Conversion?

Does *"all things have become new"* mean that after conversion, you have been given a new physical body? Think back on your own born-again experience.

• Did you receive new skin, organs, brain, muscle, and a new nervous system when you made Jesus Lord?

• Did the ailments like arthritis, hair loss, and belly fat suddenly disappear when you got saved?

• Did your vision return to 20/20 when you converted?

I would say that, while possible (miraculous physical healings can and do happen during radical conversions according to God's sovereign good pleasure), these things most likely *did not* happen. In fact, the most likely scenario is that you had the same physical body issues *after* your conversion that you had a few seconds prior to your conversion to Christ.

So even though 2 Corinthians 5:17 clearly says, "**all** *things have become new*," we clearly see that the physical body isn't necessarily one of those things that becomes brand new.

## Did God Give You a New Soul at Conversion?

Did you receive a new soul upon your born-again experience? First, let's remember what the soul is. We saw earlier that the New Testament Greek word for soul is *psuché*. From this word, we get our modern words "psyche" and "psychology." According to Wikipedia, "Soul or psyche…comprises the mental abilities of a living being: reason, character, feeling, consciousness, memory, perception, thinking, etc."

## The Children's Bread

The soul is the mind, the heart, the will, our thoughts, feelings, and emotions. The soul is our "psychology." In fact, according to the *Penguin Dictionary of Psychology* (1995), the term "soul" is an obsolete secular term for the mind (page 739).

Therefore, I teach my students that the soul is the mind. Our soul is our thoughts, our feelings, our emotions, our consciousness, and "the heart." The soul is something that we can't fully define or comprehend scientifically. Regardless, the soul is the mind. The mind is the soul.

Now back to our question. Did you receive a new soul, or a new mind, when you were born again? If you are unsure, ask yourself the following questions:

• After I was born again, did every mental illness go away?

• Did the trauma of abuse, rejection, and molestation that I experienced as a child suddenly heal?

• Has my depression, impatience, fear, and anxiety disappeared?

• Has doubt and pride vanished from my mind?

• Did I gain back all the memories that I have lost over the years?

• Did my cognitive function increase after I was born again?

• Do I still experience unwanted evil thoughts, like thoughts of revenge, unforgiveness, blasphemy, and sexual perversion?

• Do I still hear those voices that discourage me and tell me to do evil things?

• Am I still being tormented in my mind?

If you are like most born-again believers, these things, if they were present beforehand, did *not* change or go away the moment you were born again. Once again, God can and does do miraculous sovereign healings of the mind at conversion according to His good pleasure. However, this is not the rule, nor is God obligated to heal every part of man's mind at his conversion. The healing of these things typically takes place over a lifetime during one's process of sanctification—which includes one's healing and deliverance.

## The Attacks on the Mind May Have Gotten Worse Since Being Born Again

If anything, things may have gotten *worse* in your mind since you gave your life to Jesus. This is also normal because when you switch sides, the devil frequently ups the intensity of his attacks. Satan is angry that you have defected and chosen to serve King Jesus now. He is trying desperately to get you back, as you were a prize for him. As a result, the battlefield of your mind might have gotten even bloodier and more violent since you repented of your rebellion against God and now serve as a soldier in His army.

In our ministry, we say it is a good thing when the attacks come. In fact, if you are *not* under attack, you need to question how much of a threat you really are to Satan. Bob Larson asks an excellent question of introspective self-analysis to his students and to those he ministers to: "Does Satan laugh or tremble when he hears your name?"

The attacks of the enemy are not without value. They serve to expose the presence of the enemy and to confirm that you are on the *right* path now. Here at Invicta Ministries, we teach the following aphorism: *If you're under attack, you're on the right track!*

People call my ministry and tell us about the different demonic manifestations that they are now experiencing, "Pastor Mark, I hear voices saying to hurt people, and I see dark shadows." To which I respond, "Good."

People are shocked to hear me say this. I then explain to them that the fact that they are experiencing and perceiving the demons is a good thing. It means that the demons are being forced out into the open and are being exposed. And this is good. We want demons to be exposed. We don't want their presence to be hidden.

*The Children's Bread*

When demons are exposed, we know we are on the correct path to expel these demons. We know that when demons are exposed, it is easier to find them, bind them, and cast them out! I also reassure them by reminding them that exposing evil is a mandate for every Christian believer (Ephesians 5:11). What we *don't* want, I tell my PRM's, is for the demons to subtly continue to do their evil handiwork unexposed and hidden. Hidden demons are much more of a danger than exposed demons.

## What Really Happens with the Soul at Conversion

So, when we are born again, we don't suddenly receive a brand-new mind (soul). What happens instead is that the Holy Spirit begins a work in us to *transform* and *renew* our minds.

*And do not be conformed to this world, but **be transformed by the renewing of your mind**, that you may prove what is that good and acceptable and perfect will of God.* Romans 12:2 (NKJV)

I teach that this transformation and renewal takes place over the course of our lifetimes as followers of Jesus. It doesn't take place all at once. It will be a process. Our transformations happen *gradually* as we submit more and more to Him. The longer we earnestly follow Jesus, the more our minds will become like His.

The following two Biblical accounts demonstrate how the born-again believer does not receive a new mind, or soul, at conversion.

### *Ananias and Sapphira*

The story of Ananias and Sapphira shows us how the born-again believer does not receive a new soul at conversion. Ananias and Sapphira were new Christians of the early church, yet they still had evil in their hearts. Remember that the "heart" is synonymic with "soul."

In the early church, new believers would sell their lands

and houses and give this money to the church. They would lay this money "at the Apostles' feet" (Acts 4:35), and this money would then be distributed to those in need.

Ananias and Sapphira were two of these new believers. They were born-again. We know this because they were part of "those who believed" (Acts 4:32). Later, Ananias and Sapphira agreed to sell a field that they owned and lay the proceeds of the sale at the Apostles' feet.

However, when it came time to deliver the pledged money to the Apostles, Ananias and his wife decided to lie and withhold some of the money for themselves. The Holy Spirit no doubt exposed this deceit to Peter, and the Apostle then rebuked Ananias. During this rebuke, Peter used language that described the literal spiritual state of Ananias's soul:

> *But Peter said, "Ananias, why has **Satan filled your heart** to lie to the Holy Spirit and keep back part of the price of the land for yourself?* Acts 5:3 (NKJV)

Ananias was a believer. He was one of "those who believed." Since this episode took place post-Pentecost, Ananias, therefore, had the indwelling Holy Spirit. Yet Peter said that Satan had "filled his heart." Again, recall that "heart" is a synonym of soul. So, how is it possible that Satan could fill the heart of a believer? I will tell you.

Just because Ananias was a believer with a regenerated spirit, his mind (his soul) still had wickedness. Even though Ananias was a new creation in Christ, he had not received a new mind. His soul still had wickedness. He was a new believer, and his mind was now being transformed by the Holy Spirit, but his mind still had evil. Peter said that Satan had "filled his heart."

In addition to his wicked mind, I believe that it is quite possible that Ananias had demon spirits in his soul. These demons "filled his heart" in order to influence him to lie. If this were the case, then Ananias would be a clear example of a Biblical Christian with indwelling demons.

*The Children's Bread*

Since we don't know about Ananias's previous life before Christ, I cannot speculate too much regarding possible points of entry for demons. Perhaps demons could have entered into Ananias because of earlier fraudulent real estate deals. Or maybe Ananias got demons the moment he lied to the Holy Spirit. Regardless, God struck down both Ananias and his wife Sapphira in judgment.

The important thing here is that both Ananias and his wife had the same soul with the same wicked thoughts after their conversion as they had before receiving Christ. While their spirits had been reborn, neither Ananias nor his wife received a new soul at conversion.

## Simon the Sorcerer

Simon the Sorcerer is another example of a Biblical character who was born again yet still had the same wicked mind that he had before his conversion. Before he was born again, Simon the Sorcerer went around amazing people with his witchcraft:

*But there was a certain man called Simon, who previously **practiced sorcery** in the city and **astonished the people** of Samaria, claiming that he was someone great.   Acts 8:9 (NKJV)*

Witchcraft is real. It existed two thousand years ago, and it exists today. Essentially, witchcraft is harnessing the power of demons to do demonic supernatural acts. It is making sacrifice to demons so that they will work for man. These demonic works are what the Bible calls "false signs and wonders" (2 Thessalonians 2:9). When witches do witchcraft, they have demons inside of them that give them the power to carry out these supernatural feats. They are sold out to Satan and have traded their eternity in order to work "miracles" as they see fit.

In my ministry, I have worked with people who used to practice divination, astrology, angel healing, shamanism, *Santería, Palería, Obeah, Voodoo, Candomblé, Umbanda, Sangoma, Eddogo, Yoruba,* Wicca, and countless other forms of witchcraft.

The one thing these individuals all have in common is that they all had demons. They had demons that permitted them to work in the dark arts of witchcraft. And Simon the Sorcerer was no different. He had demons too. Then Simon heard the Gospel and got born again:

> *Then **Simon himself also believed**; and when he was baptized he continued with Philip, and was amazed, seeing the miracles and signs which were done.* Acts 8:13 (NKJV)

I can say without a doubt that in order to be able to "astonish the people" (again, Acts 8:9) with magic, Simon had to have had demons. No question. There is no way he could have been so advanced in the magic arts and not have had indwelling demon spirits to facilitate his magic. He very well could have had spirits of Witchcraft, Jezebel, Hecate, Illusion, Python, and perhaps Divination or Psychic Power.

And since demons don't all just fly out at conversion, this means that Simon most likely still had holdover demons from his witchcraft past, even after he was born again. Unless Simon received some form of Sovereign Deliverance upon being born again—the Bible doesn't say—he could be yet another example of an early Biblical Christian with demons.

Regardless, Simon still had a wicked mind. Even though Simon was a Christian with a new spirit, his mind had not yet been transformed. Even though he had believed and been baptized and now followed the Apostles, there was still wickedness in his soul.

We know that Simon still had wickedness in his soul because when Simon saw the Apostles laying hands on folks to baptize them in the Holy Spirit, he envied this power and offered them money to be able to do it too:

> *And when Simon saw that through the laying on of the apostles' hands the Holy Spirit was given, **he offered them money**, saying, "Give me this power also, that anyone on whom I lay hands may receive the Holy Spirit."* Acts 8:18-19 (NKJV)

Here we can see that Simon's heart was just as wicked as it was before believing on Jesus for salvation. He still had the Satanic thinking pattern of being able to make deals for spiritual power. This method works with Satan, but not with God.

While his spirit was indeed reborn, he still had the same wicked heart as before. In other words, Simon didn't get a new soul at conversion. His heart, like every born-again believer's heart, would need to undergo a lifelong process of transformation by the Holy Spirit. It would take conviction by the Holy Spirit and time for Simon's mind to be transformed into the mind of Christ. Now, let's look at what *does* become new at conversion.

## We Are Given a New Spirit at Our Conversion

At our spiritual rebirth in Christ—when we repent of sin and confess Jesus as Lord—we receive a new Spirit. Our *spirit* is what is made new when we are born again. When we are born again, we are born of God's Spirit. Our new spirit is God's Spirit, the Spirit of Jesus, the third Person of the Holy Trinity. The God of the universe now fills us, regenerates our own spirits, and inhabits us. Thank You, Jesus!

There are many reasons why God gives us His Spirit. He does it to mark us as His, to seal us, to guide us, to equip and empower us to carry out the assignments He has for us, and to teach us how to live our new lives in the imitation of His Son.

This Spirit allows us to hold captive those thoughts that are obscene, violent, and blasphemous and to refocus our minds on Christ. The Holy Spirit even enables us to have the mind of Christ Himself, which means to think like Jesus.

The indwelling Holy Spirit begins to influence our souls, changing our hearts from stone to flesh (Ezekiel 36:26) even changing our wills. Take a moment now to observe the cover of this book. You can see how the Holy Spirit (depicted as the brilliant white light) emanates into the other parts of our tripartite being—into our bodies and souls. By doing this, He is influencing, healing, and transforming our bodies and souls. The red lights, incidentally, represent the indwelling demons.

God's indwelling Spirit allows us to overcome our love of self, our self-righteousness, self-sufficiency, and our self-justification. God's indwelling Spirit is what allows us to have the same ministry as Jesus and to do even greater things than He did.

The Holy Spirit gives us a new purpose for a new life. And with His Spirit, His word, the Bible, begins to make sense in a way that it never did before. Clearly, at conversion, we receive a new Spirit. **This new Spirit is what makes us a new creation!**

Now, back to the original question. Does the fact that we are new creations mean that we can no longer have demons in our bodies and minds? No, of course, it doesn't mean this.

The fact that we are new creations means that we have been given a new Spirit. We now have God's Spirit in us. This new Spirit changes us, influences us, and makes us look more like Jesus. Paul's statement that we are new creations does not mean that we suddenly become demon-free the moment we confess Christ. Nowhere in the Bible does it say that when a person is born again, every demon instantly vanishes. No Bible verse says that conversion is a substitute for exorcism. Instead, the deliverance of Jesus will take place *little by little. The Little-by-Little Verse*:

*And the Lord your God will drive out those nations before you **little by little**; you will be unable to destroy them at once, lest the beasts of the field become too numerous for you.*
Deuteronomy 7:22 (NKJV)

A born-again believer is indeed a new creation. He is a new *spiritual* creation. His old dead spiritual self has been regenerated, and now the Spirit of the living God dwells within him. However, just because the Christian is a new creation doesn't mean that he is exempt from the need for deliverance from demons. Therefore, the New-Creation-in-Christ Argument is false.

# Chapter 8

# Objection #4:

# A Christian Can't Be "Possessed" by a Demon

(Christians-Can't-Be-Possessed Argument)

When some NDMC's hear about the type of ministry I do, they respond by affirming, "The people you deliver from demons can't be born again since a born-again Christian cannot be *possessed* by a demon." This is the *Christians-Can't-Be-Possessed Argument*.

It is one of the more frustrating objections to deal with since overcoming it requires not only an understanding of theology but also of semantics and *Biblical translation*.

The (mis)use of the word "possessed" in our modern English Bibles can be traced back to two early English-language Bibles. These are the Tyndale Bible (1535) and the King James Bible (1611). Both translations utilized the word "possessed" in certain New Testament verses regarding demonization and deliverance.

In these early English versions of the Bible, the writers

chose to translate certain ancient Greek expressions as "possessed" and "demon-possessed" and "possessed by a demon" instead of opting for more literal translations such as "demonized," "to have a demon" or "to be troubled by a demon."

I believe that as a result of the Tyndale and King James Bibles, many modern English translations followed suit and began to use the word "possessed" in their versions as well. I don't believe that anyone ever questioned it. Translators, scholars, and readers just assumed that "possessed" was the best word for the job when it came to describing people with demons. They conjectured that where there are demons, there must be possession.

Interestingly, an even earlier English translation Bible, the Wycliffe Bible (1382-1395), did not use the word "possessed."

To illustrate how the first English-language Bibles dealt with describing people with demons, I have compared one "demon possession" verse in all three early English translations. Then I will show the same verse in the original ancient Greek.

## Matthew 8:28

As I mentioned, the editors of the oldest English language Bible, the 14th-century Wycliffe Bible, chose not to use the word "possessed." Instead, they opted for *hadden deuelis* which is Old English for "had devils." Here is the entire verse:

> *And whanne Jhesus was comun ouer the watir in to the cuntre of men of Gerasa, twey men metten hym, that **hadden deuelis**, and camen out of graues, ful woode, so that noo man myyte go bi that weie.* Matthew 8:28 (Wycliffe Bible)

Later, in the 16th century, the Tyndale translators decided to adopt the word "possessed." I believe that by them opting for this word, the *linguistic* seed of the modern debate of whether a Christian can have a demon was sown:

> *And when he was come to ye other syde in to ye coutre of ye Gergesites ther met him two **possessed** of devylles which came out of the graves and were out of measure fearce so yt no ma myght go by that waye.* Matthew 8:28 (Tyndale Bible)

## The Children's Bread

And then in the 17th century, the King James Bible continued the Tyndale custom of using the word "possessed":

*And when he was come to the other side into the country of the Gergesenes, there met him two **possessed** with devils, coming out of the tombs, exceeding fierce, so that no man might pass by that way.* Matthew 8:28 (King James Bible)

I believe that the King James Bible has had the greatest influence on the modern translations that we use today. Many modern translations, such as the NIV, have since continued the use of the word "possessed":

*When he arrived at the other side in the region of the Gadarenes, two **demon-possessed** men coming from the tombs met him. They were so violent that no one could pass that way.*
Matthew 8:28 (NIV)

However, when we return to the oldest Greek manuscripts that we have—the codices—the word "possessed" is not present. For example, in the 4th century ancient Greek of the *Codex Sinaiticus*, we see that Matthew 8:28 does not contain the Greek word "possessed," nor does it contain any word that should be translated as "possessed." Here is Matthew 8:28 in the *Codex Sinaiticus*:

και ελθοντων αυ των εις το περα εις την χωραν τω γαζαρηνων υπη τησαν αυτω δυο **δεμονιζομενοι** [*daimonizomenoi*] εκ των μνημιω εξερχομενοι χα λεποι λιαν ωστε.
Matthew 8:28 (*Codex Sinaiticus*)

As can be seen, the *Codex Sinaiticus* does not use the word "possessed." Instead, it utilizes a form of *daimonizomai* (Strong's Concordance Word #1139) which means "demonized" or "under the power of a demon." More on this excellent word later.

*Mark Chase*
## *The Word "Possessed" Creates Confusion Since Christians Are Possessed by God*

I can say from experience that the modern use of the word "possessed" in the Bible has created much confusion among the NDMC's. It even causes misunderstandings among those who work in the ministry of deliverance. The use of this word muddles the subject of who exactly needs deliverance. Do nonbelievers need deliverance? Believers? Both?

Most Bible readers know that Christians belong to God. They know that they are possessed by *Him*. They know that they were bought at a price (1 Corinthians 6:20) and are, therefore, no longer their own. They know that they were ransomed (1 Timothy 2:6).

So, when the average Christian sees the word "possessed" printed in his Bible, confusion arises. Since he knows he is possessed by God, he, therefore, assumes that anyone who is possessed by a demon is not, and cannot, be possessed by God. He would say, "One cannot be possessed by both God and Satan at the same time. Possession implies singular ownership."

Then he makes the connection with *deliverance* from demons. If the people who are possessed by demons are not possessed by God, then deliverance from demons can only be for those who are not possessed by God. In other words, deliverance must only be for the *nonbelievers*. Therefore, only the nonbelievers need to be delivered from demons since only the nonbelievers can be possessed by demons.

In this way, the use of the word "possessed" causes great confusion. The use of this bad word strengthens the misconception that deliverance is only for nonbelievers since they believe the Bible itself, which is the literal word of God, is clearly telling them that only nonbelievers can be possessed by demons.

## *The Word "Possessed" Creates Antagonism Toward the Ministries of Deliverance*

In addition to the above confusion, the word "possessed" has also created an antagonism towards the ministry of deliverance by the "mainstream" North American NDMC church.

The antagonism begins when we deliverance ministries try to tell these churches, "Hey NDMC church, we work with Christians who have demons. There might even be members of your own church that need deliverance." The NDMC church responds with, "Hey deliverance ministry, what you are saying is not sound doctrine. No one in our church needs deliverance since no one in our church can be possessed by demons. Everyone in our church is possessed by God." They then quote Scripture to show their point:

> *And **you are Christ's**, and Christ is God's.*
> 1 Corinthians 3:23 (NKJV)

And:

> *My Father, who has given them to Me, is greater than all; and **no one is able to snatch them out of My Father's hand**.*
> John 10:29 (NKJV)

As a result, the NDMC church dismisses the deliverance ministry as unscriptural, heretical, and maybe even blasphemous. In hurt and anger, the NDMC church snaps, "How dare you accuse some of our members of being possessed by demons! And what do you mean that you *sit with Christians* to cast out their demons?" At this point, the NDMC church breaks fellowship with the deliverance ministry. All this over an incorrectly translated word from the original Greek. Satan is celebrating.

In North America, you will rarely see deliverance ministries invited into churches to teach or to conduct deliverance. Most deliverance ministries must create their own space by renting a dedicated location, starting their own church, working out of home, or by utilizing hotel meeting rooms. Here in the U.S.A., I know of only a handful of established deliverance ministries that are allowed to work out of, and be officially associated with, an actual physical church.

## Every Deliverance Minister Knows That Christians Are Possessed by God

No deliverance minister that I know of would ever claim that a born-again Christian is not possessed by God. Those in the ministry of deliverance know that we are possessed by God. We praise God that He possesses us. Likewise, we know that no demon can *possess,* or own, a born-again Christian. Jesus paid our ransom. He owns us. We are held securely in the Father's hand. Thank You, Jesus! However, Christians can *have* demons on the inside that need to be cast out. These demons can be in the Christian's mind or body—but not in their regenerated spirit.

## Possessed Is an Extreme Word

Another great problem with the word "possessed" is that for the modern English speaker, it is such an extreme word. By using the word "possessed," people don't just *have* a demon; they now must be *possessed* by a demon. They must be fully taken over by the demon. They can't just be troubled by demons or tormented by demons; they need to be *possessed* by them.

When the word "possessed" is utilized, there can be no middle ground. The individual is either possessed or they do not have any demons at all.

## Subtle Demonization

When the word "possessed" is used, there is no room for, what I call, *subtle demonization*. Subtle demonization describes the bulk of our deliverance cases in the modern ministry of deliverance.

We see in the modern ministry of deliverance that most

demons work subtly, quietly, and insidiously in their victims to carry out their assignments.

These assignments include ruining relationships, marriages, finances, health, ministries, as well as hindering emotions and destinies. We rarely see raging, foaming-at-the-mouth, chair-throwing, screaming, growling, red-eyed zombies. We do see cases of extreme demonization from time to time; however, these cases are much fewer in number. What we do see is a lot of subtle demonization. Some common symptoms of subtle demonization include the following:

- Difficulty reading and understanding the Bible
- Difficulty worshiping God
- Unreasonable fear or rage
- Thoughts of suicide
- Constant strife in relationships
- Separation and alienation within families
- Patterns of divorce
- Unexplainable sicknesses
- Sensation of choking or heaviness on the shoulders or chest
- Repeating patterns of failure in life
- And many, many others…

Demonization can be so subtle that we see pastors, grandmothers, and even young children get set free from demons that they didn't even know they had. Many Christian victims of demonization don't know for sure that they have demons until a deliverance minister forces their demons up into open manifestation during a deliverance session. Yes, the raging demoniacs are out there, and we minister to them. But in our caseloads, they are the exception, not the rule.

## *Semantics*

The problem with the word "possessed" is not so much theological as it is semantic and translational. It is a problem of bad word selection. The word "possessed" creates a linguistic hang-up that throws a wrench into the system. I personally believe that the enemy threw that wrench, knowing the problems it would create.

However, when we remove this poorly translated word and use literal and correct translations like "have a demon," "to be troubled by a demon," or "demonized," the problem instantly vanishes. The confusion evaporates like dew on a summer morning.

We can then move on and make our case: Born-again Christians are indeed possessed by God, and no one can snatch a Holy Spirit-filled, born-again Christian from God's hand; however, a Holy Spirit-filled Christian can also have a demon on the inside too. A Holy Spirit-filled Christian can be demonized. A Christian with the Holy Spirit can have a need for deliverance.

We understand this since the Holy Spirit is in the born-again believer's spirit while the demons are in the separate locations of the body and mind (soul).

## *The P-Word*

Here at my ministry, I refer to the word "possession" as the "p-word." I treat it almost as if it were a vulgar, unclean word. In fact, it is a word that I do not permit to be used within the walls of my ministry as a synonym for "to have a demon." I do not permit my ministry Leaders to use this word, and I teach my students to avoid this word if at all possible.

The word "possessed" is not part of my own personal understanding of how deliverance works. There are four reasons why I do not use the p-word in my ministry:

1. By using the extreme p-word, great confusion arises as to who truly possesses the born-again believer. After all, if God possesses the Christian, how is it be possible then for a demon spirit to now possess this same believer? This confusion hinders the members of the Church from receiving the deliverance that they need.

2. Using the p-word creates antagonism between the NDMC's and the ministries of deliverance. This antagonism stems from the misunderstanding that the NDMC thinks we are calling anyone who has a demon "demon-possessed." Since they rightly know that they are possessed by God, the NDMC then rejects the ministry of deliverance altogether as teaching unsound doctrine.

3. The p-word doesn't describe the majority of the demonization that we deliverance ministries see in day-to-day ministry. Most demonization that we see in our daily caseloads are manifestations of subtle demonization, not raging, over-the-top demonization.

4. And finally, the word "possessed" is not in the original ancient Greek of the New Testament. God simply didn't use this word.

## *Linda's Pastor Says She Can't Be Possessed*

Before we delve deeper into the original ancient Greek of the New Testament, let's read about a precious Christian woman named Linda. Her pastor, Pastor Rick, is definitely hung up on the p-word—so much so that it causes him to misdiagnose his church member's problem.

Linda is a born-again believer from Miami, Florida. She knows she is born again because fifteen years ago, she repented of her sin—mostly sexual immorality and drug use. When Linda was a teenager, she was molested by her own father. This caused her to spiral into a life of depression, promiscuity, drug use, and even some stripping and prostitution.

In her late 20's, God gave her the grace of repentance, and she broke out of her old lifestyle and made Jesus Lord and Savior. She was baptized in water at a Spirit-filled church headed by Pastor

Rick. She has been at this church ever since.

Although Linda has not backslidden into sexual sin, she does suffer heavily from anxiety and depression, for which she takes an anti-depressant called Effexor. She also has suicidal ideation. And there is something else she deals with that is so embarrassing that she can't even muster the courage to tell her female accountability partner at church.

Linda secretly suffers from *demonic sexual harassment and violation* (DSHV). Some nights when she is alone in her bed, she feels something touching her private area. Occasionally, she feels as though something totally unwanted were even penetrating her. She cries out in angry, shameful disgust and pleads the Blood of Jesus. The attack goes away—for a while.

After reading an online article about spiritual warfare, Linda began to suspect that she might be dealing with demonic torment, specifically, something called "spiritual husband" or "Incubus." But she wasn't sure since she had never heard Pastor Rick teach on this topic or *any* topic related to demons for that matter.

One night, she began to Google "freedom from demons" and "How do you know if you have a demon?" and ultimately, "Can a Christian have a demon?" Linda came across a deliverance ministry called Invicta Ministries, which was located about twenty-five miles north of her in Fort Lauderdale. After praying and consulting the Holy Spirit, she decided to make the trip up and attend Invicta's Friday night public deliverance meeting.

At this meeting, two things impacted her. First, during the teaching portion of the meeting, she learned that deliverance ministry is for *Christians* just like her. The leader of the ministry, Pastor Mark, even called deliverance "the children's Bread." He was referring to the story of the Syrophoenician Woman's Daughter, where Jesus metaphorically used this term to refer to the fact that deliverance from demons is the spiritual "bread" that is meant first and foremost for the children of God. You will learn about this story in Chapter 10.

## The Children's Bread

Pastor Mark reminded those in attendance that under the current Covenant of Grace, the children of God are those that call on the Name of Jesus for salvation. In other words, the Christians.

Linda thought this was interesting because before going to this public deliverance meeting, Linda would have assumed that a Christian simply couldn't have any bad spirits by virtue of being a Christian. She would have thought that having demons was for the "evil people"—rapists, child molesters, murderers, terrorists, kidnappers, Satan worshipers, Hitler, drug dealers, and such.

The second thing that impacted Linda was that she witnessed, with her own eyes, demons speaking, cursing, hissing, and manifesting in other ways—*through Christians*.

Linda knew that they were Christians because she could discern it. Some spoke in tongues after their healing, while others went into spontaneous prayer of thanksgiving and worship after their demons were cast out. Others quoted Scripture in celebration.

The following week, Linda made an appointment with Pastor Rick to ask him about what he thought about her experience at this deliverance ministry. She also wanted to know if he thought that she should receive deliverance herself. She thought that certainly, her pastor should be the one to help her if she did have demons.

"Linda," her pastor explained, "you are born again. God has forgiven you. There is, therefore, now no more condemnation for those who are in Christ Jesus. It is possible that Satan is attacking you from the outside, tempting you to sin, accusing you, and reminding you of your past life of sin. But you don't need deliverance. No Christian does. Deliverance is only for the demon-possessed people who don't have Jesus in their hearts. If you want to see people who are really possessed by demons, sign up for our upcoming church mission trip to the Dominican Republic. That's where you'll see real demonic possession."

Then Linda explained what she saw and learned at the public deliverance meeting. She even mustered the courage to mention the demeaning and humiliating sexual attacks that she experiences at night.

Pastor Rick responded that Linda was probably just having flashbacks of her father's sexual abuse. Then he continued, "What you are saying is spiritually impossible. A born-again believer cannot be possessed by a demon. Do you know why? God's word says that He possesses us and therefore no demon of Hell could ever possess us." Pastor Rick continued, "Linda, you are a Christian. You don't act like the possessed people in the Bible. When people are possessed, everyone can tell. It is obvious. Possessed people roam around in graveyards, murder people, foam at the mouth, and fall into fires. You don't do these things. Everyone can tell just by looking at you that you are a sweet and quiet person—not a demon-possessed person. Therefore, you can't be possessed by a demon. You don't need some exorcism." Pastor Rick then opened his Bible and quoted the words of Jesus:

> *And I give them eternal life, and they shall never perish;* **neither shall anyone snatch them out of My hand.**   John 10:28 (NKJV)

"You see, God possesses you, not Satan. And you can't be possessed by both God and Satan at the same time. If Satan did possess you, then you would be a slave to him. But the fact of the matter is that now you are a slave to God." Then he flipped over to Romans and quoted Paul:

> *But now that you have been set free from sin and have become **slaves of God**, the benefit you reap leads to holiness, and the result is eternal life.*   Romans 6:22 (NKJV)

"There is your proof Linda. God owns you. You are His slave. You were bought at a price. You can't be possessed by a demon because you are already possessed by God."

Pastor Rick continued, "Linda, you just need to spend more time in the word. I strongly recommend that you attend our Wednesday night Bible study. You will be happy to know that we even teach on spiritual warfare once a month. There, you will see what real, Biblical, spiritual warfare is. Real spiritual warfare is not about chasing *demons*. Real spiritual warfare is about casting out the *Satanic thinking patterns* that are in your mind. These are the real demons—the Satanic beliefs that have been permitting to exist in your head. Also, once you get more into God's word, your mind won't be so fixated on demons. You will start learning self-control, and I guarantee you'll be able to get over all this."

At this point, Linda was becoming confused. That night, Linda went home and Googled again. This time she searched, "Can a Christian be *possessed* by a demon?" She was surprised to see so many websites that addressed this precise question. And most of what she saw online clearly said that NO, a Christian cannot be possessed by a demon.

Linda thought to herself, "I guess Pastor Mark over at Invicta Ministries was wrong. Pastor Rick is right. I can't be possessed by a demon since I am possessed by God."

Later that night, while she slept, Linda suffered a major spiritual attack. At around 3:00 AM, she felt her whole body become paralyzed. She felt a heavy weight on her chest. Linda could feel someone, or something, breathing by her ear, and something invisible was violating her private area.

## *The Ancient Greek of the New Testament*

For whatever reason, God chose Greek as the language of the New Testament. In other words, the oldest versions that we have today of the New Testament were written in ancient Greek. Two of these are the *Codex Vaticanus* (circa 300-325) and the *Codex Sinaiticus* (circa 330-360).

The early English Bibles (Wycliffe, Tyndale, King James), as well as our modern Bibles, are essentially translations that come directly or indirectly from these ancient Greek codices.

*Mark Chase*

## *How the Original Greek New Testament Writers Wrote About People with Demons*

In the original ancient Greek of the New Testament, there are exactly four different ways that the Scripture writers used to describe people who had demons:

1. ***Daimonizomai*** (Strong's Concordance Word #1139)

This word literally means "demonized," "to be under the influence of a demon," or "to be under the power of a demon." I believe that *daimonizomai* describes an indwelling demonic presence precisely. Someone who has an indwelling demon is demonized. She is under the influence, or power, of that demon. *Daimonizomai* can also be inflected to mean "demoniac," depending on the grammatical context.

An example of the King James writers using the word "possessed" in the place of a form of the ancient Greek *daimonizomai* is the following:

*And at even, when the sun did set, they brought unto him all that were diseased, and them that were **possessed** with devils.*
Mark 1:32 (King James Bible)

And the older Tyndale Bible, which also utilizes the word "possessed":

*And at even when the sunne was downe they brought to him all that were diseased and them that were **possessed** with devyls.*
Mark 1:32 (Tyndale Bible)

The even older Wycliffe Bible doesn't use the p-word but uses the Old English *hadden*, which we saw earlier. It means "had" in modern English. The word after *hadden* is *fendis* which signifies our modern word "fiends," which is synonymic for "demons":

*But whanne the euentid was come, and the sonne was gon doun, thei brouyten to hym alle that weren of male ese, and hem that **hadden** fendis.* Mark 1:32 (Wycliffe Bible)

2. **Echó** (Strong's Concordance Word #2192)

This word means "to have" or "to hold." Thankfully, the writers of the King James Bible translated *echó* only once as "possessed." This happened in the Book of Acts:

*And it came to pass, as we went to prayer, a certain damsel **possessed** with a spirit of divination met us, which brought her masters much gain by soothsaying.* Acts 16:16 (King James Bible)

However, *echó* is frequently translated by modern Bible editors as "possessed." For example:

*Many of them said, "He is **demon-possessed** and raving mad. Why listen to him?"* John 10:20 (NIV)

And:

*Some said, "He's **demon possessed** and out of his mind. Why listen to a man like that?"* John 10:20 (NLT)

The English Standard Version translates this verse correctly and avoids the confusion of the p-word:

*Many of them said, "He **has a demon**, and is insane; why listen to him?"* John 10:20 (ESV)

3. **Ochleó** (Strong's Concordance Word #3791)

This is a wonderfully descriptive word that means to be troubled, tormented, or vexed. I like this word because it describes very well what demons do to people. Demons trouble people, they torment people, and they vex them. Here the King James Bible, as do most of the modern translations, do a good job:

*There came also a multitude out of the cities round about unto Jerusalem, bringing sick folks, and them which were **vexed with unclean spirits**: and they were healed every one.*
Acts 5:16 (King James Bible)

Also, well-translated from the original Greek:

*Crowds gathered also from the towns around Jerusalem, bringing their sick and those **tormented by impure spirits**, and all of them were healed.* Acts 5:16 (NIV)

However, the editors of the New Living Translation bring back the confusion:

*Crowds came from the villages around Jerusalem, bringing their sick and those **possessed** by evil spirits, and they were all healed.* Acts 5:16 (NLT)

4. The Greek structure **man + demon**.

In these cases, there is an absence of any special word. This is simply an old Greek syntactic structure of putting two words together that conveys the meaning of someone having a demon.

Thankfully, there are no examples of this structure being translated as "possession" in the King James Bible. However, some modern translations can't stay away from the p-word and do translate this structure as "possessed." Let's look at Mark 1:23. First, here it is in the King James Bible translated properly:

*And there was in their synagogue a **man with an unclean spirit**; and he cried out.* Mark 1:23 (King James Bible)

Then, some popular modern translations add the p-word, causing confusion:

*Just then a man in their synagogue who was **possessed** by an impure spirit cried out.* Mark 1:23 (NIV)

And:

*Suddenly, a man in the synagogue who was **possessed** by an evil spirit began shouting.* Mark 1:23 (NLT)

*The Children's Bread*

## *Summary of Linguistic Examples*

For those who would like to examine this issue in more detail, here are most of the New Testament verses that refer to someone having a demon, organized by the original Greek terminology.

Keep in mind that while many of these have been translated as "possessed" by either the King James authors or the editors of the modern Bible translations, the word "possessed" is not in the original Greek New Testament codex manuscripts.

| **echó** to have or to hold | **daimonizomai** demonized; to be under the influence or power of a demon | **ochleó** to disturb; to trouble; or to vex | **man + demon** |
|---|---|---|---|
| Mark 7:25 | Matthew 4:24 | Acts 5:16 | Mark 1:23 |
| Mark 9:17 | Matthew 8:16 | | Mark 5:2 |
| Luke 4:33 | Matthew 8:28 | | Luke 7:21 |
| Luke 7:33 | Matthew 8:33 | | |
| John 7:20 | Matthew 9:32 | | |
| John 10:20 | Matthew 12:22 | | |
| Acts 8:7 | Matthew 15:22 | | |
| Acts 16:16 | Mark 1:32 | | |
| Acts 19:13 | Mark 5:15 | | |
| | Mark 5:16 | | |
| | Mark 5:18 | | |
| | Luke 8:36 | | |
| | John 10:21 | | |

## *Semantic Change?*

Why did the original Tyndale and King James translators get it wrong by introducing the p-word into the English language Bible? It is quite possible that in 16th and 17th century English, the word "possessed" had a different connotation than it has today. This is certainly plausible as the meaning of words does evolve over time. In the study of linguistics, this phenomenon is known as *semantic change*. Therefore, it is quite possible that the whole problem of the p-word has to do with how the modern ear hears the word "possessed" versus how the 16th and 17th-century ear heard this same word.

In addition, we need to keep in mind that the Tyndale and King James Bibles were written long before Hollywood popularized the word "possessed." Hollywood brought this word to pop culture when they started making their exorcism horror movies. These movies heavily utilized the p-word and made a mockery of the real ministry of deliverance.

Perhaps by using the word "possessed," the King James writers meant to say that an individual possessed the demon and not the other way around. Sort of like how we say now, "I *have* (possess) a cold." Certainly, we would never say that a cold *has* us!

This would make sense grammatically. However, the problem with using the p-word is that the modern English-speaking brain hears this word and automatically assumes that if a person is "possessed," then he must be a raging, evil monster who, in no way, could ever be a real Christian. Like Pastor Rick alluded to, he must be like the Demoniac of Gadara, wandering around naked in the tombs, cutting himself with stones, and breaking the chains that he was restrained with.

## *The King James Bible Rationale*

Why did the Tyndale and King James translators use the p-word? I will give my opinion; however, I might offend some of the King James-only crowd.

I believe the King James writers got it wrong for the same reason that the editors of the new versions get it wrong today. I believe that Bible translators, both four hundred years ago and today, get it wrong for the same simple reason:

## The Children's Bread

*Bible translators and Bible editors most likely know **nothing** about the practical ministry of deliverance. Most Bible translators and Bible editors of today and centuries past are surely NDMC's.*

In other words, most Bible scholars, Bible translators, and Bible editors are very likely NDMC's. NDMC's are people who do not sit with individuals to conduct Session Deliverance and most likely do *zero* deliverance ministry at all. I strongly doubt that the Tyndale and King James Bible writers had any practical demon-casting experience. I would make the same assumption about the editors of the NIV, the ESV, the NKJV, etc.

For the Tyndale and King James writers, as well as the majority of modern Bible editors, the casting out of demons is surely a mysterious theological subject that can only be studied academically. They would most likely say that the casting out of demons was something that Jesus and His disciples did "back in the days of the Bible" and probably not something that belongs to the contemporary church—either the 16th or 21st-century church.

## *The Solution*

If we just remove the p-word from our Bibles and use more literal translations such as "demonized," "to have a demon," "a man with a demon," "tormented by a demon," etc., then I believe great progress can be made.

Without the p-word, we can eliminate the confusion about who actually possesses the born-again believer. And by doing this, we can bring the revelation to the Church that while Christians can *have* demons, they cannot be *possessed* by them. And since they can have demons, they, therefore, need deliverance from these demons.

Without the p-word, we can heal the antagonism between the mainstream NDMC church and the ministries of deliverance. Without the p-word, the NDMC's will not think that we deliverance ministers are calling them "possessed by demons" just because we recommend that they receive deliverance ministry.

Without the p-word, we can succeed in putting the ministry of deliverance into the churches where they belong.

Without the p-word, we can get on to accurately describing the subtle demonization which constitutes the majority of the cases of demonization that individuals suffer from. Without the p-word, we can begin to accurately translate the Bible with regards to verses relating to demonization.

If we delete the word "possessed" from our Bibles, the members of the NDMC churches who need spiritual healing have a better chance of overcoming the theological hurdle of Christian demonization. Perhaps then, they can finally begin to receive the spiritual relief—the deliverance from demons—that so many believers need.

And perhaps also, Christians will understand that having a demon is not the end of the world. Having a demon does not mean that he or she is unsaved. By eliminating the p-word, indwelling demons can be dealt with for what they are—a spiritual sickness that just needs the healing of Christ. And as this spiritual sickness is healed, the Christian can get on to doing what is really important, which is being obedient to the Great Commission.

So, if the original Greek says *echó*, then translate it, "to have a demon." If the Greek says, *daimonizomai*, then write, "under the influence or power of a demon" or "demonized." If the original text says *ochleó*, then translate it as "tormented by a demon." But please, let's stop using the word "possessed"!

## *Which Translation is Best?*

I do not endorse any one Bible version or translation. In fact, I use a variety of different translations—even translations that use the p-word—during my teaching and preaching. I use whatever does the best job in a given situation.

For example, I personally use different versions of the King James in my own ministry—even though the p-word is used in these versions. Its poetic beauty is stunning and powerful. There is wonderful tradition behind it. For me, classic Scriptures like

## The Children's Bread

Psalm 23 and the Lord's Prayer sound best when read from the classic King James.

The only point that I want to make here is that the word "possessed" is just not an appropriate translation for certain ancient Greek linguistic structures. It hurts the Church, and it certainly undermines the ministries of deliverance.

I have found in my own research that the following three modern English translations do the best job of NOT using the p-word in their texts:

*Young's Literal Translation (YLT)*, 1862-1898 by Robert Young

*Good News Translation* (GNT), 1976 by the American Bible Society

*Contemporary English Version* (CEV), 1995 by the American Bible Society

### Loaded Questions

A serious concern arises when the word "possessed" is used in a question related to demons and deliverance. When the p-word is used to ask a question about these topics, it automatically creates a loaded question.

A loaded question is a question that uses terminology that presupposes a certain fact or a certain answer. The classic loaded question goes like this, "Have you stopped beating your wife yet?" It is loaded since whether the husband answers yes or no, he is still implying that he beats or has beaten his wife.

Another example of a loaded question occurs when someone asks, *"Can a Christian be **possessed** by a demon?"* This question is loaded since it makes a dangerous, confusing, and fellowship-breaking presupposition. It presupposes only two possibilities: That one can be either *possessed* by a demon or that one is *not* possessed by a demon. There is no middle ground, no room for subtle demonization, and no other options. As a deliverance minister, I estimate that most (>90%) demonization that I encounter is subtle, sneaky, and can be quite difficult to observe. This is the *subtle demonization* that I spoke of earlier.

Asking if a Christian can be possessed by a demon is asking a loaded question. It makes an inaccurate assumption even before the question is answered. Already in Chapter 2, we saw how an excellent apologetics website uses the word "possessed" in its online teachings. In the next chapter, you will see how a major denomination uses this loaded question as the title to its position paper on the subject of whether a Christian can have a demon.

I do not believe that individuals ask this loaded question maliciously. I think they ask it from the standpoint of a simple lack of knowledge. Those who do not know about deliverance are typically the NDMC's. And NDMC's simply do not have practical experience or revelation in the area of deliverance ministry. NDMC's cannot appreciate the nature of real demonization, which is mostly subtle. NDMC's do not practice Session Deliverance, and most likely, conduct no deliverance whatsoever. If these NDMC's ever began to work in the ministry of deliverance (which I exhort them to do—see the final chapter of this book), I doubt that they would want to continue using the non-Biblical term "possessed" when asking about whether or not someone has a demon.

Here, I want to pause and remind the reader and the student of deliverance about something that I made clear in Chapter 1: We are never against the NDMC. We *are* against the devil. We must not fall into the trap of spiritual pride. Just because we have received the revelation that Christians can need deliverance doesn't mean that we are in any way superior to other Christians who haven't yet received this revelation. I teach my students to be humble and to bless the NDMC and thank the Lord for the great works for God's Kingdom that the NDMC churches and ministries do. Personally, I have been blessed countless times by different NDMC ministries. I have even attended and been blessed by NDMC churches.

I am even thankful for the NDMC apologetics websites that

affirm that Christians can't have demons. Perhaps they don't know about deliverance, but they do have many other great teachings on other important topics that have blessed me, and surely, countless others. As long as their teachings glorify Jesus, that is all that really matters. Therefore, gently instruct the NDMC, but always bless him!

## *So, Can a Christian Be Possessed by a Demon?*

Absolutely not. A Christian is already possessed by God. A Christian is a slave to God (Romans 6:22). And slaves are owned, or possessed, by their masters. Paul knew who possessed him. He knew that he was slave, or bondservant, of Jesus:

> *Paul, a **bondservant** of Jesus Christ, called to be an apostle, separated to the gospel of God.* Romans 1:1 (NKJV)

Therefore, a demon can never *possess* a Christian in any way. However, a Christian can certainly *have* a demon on the inside. Perhaps it can be said that a Christian *possesses* the demon, but I still won't use this word. It just sends the wrong message in our 21$^{st}$ century English.

For some reason, the Wycliffe writers knew not to use the word "possessed." They used the Old English *hadden* instead. It was the Tyndale, and later the King James writers, who set in motion the damaging practice of using the p-word. And since then, the practice of using this term has been heavily imitated by various modern Bible editors, Christian teachers, and Christian writers in general. The Tyndale and King James use of the word "possessed" has influenced the theology of countless multitudes of Christians regarding demons and how they indwell men. The use of this word has influenced many to believe that a Christian cannot have a demon on the inside.

However, the fact remains that a Christian *can* have a demonic spirit in his mind or body. A Christian *can* have a need for deliverance from this evil spirit. A Christian *can* be infected with a spiritual sickness that can only be cured by the words, "Go in the Name of Jesus Christ of Nazareth!"

## Can a Nonbeliever be Possessed by a Demon?

Maybe it is possible that a nonbeliever could be truly taken over, or possessed, by a demonic spirit. *Perhaps* demons can dwell in the spirit of an unsaved person (although I don't believe this to be possible). Perhaps without the Holy Spirit, a person could get to the point where a demon truly does *possess* an individual. I will leave this possibility open. After all, the Bible does say that those without salvation belong to the devil. Speaking to the Pharisees who wanted to murder Jesus, He said:

> ***You belong to your father, the devil****, and you want to carry out your father's desires. He was a murderer from the beginning, not holding to the truth, for there is no truth in him. When he lies, he speaks his native language, for he is a liar and the father of lies.*
> John 8:44 (NIV)

However, I will not delve into the issue of nonbelievers being possessed by demons since no one really makes an issue out of this. The issue that needs to be resolved is whether we should use the word "possessed" when referring to *Christians* with demons.

The deliverance ministries know that Christians can have demons and the Christians who come to the deliverance ministries for healing know that Christians can have demons. It is only the NDMC that refuses to confront this spiritual reality.

It is only the NDMC's—the ones who do not do Session Deliverance and most likely do no deliverance ministry at all—who equate "having a demon" with being "demon-possessed." And it is only the NDMC's who correlate demonization with a lack of salvation. The NDMC is technically correct, however, when he says, "A Christian cannot be *possessed* by a demon."

## Conclusion

The result of the introduction of the word "possessed" into some English versions of the Bible has been a victory for Satan and a setback for Christians who need deliverance. Whenever anyone equates "possessed by a demon" with "having a demon," a lot of confusion ensues.

Educated Christian NDMC teachers correctly proclaim that born-again Christians can't be possessed by a demon since they are already possessed by God. They also teach correctly that it is impossible to be possessed by both God and Satan at the same time.

However, the problem is not the NDMC's logic. The problem lies instead in their vocabulary. "Possessed by a demon" is not the same thing as "having a demon." The term "possessed" is not how God chose to describe indwelling demons when He inspired the original Greek New Testament texts. God used "demonized," and "to be troubled by a demon," and "to have a demon." God did not use the word "possessed." The term "possessed" is a later linguistic addition to the Bible. It is not in the original texts.

When the NDMC uses the word "possessed" in his argument, he is utilizing a word that God Himself did not use. When this word is utilized, great confusion and discord arise. As a result, many Christians with demons never get the precious deliverance that they really need. They can never break out of the semantic trap that Satan has them in. And in the case of Pastor Rob in Chapter 3, whole ministries can be destroyed.

In addition, the word "possessed" creates much disdain towards the ministries of deliverance by other Christians. It creates a division and antagonism between the NDMC's and the deliverance ministries. The NDMC's feel that we deliverance ministers are accusing fellow Christians of being *possessed* by demons when all we are saying is that it is possible for Christians to have demons and therefore have a need for deliverance. We ministers of deliverance are just saying to the NDMC church:

*"Look, you are saved. You are born again. But because of the spiritual symptoms that you are exhibiting, you might have demons too. And if you do have demons, we are not saying that you have lost your salvation. We are not implying that you never had salvation, to begin with. We are just saying that if you do have demons, then your demons need to be cast out in the Name of Jesus. All your demons didn't come out when you got saved. So, now as a believer, you need to be delivered from them. Only in this way can you start walking in the abundant spiritual life that God has ordained for you. Only in this way can you get on unhindered with the ministry that God has called you into."*

Perhaps if the word "possessed" were really in the Bible, we deliverance ministries would have to rethink our paradigms, practices, and theologies. After all, Pastor Rick's correct logic above would then make perfect sense: We couldn't be possessed by both God and a demon at the same time. However, the word "possessed" simply isn't in the Bible.

Therefore, the Christians-Can't-Be-Possessed Argument fails to prove that it is impossible for Christians to have indwelling demons that need to be expelled.

# Chapter 9

# Objection #5:

# My Denomination Says That Christians Can't Have Demons

By affirming that a Christian cannot have a demon, one is making a statement of *doctrine*. One is not quoting Scripture. One is not repeating the words of Paul or Peter. And one is certainly not quoting the red-lettered words of Christ.

There is no one verse or passage of Scripture that says, "A Christian can't have a demon." Nor is there a verse that reads, "The moment a person is born again, every demon flies out instantaneously."

When an NDMC (an individual, a ministry, a church, a seminary, or an entire denomination) professes that a Christian cannot have a demon, this NDMC is stating its *doctrine*. They are expressing their interpretation of Scripture that is projected through the lens of their personal opinion, personal experience, theological understanding, revelation received, and wishes about how things should or shouldn't be.

The Pharisees demonstrated their doctrine to Jesus. They were absolutely sure that they had never been in bondage to anyone. This was their doctrine. They told Jesus that by virtue of the fact that they were Abraham's descendants, it was therefore impossible for them to be in bondage (John 8:33). However, this was only their *interpretation* of how things were. It was their opinion. The Pharisees had not received the revelation of their bondage because they never invited the Holy Spirit to show them. Because we have the Bible, we know that the Pharisee's doctrine was wrong. Jesus knew they were wrong, and He corrected them.

When an NDMC declares that a Christian can't have a demon, he, like the Pharisees, is giving his *interpretation* of Scripture, and in a broader sense, he is giving his interpretation of reality itself. He is like the doctrinally proud Pharisees.

Interpretations of Scripture can also be influenced by not having all the facts. Lack of first-hand experience casting out demons can certainly influence a Bible teacher's opinion on the issue of whether or not a Christian can have a demon. This lack of experience doesn't build wisdom in the area of deliverance. It builds foolishness. It is foolish not to engage in the Great Commission mandate to deliver people. And it is foolish, not wise, to affirm the haughty position that a Christian can't have a demon on the inside.

I call on the NDMC's to just get out there and start casting out demons. By doing so, they will quickly see that the majority of those whom the Lord brings to them for deliverance will be *Christians*!

When NDMC's declare their doctrine that Christians cannot have demons by virtue of being Christian, they are demonstrating pride. They are also showing their unwillingness to see God's overriding pattern in all of Scripture:

### *God delivers those who belong to Him*

God's pattern was, is, and always will be that He delivers those who belong to Him. While it is true that God can and does deliver the unsaved as a sign to confirm His Word, this is not the prevailing pattern. The overriding pattern we see in the Bible is

## The Children's Bread

that God delivers *His* people. We see this Big Idea pattern throughout both Testaments of the Bible.

### Old Testament Examples of God Delivering His People

- We see it as Joseph, whom the Lord was with, was delivered from Pharaoh's prison (Genesis 41).
- We see it in the story of the Parting of the Red Sea and how God delivered Moses and the Israelites, who were the apple of His eye, from Pharaoh's chariots (Exodus 14).
- We see in the story of Esther how God delivered His people, the Jews, from the evil plan of Haman the Agagite (Esther 8-9).
- We see it in the story of Shadrach, Meshach, and Abednego, where He delivers His faithful servants from the fiery furnace of the King of Babylon (Daniel 3).
- We see in the story of the Battle of Mount Tabor how God delivered Deborah, her general Barak, and the Israelite army from 900 iron chariots of the Canaanite army led by Sisera (Judges 4).

### New Testament Examples of God Delivering His People

- We see it in the story of the deliverance of the Daughter of Abraham, who was delivered from a demon of infirmity (Luke 13).
- We see it in the story of the Multiplication, where more than 5,000 people were delivered from hunger (John 6).
- We see it in the story of Lazarus of Bethany, who Jesus loved and raised from the dead after being dead for four days (John 11).
- We see it in the story of the Lord using an angel to deliver one of the pillars of His Church, Peter, from Herod's prison (Acts 12).
- We see how God delivered the Philippian Jailer from suicide. Then God delivered him and his entire household from unbelief in God, and ultimately from Hell itself (Acts 16).

- We see how God delivered His chosen vessel, the Apostle Paul, from the venomous bite of the viper on the island of Malta (Acts 28).

The NDMC's maintain their doctrine that Christians cannot have demons because they are unwilling to look at Scripture with an open mind. When they look at Scripture, they do so with preconceived ideas about how things should be. They don't allow the Holy Spirit to show them.

NDMC's are not willing to see the Big Idea that God delivers His people. They never sit with Christians in Session Deliverance, so they never test their doctrine. They just make their doctrinal statements that Christians can't have demons in the vacuum of inexperience and unwillingness to look deeply into God's word. They keep their doctrine because it aligns with, and is accepted by, other NDMC's. They keep their doctrine because it is inoffensive to them.

When the NDMC confesses his doctrine that Christians can't have demons, he is not stating truth, but rather, he is declaring his view in light of his personal opinions, personal experiences, theological understandings, revelation received, and wishes about how things should or shouldn't be.

## Doctrine

Wikipedia, in its article entitled "Doctrine," says that doctrine is "a body of religious principles as promulgated by a church." The website *thefreedictionary.com* says that religious doctrine is "the written body of teachings of a religious group that is generally accepted by that group." I teach that doctrine is man's interpretation of spiritual truth.

In and of itself, doctrine is not wrong or sinful. In fact, the Bible exhorts us to have *sound doctrine*. For example, Paul tells Titus that bishops are to have sound doctrine:

> *7 For a bishop must be blameless, as a steward of God, not self-willed, not quick-tempered, not given to wine, not violent, not*

*greedy for money,* **8** *but hospitable, a lover of what is good, soberminded, just, holy, self-controlled,* **9** *holding fast the faithful word as he has been taught, that he may be able, by* **sound doctrine**, *both to exhort and convict those who contradict.*
Titus 1:7-9 (NKJV)

The problem arises when one holds to a doctrine that is contrary to God's heart. What is God's heart? We see it demonstrated over and over in Scripture, so I will keep repeating it as well:

### God delivers those who belong to Him

Therefore, if our doctrine does not include a provision for delivering God's people, then we are confessing doctrine that is contrary to God's heart. And doctrine that is contrary to God's heart is not sound doctrine. Doctrine that is contrary to God's heart is bad doctrine. And bad doctrine hurts God's people.

## Three Examples of NDMC Doctrines that Affirm That Christians Can't Have Demons

### Example #1: Assemblies of God

*It would seem contradictory for demons to indwell our bodies now that our bodies are temples of the Holy Spirit...For a Christian to have a demon would bring division that Jesus refused to admit...The idea of a true believer being inhabited by a demon also erodes the biblical concept of salvation and peace...We also believe that the gift of the discerning of spirits is for the purpose of discerning the spirit that may motivate people who are not indwelt by the Holy Spirit, not the discerning of supposed demons in believers...* (Official Assemblies of God 1972 Position Paper on the subject, "Can Born-Again Believers Be Demon Possessed?")

*...While believers will engage in spiritual warfare and be oppressed, they cannot be possessed by demonic forces...*

(Official Assemblies of God 2019 Position Paper on the subject, "Spiritual Warfare and the Believer")

### Example #2: Southern Baptist Convention

*...Yet to think of now in Christ those who are forgiven of sins and born of the Spirit and have new life as being then possessed by an evil spirit, a demonic spirit is quite unthinkable. In a fallen state yes, but in Christ, no... So, can a Christian be demon-possessed? No. To be demon-possessed would mean one is outside of Christ one is dead in their sins one is under the power of the evil one...* (Official Southern Baptist Theological Seminary video at *equip.sbts.edu*: "Can a Christian be Demon Possessed?" by Stephen J. Wellum, Professor of Christian Theology at The Southern Baptist Theological Seminary and editor of The Southern Baptist Journal of Theology)

### Example #3: Christ for all Nations

Christ for all Nations (CFAN) was founded by the late Reinhard Bonnke. This ministry is beyond a doubt one of the most powerful evangelism ministries of all time. God has used and continues to use this ministry to do mighty works for the Kingdom. I am thankful to CFAN as I have personally learned much about evangelism and the baptism of the Holy Spirit through the sermons of Evangelist Bonnke.

However, in terms of *deliverance*, CFAN is an NDMC. Now headed by Daniel Kolenda, CFAN maintains that Christians cannot have demons. In his book about spiritual warfare, *Slaying Dragons* (2020), Daniel Kolenda says:

*I do not believe that Christians can be demonized. When a person is saved, the Holy Spirit comes to dwell within him or her. So I don't see how a believer's "house," inhabited by the Holy Spirit, can be shared with demons.* (page 165)

Daniel Kolenda is an NDMC evangelist. He does not sit with people one-on-one to engage in Session Deliverance. He has a powerful evangelism ministry that is full of the fire of the Holy Spirit, but he is not a deliverance minister.

However, Daniel Kolenda does not fit the profile of the average NDMC who does no deliverance at all. Kolenda, like his predecessor Bonnke, does do deliverance—just not Session Deliverance. His ministry embraces Sovereign Deliverance in the form of Evangelistic Deliverance. And this is great news! People are being set free from demons through his ministry.

In his book, Kolenda describes how he does Evangelistic Deliverance. At his crusade events, he has a deliverance tent set up called "The Snake Pit," where he delivers the unsaved from demons and then helps them get born again. One unsaved woman at an evangelism event manifested a demon while Kolenda was preaching and was taken to The Snake Pit:

*The deliverance team cast out the demons out of her, and she came to her right mind and received Jesus as her Savior.* (page 3)

Kolenda is conflicted, however. While he clearly teaches the NDMC doctrine that Christians can't have demons, he also admits that what he sees in real-life ministry operations contradicts his own doctrine:

*On the other hand, I have seen people who by every outward indication were in fact Christians. Yet they clearly manifested demons and received deliverance. This is something I have witnessed not once or twice but many times—even hundreds of times. I don't fully understand how this is possible, but I cannot deny what I have seen.* (pages 165-166)

Daniel Kolenda is a dedicated and anointed servant of God, no doubt. I believe that if he were to receive the revelation of the tripartite nature of man, which was discussed in Chapter 5, he would quickly understand how it is possible for a Christian to have both the Holy Spirit and demon spirits in the same "house." Until he receives this revelation, I will continue to bless him and his ministry. Thank You, Jesus, for CFAN.

## The Christians-Can't-Have-a-Demon Doctrine Is Bad Doctrine And It Hurts the People in the Church

Saying that a Christian can't have a demon is not sound doctrine. And as you learned in the previous chapter, saying that Christians can't be "possessed" by demons is not sound doctrine either (not to mention that it is terrible Bible translation also).

By teaching that Christians cannot have demons, God's Biblical pattern of delivering His people is partially ignored. Yes, God's people are delivered from the fires of Hell (Big Deliverance) through the preaching and receiving of the Gospel. But if we don't deliver the Christians from the demons (Little Deliverance) that got in before they got saved, we are blocking them from living the full and abundant spiritual life that should be theirs as sons and daughters of the Most High. And this is the problem. The NDMC's rationalize that once someone is saved, there is nothing else that this individual must ever be delivered from.

*The NDMC's believe that salvation is the final deliverance that a Christian will receive in his or her lifetime.*

However, as Pastor Sam Alcime stated in his testimony, "Christians still need to live on this Earth." This Haitian deliverance minister was referring to the fact that we all have a mission to accomplish here on Earth serving the Lord. If we are hindered and weighted down by indwelling demons, we just can't do this mission as effectively as God wants us to.

The doctrine that Christians can't have demons is hurtful to the Church as it blocks Christians from performing their assigned ministries to the fullest.

Deliverance for Christians isn't offered in most churches since this ministry was not included in their church's doctrine or catechism. The NDMC church's doctrine states implicitly or explicitly that Christians do not and cannot need deliverance from demons.

Perhaps deliverance cannot be offered in the NDMC church since deliverance might expose demonization *within* the congregation. And demonization within the congregation would violate the church's doctrine that Christians can't have demons.

Or perhaps deliverance is not offered since an individual manifesting a demon might frighten the first-time visitors or even affect giving. Recall how Reverend Mike in Chapter 3 felt about this. The fact is, is that demonic manifestations can be an inconvenient truth for the NDMC church:

> *Many evil spirits were cast out,*
> ***screaming*** *as they left their victims...* Acts 8:7 (NLT)

## *Saying that Christians Cannot Have Demons Is Rooted in Pride*

The doctrine that Christians are immune to demonization is rooted in pride. I have already made the parallel to the pride of the Pharisees who said that they could never have been in bondage to anyone (John 8:33).

The pride of the Pharisees and of the NDMC's who say that Christians can't have demons stems from man's sinful nature to think more highly of himself than he should. The Pharisees needed to overcome their pride, and Christians are no different. In fact, when the wise Christian reads the Bible, he knows that *he is* the Pharisees. And for that matter, he knows that *he is* Judas. *He is* Peter, denying Jesus. Can anyone who reads this deny his prideful state? Can any reader honestly claim that he has never denied or betrayed Jesus?

The wise Christian knows that it is arrogant for the Christian to believe that we cannot have demons in our bodies and emotions just because we are God's people. It is tantamount to the Christian saying that he cannot have anger, hatred, lust, or fear just because we are Christians.

*Mark Chase*

Being a Christian does not make us immune to anger, hatred, lust, and fear. Being a Christian gives us *authority* to overcome anger, hatred, lust, and fear in the Name of Jesus.

## Spiritual Sickness Requires Healing By the Great Physician

Countless Christians in the church today are spiritually sick. They are like patients in a hospital (their church). Except that the hospital that they are in is not properly treating their sickness. Their hospital is guilty of neglect and malpractice, albeit unintentionally.

These patients continue to suffer because their doctor (their pastor) does not offer them the correct remedy. They are not offered the remedy because the FDA (their denomination) hasn't approved the treatment. To make matters worse, the doctor doesn't believe that his patients are sick anyway. He believes that all his patients have already been vaccinated (been born again) and therefore cannot have any sickness to begin with. As a result, the doctor in the hospital does not make any referrals for his patients to see the Great Physician for additional screening and treatments (Christ-centered deliverance ministry) since he views these treatments as medically unnecessary.

Because of the general lack of available deliverance ministry in the churches, God raises up independent deliverance ministries like mine and perhaps yours. Perhaps you are reading this book because you desire that God train you up to operate in this ministry. Your goal might even be to become an Invicta-Certified Deliverance Minister and Inner Healer. Our online school, Invicta University, offers this certification.

Consider the ministries of deliverance to be the urgent care clinics of the modern church. We accept walk-ins at our public meetings, and we make appointments for one-on-one consultations. Either way, we are aware of the spiritual epidemic and what needs to be done about it. We are ready, willing, and able to deal with the spiritual problems of the hurting members of the

Church and even of those outside the church when God calls us to conduct Sovereign Deliverance.

As I alluded to earlier, deliverance ministries should not have to exist at all. The ministry of deliverance and healing should be taking place in the *churches*. But due to doctrinal red tape in the churches and denominations, small independent deliverance ministries naturally begin to spring up to fill the obvious and undeniable need—the need for Christians to be delivered from demons.

Let's stop denying the hurting and tormented Christians the deliverance they need, and let's bring deliverance back to the church local. Let's teach the reality of the spiritual war and the authority that every Christian has been given to cast out the devil—even out of other Christians!

## Church Tradition

Doctrine can also form part of church tradition. Sometimes men elevate their doctrines to the status of divine commandments. This is what happens when religious men proclaim the doctrine that Christians cannot have demons. The man-made tradition of washing cups and pitchers becomes the man-made tradition of excluding the ministry of deliverance from the churches.

We need to be especially careful that our man-made church traditions and doctrines do not hinder our obedience to the real commandments of God:

> **7** *'And in vain they worship Me, teaching as doctrines the commandments of men.'* **8** *For **laying aside the commandment of God, you hold the tradition of men**—the washing of pitchers and cups, and many other such things you do.* Mark 7:7-8 (NKJV)

And what is the commandment in question? Examine this verse from Mark's Great Commission passage:

*Mark Chase*

*And these signs will accompany those who believe: In my name they will **drive out demons**; they will speak in new tongues.*
Mark 16:17 (NIV)

Jesus commands that those who believe (that is *us*, the born-again Christians) be casting out demons as a part of our faith.

And what is the man-made (and un-Biblical) church tradition in question? That Christians could never have a demon and, therefore, could never be in need of deliverance from demons. Recall in Chapter 3 how Pastor Gary informed Michelle that their denomination had been around for more than a century and never had to do any deliverance. This is church tradition.

The problem with the Christians-can't-have-a-demon tradition is that it hinders obedience to Christ's command to cast out demons. It stops people from being obedient to this command.

It does this since now, "those who believe" (once again, "those who believe" are the present-day, born-again Christians) are only permitted to focus their attention on casting out demons out of *confirmed* non-Christians. Now, the pastor needs to decide who is really a Christian before he will pray deliverance prayer. Recall the humorous anecdote that Derek Prince told about Brother Jones (Chapter 2).

But what if the pastor makes a mistake? What if he thinks someone is born again but really, she is not? In a case like this, he could miss the opportunity to heal someone who needs it.

Another problem with the Christians-can't-have-a-demon tradition is that a pastor will confine his deliverance activities (that is, *if* he does any deliverance at all) to evangelism events and to the mission field in the developing countries. He will assume that only during these activities will there be people with actual demons. Pastor Rick in Chapter 8 probably feels this way. Recall that the prevailing attitude of the average intellectual and arrogant North American Christian is that demons mostly inhabit the unsaved heathens who live in places like Latin America and Africa.

However, I can assure my readers that even in socially and intellectually sophisticated South Florida, where I live, there are massive hordes of demons that indwell God's faithful. And these demons need to be crushed and cast out.

## There Are No Limitations Listed In the Great Commission

The command of the Great Commission in Mark 16:17 to cast out demons does not say, "In My Name, they will cast out demons out of non-Christians during evangelism and missions work."

The Great Commission does not limit who is to receive deliverance from demons. The Great Commission simply informs all Christians that they should be engaged in the casting out of demons.

## The Correct Attitude about Deliverance

I believe that the correct attitude that we Christians should have is the following: God wants us to cast out demons out of anyone who has demons, not just out of one subgroup (seekers, heathens, pagans, atheists, the backslidden, the unsaved, the saved, etc.).

While it is God's overriding pattern and heart to deliver those who belong to Him, He can and does deliver those who have not yet confessed Jesus as Lord. For example, Paul sovereignly cast out a Python spirit, a type of witchcraft demon, from a non-Christian, non-Jewish, fortune-telling girl in Asia:

> **16** *Once when we were going to the place of prayer, we were met by a female slave who had a spirit by which she predicted the future. She earned a great deal of money for her owners by fortune-telling.* **17** *She followed Paul and the rest of us, shouting, "These men are servants of the Most High God, who are telling you the way to be saved."* **18** *She kept this up for many days. Finally Paul became so annoyed that he turned around and said to the spirit, "In the name of Jesus Christ I command you to come out of her!" At that moment the spirit left her.* Acts 16:16-18 (NIV)

God delivers people according to His good pleasure. His deliverance is primarily for those who belong to Him. However, God also delivers nonbelievers in order to demonstrate His power, to show who He is, and as a sign to confirm His word.

The tradition and doctrine that deliverance is only for the unsaved and unregenerate is false. As a church, we need to stop laying aside the commandment of God and start delivering whoever the Holy Spirit brings to us to be delivered.

When God brings us a Christian believer to be delivered, we will confront and challenge their demons. We will not turn them away just because they have already been born again.

And if God brings us a Muslim, a Jew, a Hindu, a Catholic, a witch, a pornography addict, an adulterer, or a liar to be delivered from demons, and they are willing, then we must do it. At least, we must attempt to do it in faith. Perhaps it will be God's good pleasure to deliver this sinner from his demons. And maybe as a result of this Power Encounter, the unsaved individual will then be convicted of sin, repent, and make Jesus Lord. When the Lord brings us these people, we must assume that He has predestined them to belong to Him.

We who work in the ministry of deliverance see that the majority of people who God brings to us to receive spiritual healing are fellow born-again Christians. The testimonies of other deliverance ministers at the beginning of this book confirm this truth.

## My Doctrine

I believe that it is sound doctrine to deliver whoever God brings to me to be delivered. Of course, the great majority of those who come to my ministry, and other deliverance ministries like mine, will already be born again. But I will not argue with God if He brings me a non-Christian to deliver. I will be obedient and let God do what He wants to do according to His good pleasure. As Pablo Bottari said, *I am a servant, not a lord.*

## The Children's Bread

## *How Did I Arrive at My Doctrine?*

My doctrine is that anyone, including Christians, can have demons and therefore require deliverance. This doctrine was arrived at systematically. I arrived at my doctrine in the same way that any life question, spiritual decision, or theological doctrine should be arrived at. The Christian decision-making process:

1. **Scripture**—First, I go into God's word to see what God is saying about the issue. The Bible is my final authority on all matters. My denomination, my church's doctrine and tradition, and my catechism are not. Regarding the topic of this book, I see that in the Bible, God delivers those who belong to Him. However, if I do not see an obvious answer to my question in Scripture, I then seek revelation.

2. **Revelation by the Holy Spirit**—Second, I ask for revelation by God's Spirit on the matter. In the deliverance ministry, I discern that the Finger of God is driving out demons from real Christians. The Holy Spirit has convicted me of the fact that Christians can be demonized. However, if I cannot understand what the Holy Spirit is showing me, I then seek wise counsel.

3. **Wise Counsel**—Third, I consult men and women of God that I know have a strong relationship with the Lord. I seek out the counsel of the wise. I engage in fellowship with other deliverance ministers as well as with mature leaders of the Church. And finally, to confirm the counsel of the wise, I see what God is showing me in my own life.

4. **Life Experience**—Finally, I see what God is showing me in my actual day-to-day ministry. I see what is happening—namely, that Christians are manifesting demons and subsequently receiving deliverance from them. I see that

among these Christians are veteran, mature believers who lead ministries and entire congregations. I have sat with many Christians who needed deliverance who had known the Lord since before I was born!

## The Christians-Can't-Have-a-Demon Doctrine Is a Learned Doctrine Taught by Men

Once I was at a church service, and the pastor was teaching on the lie of cessationism. He said something that really resonated with me.

He said that if some nonbeliever who had never read the Bible were given a copy of God's word, and this nonbeliever read the entire New Testament, that he would never come to the conclusion on his own that the Gifts of the Holy Spirit had ceased. There just isn't any Biblical evidence for cessationism. He went on to say that the only way that an individual could come to the conclusion that cessationism was true would be if someone *taught* him this doctrine. I immediately knew that this same concept applied to the *Christians-Can't-Have-a-Demon Doctrine* as well.

I realized that if the same nonbeliever read the Bible for the first time, he would never arrive at the conclusion on his own that Christians can't have demons either. As with the doctrine of cessationism, there just isn't any Biblical evidence for this. In fact, the only way that people do arrive at the conclusion that Christians can't have demons is when these individuals are *taught* this doctrine by an NDMC.

The Christians-Can't-Have-a-Demon Doctrine is not naturally derived from reading the Bible alone. Instead, it is an artificial doctrine that takes root only after it is *taught*. The NDMC's are the ones who teach this doctrine, and Satan is the one who concocted it. Satan made this doctrine up in order to remain undetected in the minds of countless Christian believers.

*The Children's Bread*

## *Summary*

If the doctrine of one's denomination, church, or seminary restricts deliverance to those who are outside of their church's doors, then this is an unsound doctrine. This is a doctrine that is man-made and rooted in pride. We must be humble and align our doctrines with the Biblical doctrine that God delivers those who belong to Him.

I believe that my doctrine—that Christians can have demons and subsequently need the deliverance of Jesus, is:

- Revealed through the repeating Biblical pattern—that **God delivers those who belong to Him**

- Supported by and even directly indicated by Scripture

- In no place prohibited by Scripture

- A revelation that the Holy Spirit has given me and many others who have been called into the ministry of Session Deliverance

- Affirmed by decades of written documented experiences of modern deliverance ministers whose ministry subjects are predominately Christians

- Opposed only by the NDMC's, the precise group of individuals that does not spend time doing this ministry at all

*Mark Chase*

# Part 3

# Scripture That Shows That Deliverance Is for The Children of God

*Mark Chase*

# Chapter 10

# *The Syrophoenician Woman's Daughter and The Children's Bread*

In Mark 7 and Matthew 15, we find the precious story of deliverance known as *the Syrophoenician Woman's Daughter*. I want to emphasize: The story of the Syrophoenician Woman's Daughter is a story of *deliverance*. This story concludes with Jesus delivering someone—a little girl—from a demon.

I frequently teach from this story in my ministry because it teaches so many practical lessons that we can immediately apply to our own modern ministries of deliverance:

- That small children can have demons
- That it is normal for parents to take their children to Jesus to be delivered
- That demons can be cast out *from a distance*—think teleministry, like Internet deliverance over Zoom or Skype

*Mark Chase*
## *Before the Cross, God's Children Were the Jews Only*

In this story, Jesus teaches this non-Jewish, gentile Syrophoenician Woman that deliverance—specifically, deliverance from demons in this case—is something that is first and foremost for *His* children. It was for the ones who knew the God of Israel as their God.

When this story took place during the earthly ministry of Jesus, "His children" would have been the Jews, or the "lost sheep of Israel," as He called them in this story. Before the Cross and the Pentecost Outpouring in the Upper Room, His people were the Hebrew Israelite Jews. We see in the Book of Exodus that God delivered **His** children out of Egypt:

*Afterward Moses and Aaron went in and told Pharaoh, "Thus says the Lord God of Israel: 'Let **My** people go, that they may hold a feast to Me in the wilderness.'*   Exodus 5:1 (NKJV)

## *His People Under the New Covenant*

Today, we Christians serve the same God as Moses and Aaron; however, we live under a different Covenant than did the Hebrew Israelite Jews. While God Himself doesn't change (Malachi 3:6), His covenants with His people do. In Jeremiah 31:31, we learn of the New Covenant that God would soon make with His people. Jesus affirmed this New Covenant in 1 Corinthians 11:25. The New Covenant, the one that we are currently under, is the New Covenant of Grace. The Old Covenant was a covenant of law.

In the New Covenant, it is the final atoning blood sacrifice of Jesus on the Cross that makes propitiation for our sins (1 John 2:2). Instead of animal blood, it is now the Blood of Jesus that cleanses us from our sins. In the New Covenant, we are not justified as a result of our own righteous works. Instead, we are justified by what He did—His life, death, burial, and resurrection. We are saved when we repent of sin and confess Jesus as Lord. We are saved by grace through faith in Jesus Christ (Ephesians 2:8).

Again, God has not changed. And He never will. God still delivers the people who belong to Him. He delivers His people. He delivers those who know His Name. He saves those who know His Name. And under the New Covenant of Grace, His people are those who call on the *Name of Jesus*:

> *For "whoever calls on the name of the Lord shall be saved."*
> Romans 10:13 (NKJV)

Under the New Covenant, the ones who call on the Name of Jesus are the Christians, the Messianic Jews, the followers of Jesus, or however you want to call those who have repented of sin and confessed Jesus as Lord (Romans 10:9).

The ones who call on His Name in the New Covenant are the ones who have been *born again*. They have been born of water and the Spirit. They are the ones with the indwelling Holy Spirit. They are the ones who have called on the only Name given to men under Heaven by which they must be saved. And *they* are the ones whom God will deliver since they know His Name.

## *God Delivers Us Because We Need to Be Delivered*

Since God delivers those who know His Name and call on His Name, a logical inference can be made. If God delivers the ones who call on His Name, then those who call on His Name must be in *need* of being delivered.

This means that the ones who call on His Name, the Christians, *need* deliverance. First and foremost, from the damnation of Hell that the wages of our sin merit. This is Big Deliverance. And secondly, Christians need deliverance from the demon spirits that entered during our rebellion against God (mainly) before having known Jesus. This is Little Deliverance.

*Mark Chase*

## The Bloodline of the Syrophoenician Woman and Her Daughter

In the story of the Syrophoenician Woman's Daughter, we see a woman who *does not* belong to God. She is not one of His people. The Syrophoenician Woman is not a Hebrew Israelite Jew. She is not an Old Covenant believer. This is another key part of the story.

By the term "Syrophoenician," we know that she was a native of Phoenicia while it formed part of the Roman province of Syria. She was of gentile Greek and Canaanite descent. This means that her ancestors on her Greek side most likely worshiped Diana, Aphrodite, and other demon gods of the Greek pantheon. And her Canaanite bloodline most certainly made sacrifice to the demons of Baal, Molech, and Asherah, which is a type of Jezebel.

This idolatrous background of her bloodline is insightful since we can safely assume that both the Syrophoenician Woman and her little daughter carried generational curses of idolatry and, probably, human sacrifice. The probable existence of all this generational sin explains why her daughter could have been suffering from such severe demonization, even at such a young age. The Syrophoenician Woman's daughter no doubt was a victim of generational curses going back to her ancestors' Satanic religious practices.

Regardless, the Syrophoenician Woman was not one of God's people. She was not Jewish. And since this story takes place before the Cross and Pentecost, she was not a Christian either.

## The Story of the Syrophoenician Woman's Daughter

The Gospel narrative tells us that while Jesus was in the region of Tyre and Sidon, the location of ancient Phoenicia, a mother comes to Jesus on behalf of her young demonized daughter who was back at home in bed suffering from severe demonic torment. The woman somehow recognizes the Lordship and Messiahship of

## The Children's Bread

Jesus and pleads with Him to deliver her daughter from her tormenting demons:

> *Behold, a Canaanite woman came out from those borders, and cried, saying, "Have mercy on me, Lord, you son of David! My daughter is **severely demonized**!*
> Matthew 15:22 (World English Bible)

However, since God first and foremost delivers His people and neither this mother nor her daughter were Jews, Jesus initially denies her request. Jesus tells the woman that He was sent only to deliver those who did belong to God—the Jewish people:

> *But He answered and said, "I was not sent except to the **lost sheep of the house of Israel**."* Matthew 15:24 (NKJV)

After the woman pleaded further and even worshiped Him (verse 25), Jesus explained His rationale:

> *But He answered and said, "It is not good to take the children's bread and throw it to the little dogs."* Matthew 15:26 (NKJV)

Speaking metaphorically, He told her that the deliverance of Jesus (the Children's Bread) was not for the gentile pagans who were not His people (the little dogs). Instead, the deliverance of Jesus (the Children's Bread) was first and foremost for the children of God (the Jews).

And who were the children of God in the time of the story of the Syrophoenician Woman's Daughter? Once again, for emphasis: The children of God up until the Cross and the Outpouring at Pentecost were the Jews, whom she was not. And post-Pentecost, in the present New Covenant, the children of God are us, the believers in Messiah Jesus, the Christians:

> *For you are all **sons of God** through faith in Christ Jesus.*
> Galatians 3:26 (NKJV)

And:

> *The Spirit Himself bears witness with our spirit that **we are children of God**.*   Romans 8:16 (NKJV)

Today, the Christians are the children of God, and as such, they are the rightful recipients of the Children's Bread, which is the deliverance of Jesus. And specific to this story, "the deliverance of Jesus" refers to the deliverance from demon spirits!

## Christians Are Hungry for This Bread of Deliverance

Therefore, deliverance from demons by the Name of Jesus is first and foremost *for* the Christians in the present Covenant. And if this bread is *for* the Christians, then that means that Christians are hungry for this bread. In other words, Christians *need* to be eating this bread. Christians need deliverance. Christians need the Bread of deliverance because they can have demons. Bread is a Biblical metaphor for Jesus:

> *And Jesus said to them, "**I am the bread of life**. He who comes to Me shall never hunger, and he who believes in Me shall never thirst."*   John 6:35 (NKJV)

In the story of Syrophoenician Woman's Daughter, Jesus makes the point that it is God's Children who are to be filled first with this Bread who is Jesus:

> *Let the **children be filled first**...* Mark 7:27

Who were these children? Once again, before the Cross, they were the Jews. The Jews are the ones who belonged to Him under the Old Covenant. The Good News of Jesus was for the Jews first and *then* the gentiles:

> *For I am not ashamed of the gospel of Christ, for it is the power of God to salvation for everyone who believes, **for the Jew first and also for the Greek**.*   Romans 1:16 (NKJV)

*The Children's Bread*

We could make a parallel statement to Romans 1:16 by declaring that: *"Deliverance from demons is for the Christian first and also for the nonbelievers."*

In this book, I have tried to make it clear that deliverance is first and foremost for the Christian believers; however, we do not limit who is to receive deliverance. We will deliver whoever God brings to us to be delivered. We will even cast out demons out of nonbelievers in the form of sovereign Power Encounter Deliverance if God calls us to do so. God delivers the nonbelievers as a sign to confirm His word (Mark 16:20, Hebrews 2:4). And this is precisely what Jesus did in the case of the Syrophoenician woman's daughter.

## *Deliverance Is for Nonbelievers Too*

While the divine Bread of Deliverance is primarily for the children of God, it is also for whomever God chooses to distribute it according to His good pleasure. In the story of the Syrophoenician Woman's Daughter, God chose to feed a gentile child with this Bread of Deliverance.

In my own ministry, I have seen that God chooses to deliver some, and others He demands additional submission before He delivers them. There is no mathematical formula to be able to determine beforehand who God will deliver and when He will deliver them. God is always sovereign, and He delivers according to His good pleasure.

## *The Faith of the Syrophoenician Woman*

The Syrophoenician Woman recognized the Lordship of Jesus and that He was the Son of David (Matthew 15:22). She somehow knew that He was God of even the gentiles, "the little dogs." After Jesus denied her initial request, this mother, in absolute humility, proceeded to "out-argue" Jesus:

> *And she said, "Yes, Lord, yet even the little dogs eat the crumbs which fall from their masters' table."* Matthew 15:27 (NKJV)

At this brilliant and humble response, Jesus made the decision to grant the mother's request for mercy and to deliver her daughter. Jesus praised her faith in who He was and then cast out the demon from her little daughter:

> *Then Jesus answered and said to her,* "*O woman, great is your faith! Let it be to you as you desire.*" *And her daughter was healed from that very hour.* Matthew 15:28 (NKJV)

Jesus didn't have to deliver this young girl. Feeding the Bread of Deliverance to the gentiles was not Jesus's primary mission. His principal mission was to feed the lost sheep of Israel. God's heart is always to feed His people first.

He chose to deliver this gentile mother's daughter after she demonstrated faith in who Jesus was. Jesus demonstrated that God is compassionate and merciful even with those who are not His. He delivered the little girl even though He was not obligated to do so.

Perhaps this woman and her daughter were predestined to know Jesus as future born-again Christians later on in their lives. Perhaps both would become active in a future Christian church in their region. Perhaps the mother would go on to deliver other demonized individuals in her country in the Name of Jesus. These are mysteries that we cannot know without specific revelation.

## Teleministry

At the beginning of this chapter, I mentioned that the story of the Syrophoenician Woman's Daughter demonstrates the validity of *teleministry*. Teleministry includes all deliverance that is conducted over communication applications such as Zoom, Skype, or WhatsApp video calls. Deliverance over voice-only calls would also be considered teleministry. Deliverance Encounters that take place over a video call are *virtual sessions*. I consider virtual sessions to be equally effective as in-person sessions.

Believe it or not, there are many who question whether demons can really be cast out from a distance. Opponents to teleministry claim that deliverance doesn't work if the one who is praying and the one who is receiving the prayer are not in the same room. This, of course, is false, and the story of the Syrophoenician Woman's Daughter proves this point. I often say that there is no time, space, or distance for the Holy Spirit to move. God can and does frequently expel demons from any distance, all according to His good pleasure.

At the time of this writing, approximately one-third of my private Deliverance Encounter appointments are Internet video call encounters. However, there is an even greater lesson than the validity of teleministry that we learn in the story of the Syrophoenician Woman's Daughter:

***God delivers those who belong to Him***

## Denying the Children Their Bread Is Wrong

It is doubtful that anyone reading this book would willfully withhold physical bread from a hungry child. Who then would deny spiritual Bread to a child of God who is spiritually hungry? I will tell you who. The NDMC's would.

It is the NDMC's who would withhold the children's Bread of Deliverance to a fellow believer due to doctrinal prejudices, church traditions, and prideful personal beliefs that Christians can't have demons. Essentially, the NDMC tells the Christian who is seeking spiritual healing:

*"You say you are hungry. I see the signs that you are hungry. But you really don't know what you're talking about. You don't really need the Bread of Deliverance. The Bread of Deliverance isn't for Christians. It is something they gave certain people in Bible times. It is something that they give to the pagans on missionary trips to Central America. It is something that might be given to atheists, Satanists, or murderers. However, as for you, reading the Bible and coming to church on Sunday is all you could possibly need. You should probably make an appointment to see a therapist too."*

*Mark Chase*

## Conclusion

     When the NDMC church refuses to deliver Christians from demons, the children of God go hungry. Many Christians in the church today are spiritually emaciated as a result. Deliverance from demons is the Jesus Bread that God offers us hungry Christians—His children, the ones who belong to Him.

     By insisting that Christians can't have demons, the NDMC is resisting the will of God to dispense this liberating Bread to those who belong to Him. And by maintaining the prideful position that once someone is saved, he can no longer hunger for the spiritual Bread of Deliverance, is to deny God's people of what has been promised to them—liberty to the captives and the opening of the prison to those who are bound (Isaiah 61:1).

# Chapter 11

# *The Man in the Synagogue And the Daughter of Abraham*

There are two stories of deliverance in the New Testament that I refer to as "The Church Deliverance Stories." I call them this because they do not take place on the dusty streets of Bethsaida or out in the rocky Judean countryside. Instead, they take place in the "churches" of Jesus's day—the Jewish synagogues.

    I believe that it is highly significant that God chose to include not one but *two* deliverance stories that take place *inside* Jewish houses of worship. This fact is worthy of attention as I believe that God is sending us a clear message that deliverance should be taking place not just out in the world where the pagans are but *in the church* where the believers congregate. In other words, the casting out of demons should be taking place where God's children assemble.

    In these two stories, God's people, the Jews, assembled in the synagogues. And we need to keep in mind that before the Cross, the Old Covenant was the only way to come into right relationship with the One True God. Before the Cross, there was no other Covenant unto salvation. There was no other way to know God. And this Covenant was taught in the Jewish synagogues during the time of Jesus's earthly ministry.

Therefore, in the Jewish synagogues, we can expect to find the people who belong to God, the Jews. Would every Jew in every synagogue be a true, spiritual Jew? Probably not. But the real Jews would definitely be found in the synagogues on the Sabbath day.

## The Man in the Synagogue

In this story, found in Mark 1 and in Luke 4, Jesus was teaching in the synagogue of Capernaum. Those in attendance were amazed at how Jesus taught with authority, unlike the teachers of the Law who just quoted other teachers. Then, while the Master was teaching, someone *inside* of this synagogue began to manifest a demon:

*Now there was a man **in their synagogue** with an unclean spirit. And he cried out.   Mark 1:23 (NKJV)*

This man was not a first-time visitor or a pagan seeker. He was not a guest. He was a man *in their synagogue*. I believe this means he was a Jew. He belonged to God.

Next, we learn that this demonized man had not only one unclean spirit, but instead, *multiple* demons. One demon, possibly the strong man, spoke for the whole group of demons:

*Saying, "Let **us** alone! What have **we** to do with You, Jesus of Nazareth? Did You come to destroy **us**? I know who You are—the Holy One of God!"   Mark 1:24 (NKJV)*

Then, in the following verse, we see deliverance, the casting out of evil spirits, taking place—right in God's house of worship. Jesus issues the forceful command by ordering the demon to go from this demonized Jewish believer:

*But Jesus rebuked him, saying, "Be quiet, and **come out of him!**"   Mark 1:25 (NKJV)*

And with that rebuke, demons were cast out of this Jewish man in the synagogue at Capernaum. Deliverance had taken place in God's house of worship, a "church" of the Old Covenant.

Incidentally, Jesus did not permit the demon to speak because he hadn't yet revealed his Messiahship (which He wouldn't do until John 4:26), and the demon was exposing this fact before the appointed time. Jesus did *not* silence the demon in order to teach us not to interrogate demons, as many NDMC's have stated. Mark 5:9 proves this point.

Finally, we see a demonic expulsion not unlike what we see in the modern ministry of deliverance. As the demons were expelled, the man's body convulsed, and the demons made a lot of noise:

*And when the unclean spirit had **convulsed him and cried out** with a loud voice, he came out of him.* Mark 1:26 (NKJV)

This is how the first deliverance in the New Testament is recorded. And I do not believe it to be a coincidence that God chose His very own synagogue to be the location of this first. The first-recorded exorcism in the New Testament happened right in God's church. Jesus started his ministry of deliverance *in a synagogue*. Could there be a deeper meaning to this? Is God telling us here that deliverance needs to start *in the church*?

Again, The Man in the Synagogue was a Jew. He was a member of this synagogue. He worshiped the God of Israel. He belonged to God. And he needed deliverance because he had demons.

## The Daughter of Abraham

In this next Church Deliverance Story, found only in Luke 13, we see Jesus once again delivering one of God's people from demons inside His church, a Jewish synagogue.

In "The Daughter of Abraham," Jesus delivers a Jewish woman from a demon that is specifically named by the Gospel writer. This named demon was referred to as a "crippling spirit," or a "spirit of infirmity," depending on the translation.

Any deliverance minister will quickly recognize these names. In the modern ministry of deliverance, we see demons named Infirmity and Sickness quite often. The Daughter of Abraham had an evil spirit that had been tormenting her with some sort of curvature of the spine for eighteen years:

*And behold, there was a woman who had a **spirit of infirmity** eighteen years, and was bent over and could in no way raise herself up.* Luke 13:11 (NKJV)

Jesus called the woman to Him to do a public deliverance. This is very similar to how we call people to the front during our modern public deliverance meetings. The purpose of these open demonstrations of God's Spirit over infinitely inferior demon spirits is to make a public spectacle (Colossians 2:15) of the demons. Jesus called her to Him and then cast out the demon from her. Jesus calls His people to Him and then delivers them:

*But when Jesus saw her, **He called her to Him** and said to her, "Woman, you are loosed from your infirmity."* Luke 13:12 (NKJV)

In the next verse, we learn that this woman was not just a churchgoer or a pew warmer. Instead, she was a *worshiper*. We know this because, after her deliverance and subsequent physical healing, she was convicted to glorify the God who healed her:

*And He laid His hands on her, and immediately she was made straight, and **glorified God**.* Luke 13:13 (NKJV)

This reminds me of multitudes of deliverances that I have done at public meetings where people who, after being delivered, began to spontaneously praise and worship Jesus after their deliverances.

For some, this means gently offering up sweet praises, "Thank You Jesus; You alone are worthy; I worship You alone; thank You for healing me today!" For others, the Holy Spirit touches them, and they begin to manifest the gift of speaking in tongues. Still, others begin to prophesy, testify, and even dance to the Lord! Many of our ministry's YouTube videos show beautiful examples of post-deliverance praise and worship.

## Was the Daughter of Abraham a Real Jew?

At this point, the NDMC might object and say that not everyone who attended synagogue was a faithful, law-keeping Jewish believer. And I would agree. As I mentioned at the beginning of this chapter, I believe that we can be certain that in this synagogue, like in any other, there were at least some hypocrites or non-spiritual Jews.

However, in the story of the Daughter of Abraham, we are given a crucial detail that shows us that this woman was not just Jewish by virtue of being inside the synagogue or Jewish by race. Instead, Jesus calls this particular Jewish woman a *daughter of Abraham*. This is highly significant.

## A Daughter of Abraham, Not Just a Descendent of Abraham

After the synagogue leader rebuked the people (and probably Jesus as well) for coming to be healed on the Sabbath, Jesus provides a very important detail regarding this woman's spiritual identity. Jesus proclaimed that this woman was not just a Jew by birth, but that rather, that she was a *daughter of Abraham*:

> *So ought not this woman, being a **daughter of Abraham**, whom Satan has bound—think of it—for eighteen years, be loosed from this bond on the Sabbath?* Luke 13:16 (NKJV)

This term, "daughter of Abraham," is highly indicative of the woman's spiritual state. It was Jesus's way of declaring that this woman was not just a holiday Jew, a cultural Jew, or a Jew by birth. Instead, she was a *woman of the Covenant.*

By saying this, Jesus is revealing to us that this woman doesn't just claim Abraham as her ancestor. Instead, she is one who does the works of Abraham. How do we know this? Because

Scripture interprets Scripture. In John 8, Jesus explains the difference between a mere *descendent* of Abraham and a *child* of Abraham. Jesus called the nonbelieving Jews mere *descendants* of Abraham:

> *I know that you are Abraham's **descendants**, but you seek to kill Me, because My word has no place in you.* John 8:37 (NKJV)

Jesus then made His point again:

> *They answered and said to Him, "Abraham is our father." Jesus said to them, "If you were Abraham's children, you would do the works of Abraham."* John 8:39 (NKJV)

Therefore, we can conclude that by using the term *daughter of Abraham*, Jesus was showing us that she was not only a physical *descendant* of Abraham, but instead, she was also a spiritual *child* of the Patriarch. For Jesus to say this, she must have shared the works of Abraham. And what were the works of Abraham? His faith. Abraham was a true man of faith:

> *And the Scripture was fulfilled which says, "Abraham **believed God** [had faith], and it was accounted to him for righteousness." And he was called the friend of God.* James 2:23 (NKJV)

Jesus places the daughter of Abraham in the same spiritual family as Abraham, the father of Isaac. She had the works of Abraham—true faith. *And yet, even with this true faith, this daughter of Abraham had a demon.* She needed deliverance, and Jesus cast out her demon right there in the synagogue. Could it be that Christians of today who have this same faith might also have demons? Yes, it can. True, born-again, saved-by-grace-through-faith Christians can have demons.

There is another Biblical account in which Jesus uses this term. In the story of Zacchaeus, the tax collector, Jesus directly correlates being a *son* of Abraham with having salvation:

### The Children's Bread

*And Jesus said to him, "Today **salvation** has come to this house, because he also is a **son of Abraham**."* Luke 19:9 (NKJV)

Therefore, we can conclude that the children of Abraham—the sons and daughters of Abraham—have salvation. Yet, in this story of the Daughter of Abraham, we see that she also had an indwelling demon spirit. She had salvation, *and* she had a demon. God delivered the Daughter of Abraham because she belonged to Him. Recall again the Big Idea that runs throughout both Testaments of the Bible:

**God delivers those who belong to Him**

## Summary

The two Church Deliverance Stories show us two individuals who received deliverance from demons in the "church" of the Old Covenant. The Man in the Synagogue was most likely a true Jew since he was "in the synagogue." Although we do not know this with 100% certainty, I think it can be safely assumed. Regardless, it is highly significant that God chose the first recorded deliverance of the New Testament to take place in His own house of worship. I believe that God is showing us by this "first" that deliverance needs to *first* take place in God's houses of worship—the modern Christian churches.

And in the case of the Daughter of Abraham, there is no question as to her salvation status. She was a true Jewish believer with salvation. We know this since Jesus assigned her a title that confirms her as a child of the Covenant.

I believe that God is trying to teach us two important messages here: First, that deliverance should be taking place in the churches. Second, that there are people in the churches who have demons and need to be delivered from these demons.

Is it possible that there are individuals in *your* church who have demons and need deliverance? Pray about this and ask the Holy Spirit to give you revelation.

*Mark Chase*

# Chapter 12

# *The Psalms of David*

David is one of the great Old Testament men of faith listed in the "Hall of Faith" in the Book of Hebrews (11:32). He was a man after God's own heart (Acts 13:22). He also had the Holy Spirit:

*Then Samuel took the horn of oil and anointed him in the midst of his brothers; and* **the Spirit of the Lord came upon David** *from that day forward. So Samuel arose and went to Ramah.*
1 Samuel 16:13 (NKJV)

He wrote seventy-five of the one hundred fifty Psalms. He was a true believer, and like every true believer, David did not live a sinless life. However, he had the salvation of God, and he knew that only God could deliver him. David frequently wrote about the fact that *God delivers those who belong to Him*. He did this by using a variety of poetic expressions in his Psalms.

## *David Tells Us Who God Delivers*

David wrote that the ones who God delivers are those who:

• Trust in Him

• Love Him

• Know His Name

- Call on Him

- Seek Him

- Pray to Him

- Those in whom He delights

- Those who are righteous

And who does all these things? What is the common denominator? The one who does all these things and is all these things are *those who belong to Him*. The one who does all these things is the one who knows that He is God. The one who does all these things is the one who serves Him. The one who does all these things belongs to Him. And God delivers those who belong to Him!

God delivers those who *trust in Him*:

*And the Lord shall help them and deliver them; He shall deliver them from the wicked, And save them, Because **they trust in Him**.*
Psalm 37:40 (NKJV)

God delivers those who *love Him and know His name*:

*"Because he has **set his love upon Me**, therefore I will deliver him; I will set him on high, because **he has known My name**.*
Psalm 91:14 (NKJV)

God delivers those who *call on Him*:

*He shall **call upon Me**, and I will answer him; I will be with him in trouble; I will deliver him and honor him.* Psalm 91:15 (NKJV)

God delivers those who *seek Him*:

***I sought the Lord**, and He heard me, And delivered me from all my fears.* Psalm 34:4 (NKJV)

## The Children's Bread

God delivers those who *pray to Him*:

*But as for me, **my prayer is to You, O Lord**, in the acceptable time; O God, in the multitude of Your mercy, Hear me in the truth of Your salvation. Deliver me out of the mire, And let me not sink;*
***Let me be delivered*** *from those who hate me, And out of the deep waters.* Psalm 69:13-14 (NKJV)

God delivers those *in whom He delights*:

*He also brought me out into a broad place; He delivered me because **He delighted in me**.* Psalm 18:19 (NKJV)

God delivers those who are righteous:

***The righteous*** *cry out, and the Lord hears, And **delivers them** out of all their troubles.* Psalm 34:17 (NKJV)

The common denominator that David conveys in these psalmic verses is that *God delivers those who belong to Him*. We know this because the only ones who can possibly do and be all these things are those who belong to Him.

## David's Deliverance

The deliverance that David spoke of in his Psalms was primarily deliverance from his physical enemies. These included King Saul and later the Philistines and the Moabites, and others. However, we are living under a different Covenant than David did. Our enemies are no longer physical, or carnal.

The weapons of our warfare are no longer carnal (2 Corinthians 10:4) as they were in David's day. We are no longer confronting and overcoming *physical* enemies. Now, our adversary is a *spiritual* enemy. Our enemy is Satan and his hordes of demons that have assignments against our lives, our families, our marriages, our ministries, and everything good that God has ordained for us. The physical enemies of David are emblematic of our spiritual enemies in the present Covenant. In fact, all the physical enemies of God's people in the Old Testament are emblematic of our spiritual demonic enemies under the New Covenant. In my ministry, we call this important concept the *Old Testament-New Testament Warfare Shift*. From the Old Testament to the New Testament, there has been a shift in the identity of the enemy, and subsequently, in the way we are to fight.

Our enemies now are the demons. And we fight these demons using the Sword of the Spirit, not swords of metal. Now we wield the superior weaponry of prayer. Reinhard Bonke understood this:

*Prayer opens up God's armory with its superior weapons. If we think we don't need to pray, then we don't know what we are up against. If we think that we can manage on our own achievements, then we simply make ourselves the devil's laughingstock. To be prayerless means to be defenseless.* Reinhard Bonnke interview on YouTube (video since removed).

Therefore, we utilize prayer to defeat our enemies, the demons. Much of this prayer is in the form of the forceful command. Now, we no longer slay enemy soldiers. Now we cast out demon spirits. We no longer conquer fortified cities. We now pull down spiritual strongholds. We no longer conquer a geographical territory. We now take possession of our spiritual promised lands. This is the essence of the Old Testament-New Testament Warfare Shift.

As we transfer the Psalms over to our modern lives under the New Covenant, we see that God now delivers us, His people, from our spiritual enemies—the demons. Those who follow Jesus are the ones who belong to Him in the New Covenant. Therefore, God now delivers us, the Christians. Everything David said remains true. The only difference being the identity of the enemy and the weapons of our warfare.

For David, he needed deliverance from *men* who were trying to physically kill him. We, on the other hand, need deliverance from evil *spirits* who are hell-bent on trying to do the same thing. We know that the demons come to steal, *kill*, and destroy (John 10:10).

## *David Probably Needed Spiritual Deliverance Too*

Even though David was a man after God's own heart, he most likely needed deliverance from demons as well. After all, David did things that could have provided clear points of entry for demons. For example, he committed adultery with Bathsheba and then murdered her husband Uriah to cover it up. Physical adultery and physical murder are very strong sins. I have seen demons use murder and adultery as legal right. Perhaps some of David's cries for deliverance were for deliverance from demons as well.

This is possible since David certainly knew about evil spirits. While David served under King Saul, he was called to do a type of musical deliverance. Earlier on, God had judged Saul and had given Saul evil spirits (1 Samuel 16:14). Saul was tormented by these spirits. David would then play his harp for Saul, and at the playing of his harp, Saul's demons would depart. Because of this, we can say that David is the first exorcist listed in the Bible:

*Whenever the spirit from God came on Saul, David would take up his lyre and play. Then relief would come to Saul; he would feel better, and* **the evil spirit would leave him***.*   1 Samuel 16:23 (NIV)

## *David Knew That Only God Could Deliver Him*

In the 10th century BC, David was made king over the united Northern and Southern kingdoms of Israel. He brought the Ark of the Covenant into Jerusalem. He had the salvation of God. Yet, David still needed deliverance. He knew that only God could deliver him. Outside of the Psalms, David cried out:

*Moreover David said,* **"The Lord, who delivered me** *from the paw of the lion and from the paw of the bear,* **He will deliver me** *from the hand of this Philistine." And Saul said to David, "Go, and the Lord be with you!"*   1 Samuel 17:37 (NKJV)

Interestingly, in the ministry of deliverance, we see *demons* called Lion, Bear, Nephilim, and Giant. Only Jesus can deliver us from these demon spirits. David had God's salvation, and he knew that only God could deliver him from evil men and maybe from demons too.

As an aside, David needed inner healing, which is the healing of the mind or soul, too:

**Bring my soul out of prison**, *That I may praise Your name; The righteous shall surround me, For You shall deal bountifully with me."* Psalm 142:7 (NKJV)

## More Davidic Psalms of Deliverance

*Keep my soul, and **deliver me**; Let me not be ashamed, for I put my trust in You.* Psalm 25:20 (NKJV)

*For **He has delivered me** out of all trouble; and my eye has seen its desire upon my enemies.* Psalm 54:7 (NKJV)

*But I am poor and needy; Make haste to me, O God! You are my help and **my deliverer**; O Lord, do not delay.* Psalm 70:5 (NKJV)

We learn in the Psalms of David two things about deliverance. First, like David, we too are to call out to God and to God alone for our deliverance. And second, deliverance is for those of us who, like David, know the Most High God as our personal God. *Deliverance was and always will be for those who belong to Him.*

# Part 4

# Two Strong Pieces of Biblical Evidence that Suggest that Christians Can Have Demons

*Mark Chase*

# Chapter 13

# *Paul's Messenger of Satan*

> *And lest I should be exalted above measure by the abundance of the revelations, a thorn in the flesh was given to me, a **messenger of Satan** to buffet me, lest I be exalted above measure.*
> 2 Corinthians 12:7 (NKJV)

In Paul's second letter to the Corinthians, I believe that God shows us something absolutely stunning that is hidden in plain sight. It is something that if you were to teach on it in the average NDMC church, you would immediately be given the left foot of fellowship and then labeled a radical heretic. You would not be returning to speak at that church ever again!

I am referring to the passage of Scripture that Bible scholars traditionally refer to as "Paul's Thorn." However, in my own understanding of this passage, I propose a renaming. I suggest a paradigm shift. Instead of focusing on the "thorn," I recommend a refocus on the second descriptor of his affliction: "Paul's messenger of Satan."

For this reason, I refer to this passage as "Paul's Messenger of Satan" in my ministry teaching materials. I believe that this name change helps us get closer to the deeper meaning of the passage.

So, what is this stunning revelation that God is giving us right in plain sight? I believe that it is highly likely that:

**Paul had a demon.**

The Apostle Paul, author of one-fourth of the New Testament and Jesus's chosen vessel to bring the Gospel of Jesus to the gentiles and to Israel, had an unclean demon spirit. While this statement would seem absolutely unthinkable to the mainstream NDMC church establishment, I believe there is no better exegesis for this Scripture. Let's look at why it is completely sensical to arrive at this conclusion.

## *Paul Was Tormented by It*

Paul's messenger of Satan *tormented* him:

> *...I was given a thorn in my flesh, a messenger of Satan,* ***to torment me****.* 2 Corinthians 12:7 (NIV)

Other translations say Paul was *buffeted* by the messenger of Satan:

> *...a thorn in the flesh was given to me, a messenger of Satan* ***to buffet me****, lest I be exalted above measure.*
> 2 Corinthians 12:7 (NKJV)

What do demons do to their victims? They torment them. They buffet them. The original Greek word in this passage that is translated as "torment" is *kolaphizó,* which literally means to strike with the knuckles of the fist. Whether the victim of indwelling demons is a Christian or not, the demons that are on the inside are there to cause torment and to beat them down with all sorts of attacks.

## *Back to the Thorn*

Bible scholar Richard C. H. Lenski, in his *Interpretation of II Corinthians* (1946) said, regarding the thorn in this passage:

*In "thorn" we have the idea of something sharp and painful sticking deeply in the flesh so it remains there and cannot be drawn out.* (page 1300)

As an experienced deliverance minister, this sounds *exactly* like the demonic fiery darts that we encounter in our deliverance sessions. We find that demons place these and other *spiritual devices* in their victims in order to torment them, manipulate them, and put sickness on them. When I am ministering to an individual, I will often command the demon to remove these darts as part of the person's deliverance.

Lenski goes on to connect Paul's messenger of Satan to an "implacable demon." He says we should not disregard the possibility that Paul's messenger of Satan is demonic. Lenski said, "The Satanic agency should not be eliminated."

## *It Was a **Messenger** of Satan*

Paul describes his thorn as being a *messenger* of Satan. What is a messenger, Biblically? A messenger in the Bible can only be one thing. A messenger is an *angel*. An angel is a messenger. This is so in both the Hebrew and the Greek.

The word in the original Greek of 2 Corinthians that is translated into the English "messenger" is *aggelos* (Strong's Concordance Number 32a). Strong's defines *aggelos* as meaning "messenger" or "angel." No other definitions exist.

Incidentally, in the Hebrew of the Old Testament, the word for angel is also "messenger." The Hebrew word for angel is *malak* which is Strong's Concordance number 4397. Like its Greek counterpart, *malak* also means "messenger" or "angel."

Therefore, the messenger that tormented or buffeted Paul was certainly an angel. The only question that remains is, what kind of angel was it? Was it one of God's holy angels, or was it one of the devil's angels, i.e., a demon? I believe that it is not reasonable to say that one of God's heavenly hosts was tormenting Paul since, as the Scripture says, it was a messenger *of Satan*. That leaves only one possibility. The messenger *aggelos* that buffeted Paul was a demon *aggelos*.

In order to demonstrate that aggelos can signify "demon," here is another New Testament verse that utilizes the same word *aggelos* (Strong's 32a), clearly referring to a demon:

> *Then He will also say to those on the left hand, 'Depart from Me, you cursed, into the everlasting fire prepared for the devil and his **angels**' [aggelos].*
> Matthew 25:41 (NKJV)

In this verse, there is absolutely no doubt that Jesus is talking about demon angels. They couldn't be holy angels because if they were holy angels, then He couldn't say, "the devil and *his* angels."

Therefore, if *aggelos* means "demon" in Matthew 25:41, then it certainly could mean "demon" in 2 Corinthians 12:7. And since it is highly implausible that a holy angel would be tormenting Paul, we can logically assume that it was indeed one of Satan's demon angels that was afflicting the Apostle.

## What if the Bible Said That Pharaoh Had a Messenger of Satan?

Imagine if Scripture told us that Pharaoh or Pontius Pilate or King Herod had a "messenger of Satan." I believe that if such a verse existed, most theologians from every denomination would be in agreement in saying that this meant that these evil people were demonized.

But, the Apostle Paul? No never! He could never have a demon since Christians cannot have demons. And certainly, Apostles cannot have demons. So, all kinds of explanations are invented for what Paul's "messenger of Satan" is. I will list some of these alternate explanations later in this chapter.

The impossibility of Paul having a demon becomes even more acute if one thinks of Paul (even unconsciously) of being sinless or of being a "Saint" in the Catholic sense. A Catholic Saint being, of course, an individual who has been approved as a Saint through the complex and lengthy process of Catholic canonization. Because, of course, it would be unthinkable in the Catholic religion to say that "Saint Paul," or any other canonized Saint, could have been demonized. Incidentally, the *Biblical* definition of "saint" is any born-again Christian believer in Jesus:

*To the church of God which is at Corinth, to those who are sanctified in Christ Jesus, called to be **saints**, with all who in every place call on the name of Jesus Christ our Lord, both theirs and ours.* 1 Corinthians 1:2 (NKJV)

A saint is a follower of Jesus. It is one whose sin has been dealt with—it has been cleansed by the Blood of Jesus. He has been set apart as a royal priesthood to continue the work of Jesus here on Earth. He is set apart in that he is in this world, but not of it. In other words, the Christians are the saints. And Christians sin. They sinned before they converted, and they still sin (albeit against their will) after their conversion.

We understand that Christians sin and that no one is righteous since Paul taught us this (Romans 3:10). In fact, Paul talked about hating his own sin. Once again:

*For what I am doing, I do not understand. For what I will to do, that I do not practice; **but what I hate, that I do**.*
Romans 7:15 (NKJV)

The only man who ever walked the face of the planet who *never* transgressed any of God's laws, who had no sin, and *never* had a demon, was Jesus of Nazareth. There was nothing of Satan in Jesus (John 14:30). These are certainly non-disputable matters.

Therefore, we ought not to think of the Apostle Paul as being some kind of sinless Christian legend who would have been immune to any demonization. In fact, we should see Paul as someone just like you and me. Paul said to imitate him as he imitates Jesus (1 Corinthians 11:1). He was a great sinner (persecuting and murdering Christians), and then he found Jesus, repented and got on fire for the Lord. Paul is a great role model as he relentlessly carried out the Great Commission, but he wasn't sinless.

Finally, we must remember that "demonized" doesn't mean that the individual is necessarily a raging demoniac. It just means "to have a demon on the inside." You already know that the majority of demonization is *subtle*.

## Could There Have Been Legal Right in Paul's Life?

Demons cannot enter into a person without legal right. This foundational concept was already discussed in Chapter 2. This begs the question. Would demons have had legal right in Paul's life? I say absolutely. And for two different reasons.

First, remember that Paul was a murderer and persecutor of Christians in his previous life before his conversion. He touched God's anointed (Psalm 105:15). Paul confesses:

> ***I persecuted this Way to the death***, *binding and delivering into prisons both men and women.* Acts 22:4 (NKJV)

Paul's persecution and murder of Christians earlier on in his life would have given more than enough legal ground for demonization to have occurred.

Parenthetically, I have learned in my own ministry that physical murder, along with witchcraft and sexual perversion, are the "Big Three" areas of legal right that we encounter. I would say that sins involving the Big Three are responsible for approximately seventy-five percent of all cases of demonization that I see in my day-to-day deliverance sessions.

Second, we know that God gave Paul this messenger of Satan in order to keep him humble:

> *"...Therefore,* **in order to keep me from becoming conceited**, *I was given a thorn in my flesh, a messenger of Satan, to torment me."*
> 2 Corinthians 12:7 (NIV)

God Himself granted permission to the messenger of Satan to keep Paul from becoming prideful. Paul said, "I was given…" Only God in His absolute sovereignty could have given this. Only God could have authorized this. God gave Paul a messenger of Satan in order to keep the Apostle totally reliant on Him.

When you are the writer of such a great portion of the New Testament, pride could easily have set in. Three verses earlier in verse four, Paul tells us he was even caught up to Paradise and experienced the sounds of Heaven. Then he revealed to us that he had "surpassingly great revelations." Not to mention all of Paul's extraordinary miracles, including people receiving deliverance just by touching objects that he had touched (Acts 19) as well as raising Eutychus from the dead (Acts 20).

Perhaps Paul's demonization is a combination of the two legal rights. Perhaps Paul had multiple demons that are not mentioned in Scripture. Regardless, Paul did not want this messenger of Satan, and he prayed a form of prayer known as *Supplicatory Deliverance* (more on this in the next session) for the Satanic messenger to be expelled from him:

*Concerning this thing I pleaded with the Lord three times that it might depart from me.* 2 Corinthians 12:8 (NKJV)

However, after Paul prayed this, we learn that it was not in God's will for Paul to be set free from the messenger of Satan. It is here again that we must remember the sovereignty of God. He delivers or doesn't deliver, according to His good pleasure. We men do not have the final say. The demons do not have the final say. God has the final say in all matters, including deliverance.

In my own ministry, I have experienced times when I couldn't cast out a demon, and I wondered why since all the legal rights had been broken. It is during these times where I just cry out, "Not my will, but Yours be done. Amen."

Regardless, God told Paul that His grace was all that he needed. According to God, grace was enough for Paul and that he did not need to be delivered from the messenger of Satan:

### Mark Chase

*And He said to me, "**My grace is sufficient for you**, for My strength is made perfect in weakness." Therefore most gladly I will rather boast in my infirmities, that the power of Christ may rest upon me.* 2 Corinthians 12:9 (NKJV)

## Supplicatory Deliverance

Paul implored God three times to be set free from his messenger of Satan. This type of deliverance where we *ask* God to remove the demon is called Supplicatory Deliverance. It is a form of Sovereign Deliverance since it doesn't involve breaking and removing legal rights, nor does it employ the exercising of one's authority over demons by issuing the forceful command. Supplicatory Deliverance does not utilize the forceful command. Instead, it involves making supplication to God to sovereignly remove a demon from ourselves, from others, or from something else.

If you are the parent of an adult child, you have probably prayed Supplicatory Deliverance on behalf of your grown son or daughter. You have probably prayed at one time or another something like, "Lord, heal and deliver my son/daughter!"

Depending on the translation, Paul "pleaded," "begged," "besought," or "entreated" God to remove his messenger of Satan. However, for whatever reason, God did not grant Paul's request. God said that His grace was sufficient for Paul. God refused to expel Paul's messenger of Satan according to His good pleasure.

We don't know why Paul didn't ask a fellow Christian to pray Power Encounter Deliverance over him. Paul could have said, "Brother Peter, please pray for me and tell this messenger of Satan to go!" And we do not know why Paul didn't attempt straight on Self-Deliverance either. He could have commanded the demon and the infirmities to go himself. Perhaps he was convicted not to. Perhaps he did, and the Self-Deliverance was inefficacious. These questions will remain a mystery.

## Was Paul's Messenger of Satan On the Inside or the Outside?

Perhaps some NDMC's would agree that Paul's messenger of Satan was of "Satanic agency," in other words, a demon. However, most NDMC's would certainly disagree that this demon was on the *inside* of Paul.

However, I believe that the Bible says it *was* on the inside of Paul. Recall from Chapter 2 that demons can only be in one of two places in relation to man. They can be on the inside of him or on the outside. In Paul's case, I do not believe that the messenger of Satan was some external harassing spirit just punching him from the outside. Examine four different translations of the supplicatory verse, 2 Corinthians 12:8:

*Concerning this thing I pleaded with the Lord three times **that it might depart from me**.* (KJV)

*Three times I pleaded with the Lord to take it **away** from me.* (NIV)

*And I begged of my Lord concerning this three times, to **remove it from me**.* (Aramaic Bible in Plain English)

*Concerning this I implored the Lord three times **that it might leave me**.* (NASB)

## Paul's Infirmities

Some argue that Paul's messenger of Satan was just a metaphor for some sickness. They may point out the fact that Paul clearly mentions his infirmities in this same passage. They then reason that his infirmities *are* the thorn and that his infirmities *are* the messenger of Satan.

There is no doubt that Paul did have physical infirmities relating to his thorn and his messenger of Satan. He testifies:

*...Therefore most gladly I will rather boast in **my infirmities**, that the power of Christ may rest upon me.* 2 Corinthians 12:9 (NKJV)

However, the real question at hand is what is at the *root* of Paul's infirmities. Are the thorn and the messenger of Satan the infirmity itself? Or, are the infirmities a *result* of the thorn and the messenger of Satan?

For me, Paul's infirmities are related to his thorn and his messenger of Satan. But I do not believe that the thorn and the messenger of Satan are the infirmities themselves. I believe that the thorn and the messenger of Satan are the *source* of Paul's infirmities. In other words, the sickness that Paul was suffering from was the Satanic fruit of his demon.

Every experienced deliverance minister can testify to the fact that demons put sicknesses on their victims. In my own ministry, we constantly see cases where demons do this. I have seen demons put all sorts of infirmities on their victims, everything from cancer to fibromyalgia to bipolar to back pain to heart failure. For example, just today, I had a Skype Deliverance Encounter session with a woman from Houston, Texas. A Jezebel spirit was cast out of her that had been putting fibroids on her.

The Bible also testifies that demons can put sicknesses on their victims. For example, in Mark 9, Jesus cast out a deaf and mute spirit that was putting epilepsy on a young boy.

As a deliverance minister, I am not prepared to say that every sickness is the *direct* fruit of a demon. However, in Paul's Messenger of Satan passage, I believe that demonization and infirmity are mentioned together in such a way to imply a cause and effect relationship. I believe Paul had a demon. I believe that this demon was putting infirmities on Paul.

Biblical scholars have debated for almost two thousand years about what kind of physical afflictions Paul suffered from. There have been many theories as to what these sicknesses were. Some have theorized that they were an eye disease or tinnitus. Others have said that they referred to a person who was doing harm to his ministry. Still, others have wondered whether Paul's thorn and messenger of Satan were some sort of self-condemnation or PTSD from his murderous life earlier on.

Whatever the theory may be, for the NDMC Biblical scholar, it would be unspeakable that the Apostle Paul could have had a demon spirit inside of him causing these sicknesses. However, for the deliverance minister, the idea of Paul having an indwelling demon is completely plausible. We would say, "Why not?"

## Other Explanations Are Possibly A Result of Theological Prejudice

I believe that one of the main reasons that other explanations exist as to what Paul's thorn and messenger of Satan are, is because of theological prejudice and lack of practical experience in the casting out of demons. For most, the possibility of Paul, or "Saint Paul," for some, having a demon spirit is simply not on the table. Suggesting that Paul had a demon would even amount to blasphemy for some.

As we saw earlier, the NDMC correlates demonization with not being saved. So, when the NDMC hears that I believe that Paul might have had a demon, they think that I am implying that Paul was unsaved, which of course, I am not implying. I would agree that saying Paul was unsaved *would* be blasphemous. Paul was full of the Holy Spirit and knew Jesus personally. Paul was the chosen vessel. Paul certainly had the salvation of Jesus Christ.

And no doubt, after reading this book, some NDMC will accuse me of claiming that Paul was *possessed* by demons! To this, I would implore this NDMC to re-read Chapter 8 since, of course, I am not saying that Paul (or any other Christian for that matter) could be "possessed" by demons.

*Mark Chase*

## *Questions*

If we modern Christians can have demons, then why couldn't ancient Christians, even great ancient Christians like the Apostle Paul? What would make Paul any different?

Why couldn't Paul have had demons? He was not sinless. He had a heart full of deceit like you and me (Jeremiah 17:9). The words of Jesus that we are *all* evil (Luke 11:13) applied to Paul as much as they apply to us. He admitted to doing that (sin), which he hated. And, before his apostleship, he had committed the heavy sin of touching God's anointed. He murdered or was a party to the murder of many members of the early Christian Church.

If other murderers get demons because of their transgression of the Sixth Commandment, then why not Paul? And remember, the NDMC argument that all demons must somehow fly out at conversion is not Biblical at all. Nothing in the Bible says that a person's demons all disappear the moment he is born again.

## *Summary*

As uncomfortable as it is for the NDMC's to accept, I believe that an indwelling demon is the best explanation for Paul's "messenger (angel) of Satan." Paul's angel of Satan was a "thorn," causing him to be afflicted with unnamed infirmities. I even think there is a strong possibility that the thorn itself was an actual fiery dart, like the ones we see in the modern ministry of deliverance.

It is possible that as a persecutor and murderer of Christians, Paul got demons earlier on. Perhaps after he was born again, he still had holdover demons. What we do know for sure is that God allowed Paul to have this messenger of Satan in order to keep him from becoming too prideful.

I can't be dogmatic about the issue of Paul having a demon. However, in my opinion, the story of Paul's Messenger of Satan is likely the clearest, most obvious example in the Bible of a post-Calvary, post-Pentecost, Spirit-filled *Christian* having a demon. Move your spiritual opinions and doctrinal proclivities aside and ask the Holy Spirit to give you revelation.

I will conclude this chapter with one final translation of the verse in question:

*Lest I be lifted up by the abundance of revelations, a thorn for my flesh was handed over to me, an **Angel of Satan** to buffet me, lest I be lifted up.* 2 Corinthians 12:7 (Aramaic Bible in Plain English)

*Mark Chase*

# Chapter 14

# *Get Behind Me, Satan!*

After Paul, the Apostle Peter is the most significant Christian teacher of the New Testament. He knew Jesus before the Cross and walked with Him as a disciple since the very beginning of the Gospel narrative. He witnessed the Transfiguration and was there in the Garden of Gethsemane when Jesus agonized. Peter was also the first to recognize Jesus as the Messiah when Jesus asked him, *But who do you say that I am?* (Matthew 16:15)

> *Simon Peter answered and said, "You are the Christ, the Son of the living God."* Matthew 16:16 (NKJV)

Without question, Peter was a follower of Jesus. However, like every follower of Jesus, Peter had sin. Sometime after Peter identified Jesus as the Messiah, Jesus told His disciples that He must suffer and be killed:

*From that time Jesus began to show to His disciples that He must go to Jerusalem, and suffer many things from the elders and chief priests and scribes, and be killed, and be raised the third day.*
Matthew 16:21 (NKJV)

Then, instead of blessing and encouraging his Master to carry out His Father's mandate to be sacrificed and then resurrect on the third day, Peter *rebukes* Jesus:

## Mark Chase

*Then Peter took Him aside and began to rebuke Him, saying, "Far be it from You, Lord; **this shall not happen to You!**"*
Matthew 16:22 (NKJV)

    Has God ever given you a daring vision for ministry that involved some kind of serious risk? Have you ever told a close ministry associate, friend, or family member about this vision? Then, instead of *en*-couraging you, this individual proceeded to *dis*-courage you by speaking fear and unbelief into your vision, perhaps by pointing out financial risks and the like? If you have experienced something like this, it is possible that Satan was using that person to attack you in order to get you to quit. The fact that Satan uses believers to discourage and instill fear into other believers is more common than most Christians realize.

    Or, have you ever listened to someone speak and thought to yourself, "I know that that is not so-and-so speaking; that is a *demon* saying those things!" Perhaps it was your spouse who looked at you with a certain demonic look when he or she was angry. Or perhaps it was your rebellious teenage child.

    If you have experienced one of the above, then I believe you have an idea of what happened during this exchange between Jesus and Peter in the above verse.

    In the next verse, Jesus answers Peter's rebuke with a rebuke of His own. But a fascinating thing happens. Instead of rebuking Peter, Jesus rebukes *Satan*:

*But He turned and **said to Peter**, "Get behind Me, Satan! You are an offense to Me, for you are not mindful of the things of God, but the things of men."* Matthew 16:23 (NKJV)

    In this verse, Jesus did something that we do during Session Deliverance every day: Jesus looked at Peter and spoke in the physical direction of Peter, yet He *addressed* a demon!

    So, how is it possible that Jesus looked at Peter and yet spoke to Satan? Most Bible commentators say that this was just a figurative way that Jesus rebuked Peter for thinking along man's line of thought instead of God's. NDMC's like Pastor Rick in Chapter 8 would say that Jesus is just rebuking Peter's Satanic thinking patterns, not an actual demon.

However, I simply can't read it that way. I believe that something far more profound happened here. I plainly believe that Jesus was speaking to whom He said He was speaking to—to Satan. How is this possible? Simple. I think that it is likely that Peter had a demon on the inside, and Jesus was rebuking this demon. For those readers who are offended, I ask that you put down your stones and hear me out.

From my experience in the ministry of deliverance, I believe that when Peter said, "This shall not happen to You!" it is likely that a *demon* was up and speaking through Peter's lips. I believe that Matthew 16:22 is likely a Biblical record of an actual demonic manifestation—albeit a highly subtle one.

## *Peter Had Subtle Demonization*

Remember that around 90% of demonization is subtle. Most demonic manifestations do not involve a raging, convulsing, screaming, eyes-turning-red, foaming-at-the-mouth demoniac. I think that Peter, like most Christians with demons, had *subtle demonization*. The demon just spoke through Peter with demonic "concern" for Jesus's wellbeing. The demon wanted to discourage Jesus from carrying out His Father's salvific plan. And Jesus sternly rebuked this demon for it.

Demonic manifestations can be extremely subtle, and that is how Satan wants it. Satan wants to do his damage without exposing himself. Satan wants to carry out his assignment without letting anyone know that he is even there. Recall the lies of the devil in Chapter 3.

In a case like Peter's, if the deliverance minister doesn't embrace and covet the gift of the discerning of spirits (1 Corinthians 12:10), he might not even know that a demon was manifesting. In Session Deliverance, the job of the deliverance minister is to discern the spirit, expose it, interrogate it, make sure all the legal rights have been broken and removed, bind it, and cast it out—via the forceful command or some other projection of Holy Spirit power.

## *Upage Satana*

When Jesus looked at Peter and said, "Get behind Me, Satan!" He was using almost the exact same phraseology that He had said to Satan, the devil himself, at the end of His Temptation in the Wilderness. Back in Matthew 4, the Bible says:

> *Then Jesus said to him, "Away with you, Satan! For it is written, 'You shall worship the Lord your God, and Him only you shall serve.' "* Matthew 4:10 (NKJV)

These two expressions, *Away with you, Satan!* and *Get behind me, Satan!* are almost the exact same words in the original Greek. The only difference between the two expressions is the use of the word *opisō* in Matthew 16:23, which means "behind":

| Matthew 4:10 | Matthew 16:23 |
|---|---|
| "Away with you, Satan!" | "Get behind me, Satan!" |
| upage satana | upage **opisō** satana |
| To Satan, the devil himself | To a demon in Peter: perhaps to a demon named Satan, to an unknown demon, or to Satan himself |

My point is that Jesus said essentially the same thing to Satan face to face in the Wilderness as He did when He spoke right to Peter's face in the Matthew 16 narrative. I believe that God is clearly showing us who the *real* target of Jesus's words was when he was "speaking" to Peter.

The intended recipient of Jesus's words was the same on both occasions. Both times, Jesus was directing His words to Satan. Perhaps when Jesus rebuked the demon in Peter, he was using "Satan" as a generic name that could signify any demon.

Jesus did precisely this when He healed the *Daughter of*

## The Children's Bread

*Abraham* in Luke 13. She had a spirit of Infirmity (verse 11). However, Jesus generically referred to this demon as "Satan":

> *Then should not this woman, a daughter of Abraham, whom* **Satan** *has kept bound for eighteen long years, be set free on the Sabbath day from what bound her?* Luke 13:16 (NIV)

We do this in the ministry of deliverance today when we don't know the name of the demon. We just say, "Satan, I bind you!" even though it might be a Jezebel spirit, a spirit of Rejection, or whatever. Or, maybe Peter had a demon named Satan. Or, maybe the actual chief of demons was in Peter. Without specific revelation, this will remain a mystery.

Some might find it hard to believe that Jesus looked at the man, Peter, and yet *addressed* a demon. However, this would not be the only time in Scripture where Jesus did this. While addressing a man, the Demoniac of Gadara, Jesus interrogated a *demon*:

> *Then He asked him, "What is your name?" And he answered, saying,* **"My name is Legion**; *for we are many."* Mark 5:9 (NKJV)

In the above verse, there is no doubt that Jesus was looking right at the Demoniac the man while asking the *demon* what his name was. At Jesus's interrogation, a demon manifested through the Demoniac and spoke through him. The demon responded by speaking through the lips of the Demoniac, "My name is Legion; for we are many."

It is my understanding, therefore, that in the case of Peter, Jesus was looking at Peter, yet He was speaking to a demon. Where was this demon that Jesus was speaking to? I believe that there is only one option. Just like in the case of the Demoniac, Peter had a demon on the inside of him, and Jesus was addressing this indwelling demon. I do not believe that Peter's demon was on the outside of him, tempting him to rebuke Jesus by whispering into his ear.

From the passage itself, we do not know if this demon left Peter after this encounter with Jesus. Maybe Jesus, according to

His good pleasure, chose not to drive it out of Peter. Or, perhaps Jesus's rebuke alone cast out the demon. This is possible since we know that Power Encounter Deliverance can indeed occur by any projection of Holy Spirit power, including the rebuke. Maybe Jesus commanded the demon to leave, and the event simply isn't recorded in the Gospel narrative. This, too, will remain a mystery.

## Could the Apostle Peter Have Had a Demon?

Yes, Peter could have had a demon. And why couldn't he? The prophet Jeremiah's words apply to *all* men. We saw in the previous chapter that Jeremiah's words applied to Paul, and they apply to Peter as well:

*"The heart is **deceitful** above all things, And **desperately wicked**; Who can know it?* Jeremiah 17:9 (NJKV)

And so do the words of Isaiah:

*But we are all like an unclean thing, And all our righteousnesses are like **filthy rags**; We all fade as a leaf, And our iniquities, like the wind, Have taken us away.* Isaiah 64:5 (NKJV)

And the words of Jesus apply to Paul, us, and to Peter as well:

*If you then, being **evil**, know how to give good gifts to your children, how much more will your heavenly Father give the Holy Spirit to those who ask Him!* Luke 11:13 (NKJV)

Peter's heart, like yours, mine, and Paul's, was deceitful, full of wickedness, filthy, and evil. Peter was just as morally and spiritually bankrupt as any other man. If you don't see this, you are missing the point of Romans 3:10.

Like all Christians, it is only by the righteousness of Christ that Peter was made righteous (2 Corinthians 5:21). It is only by the Blood of Jesus that Peter's sins were cleansed. Peter himself understood his own sinfulness:

### The Children's Bread

*When Simon Peter saw it, he fell down at Jesus' knees, saying, "Depart from me, for I am a sinful man, O Lord!"*
Luke 5:8 (NKJV)

If you cannot recognize that your heart (or Peter's) is sinful and totally depraved before God's perfect standard of holiness and morality, then you need to ask the Holy Spirit to show you. The following verse also applies to you, me, Paul, as well as to Peter:

*If we say that we have no sin, we deceive ourselves, and the truth is not in us.* 1 John 1:8 (NKJV)

Peter needed a Savior just as much as you and I do. Surely, he had sin that could have given demons point of entry. Certainly, it was sinful of Peter to tell the Savior to disobey the Father by rebuking him:

*But Peter took him aside and began to **reprimand** him for saying such things. "Heaven forbid, Lord," he said. "This will never happen to you!"* Matthew 16:22 (NLT)

And this wouldn't be Peter's only sin. Earlier, he had doubted Jesus and fearfully began to sink into the waves on the Sea of Galilee (Matthew 14:30). Later, he would later personally sin against Jesus by denying knowing Him three times. And again, in yet another vain attempt to "save" Jesus from the Crucifixion, Peter sinfully took his sword and cut off the ear of Malchus (John 18:10), for which Jesus also rebuked him.

Jesus telling Peter to his face, *"Get behind me, Satan!"* would be consistent with Peter having a demon on the inside. This is what it looks like in the modern ministry of deliverance. The deliverance minister looks at the PRM and speaks in the authority of Christ—*to the demon.*

## Peter Was a True Disciple

Judas Iscariot had a demon (Luke 22:3), but perhaps Judas wasn't a real disciple with the Holy Spirit. Peter, on the other hand, certainly was a true disciple who had power and authority over demons and even raised the dead (Acts 9:40). One cannot say that Peter wasn't a true disciple of Christ. Later, we see that Peter was filled with the Holy Spirit:

> *Then Peter, **filled with the Holy Spirit**, said to them, "Rulers of the people and elders of Israel.* Acts 4:8 (NKJV)

Peter was a real disciple of Jesus, and after Pentecost, a real Spirit-filled Christian. From his encounter with Jesus in Matthew 16, I believe that it is reasonable to say that he had a real unclean spirit too. Peter's demon wasn't in his spirit, though. Instead, it was in his mind or body. The fact that he had a demon does not mean that Peter wasn't a true disciple or that he didn't have salvation. There is no correlation between demonization and salvation. Peter certainly knew the Lord and had His salvation.

## *Declaring "Get Behind Me Satan!" Is Anointed Deliverance Prayer*

In my own ministry, when I confront demons in public and in private sessions, I will many times look the PRM right in the eyes and speak the same anointed words of Jesus: "Get behind me, Satan!" These are powerful words that make demons shudder. In fact, Demons manifest and flee just by hearing these anointed words! Speaking a verse such as this while conducting deliverance ministry is also an example of projecting Holy Spirit power. It is also an example of declaring God's word.

## *Jesus Was Not Calling Peter the Devil*

When I am in session, and I look at the PRM in the eyes and say, "Get behind me, Satan!" I am not calling the PRM Satan. The PRM is precious and made in God's image. I am not calling the PRM Satan; I am calling the *demon* Satan.

Like Jesus, when I look at an individual and speak those words, I am challenging the *demons*, not the man. I am forcefully confronting demonic spirits. I want the demon to manifest and be exposed. My will has aligned with God to resist this demon!

## *The Liberation of Peter: Symbolic of Deliverance?*

It is interesting to note that later in Acts 12, Peter is imprisoned by King Herod Agrippa as part of his crackdown on the new Christian Church. While Peter slept in the prison, an angel of the Lord came and loosed the chains from Peter's wrists and led him to freedom while all the prison guards slept.

Perhaps the Liberation of Peter from Herod's prison is emblematic of Peter's eventual *spiritual* freedom. Perhaps God is telling us that Peter was delivered from demons at this point. This is yet another mystery. I do believe, however, that God is showing us that He uses His holy angels to aid us in our deliverance process. This is a clear example of angelic assistance.

For the deliverance ministry student who is interested in learning more about the role of holy angels in the ministry of deliverance, it is recommended that you enroll in our online school, Invicta University. The little-understood topic of angelic assistance during deliverance is taught there.

The fact that the Gospel writer tells us that Jesus addressed Peter yet spoke to a demon is, in my opinion, strong evidence that Peter had a demon on the inside. As in the case of Paul's messenger of Satan, I will not be dogmatic. However, understand that I am looking at this story from the perspective of a deliverance minister who confronts demons in Christians daily, including Christian church leaders, worship leaders, pastors' wives, etc.

I know that the NDMC will scoff at my perspective, but the NDMC doesn't spend time day in and day out sitting with Christians, and even ministry leaders, to cast out their demons either. The NDMC has little or no experience commanding demons to go. The NDMC is convinced that Christians are immune to indwelling demons simply because of their salvation status. The NDMC is sure that if anyone ever manifests a demon, then that is proof positive that he wasn't really saved, to begin with. The NDMC believes that all demons fly out of an individual at the moment of salvation. And above all, the NDMC doesn't see the overriding pattern in Scripture that *God delivers those who belong to Him.*

And, just like I mentioned in the previous chapter about Paul, if an NDMC claims after reading this chapter that I am saying that Peter was "possessed" by demons, he needs to re-read Chapter 8. Peter, like all Christians, was possessed by God and by God alone.

Deliverance ministers see that it is plausible that Peter the Apostle had a demon. Jesus addressed a demon while looking directly at Peter. The story of Peter in Matthew 16 is another strong Biblical evidence that a true follower of Jesus, or even a Spirit-filled Christian, can indeed have a demon on the inside.

# Part 5

# *Conversion vs. Deliverance*
# *Promise vs. Possession*
# *&*
# *Challenges for the NDMC*

*Mark Chase*

# Chapter 15

# *Conversion and Deliverance Are Two Separate Events*

In the Bible, conversion to Christ and deliverance from evil spirits are described as two separate events. While both are a *form* of deliverance, they are still separate. Conversion is deliverance from Hellfire. This is Big Deliverance. Deliverance is being set free from demons. This is Little Deliverance. There are clear stories of conversion in the Bible:

> *Now when he had brought them into his house, he set food before them; and he rejoiced,* **having believed in God** *with all his household.* Acts 16:34 (NKJV)

And we see separate stories of deliverance:

> **He said to them,** *"Go!" So they came out and went into the pigs, and the whole herd rushed down the steep bank into the lake and died in the water.* Matthew 8:32 (NIV)

When we comprehend that conversion and deliverance are two distinct events, we understand that demons do not instantly leave the newly converted Christian. The newly converted Christian still has the same holdover demons that he had a second earlier, right before he confessed Jesus as Lord. Nowhere in the Bible is it taught that demons leave their human hosts at the moment of their conversion. In fact, nowhere in the Bible is it taught that conversion is an alternative method of driving out demons. The Bible gives us two separate mandates. One to preach the Gospel, and another to take authority over demons and cast them out in the Name of Jesus.

I believe that if conversion and deliverance were one and the same, we would not have two separate mandates in the Great Commission—one mandate to bring sinners to faith in Christ by preaching the Gospel, and another separate mandate to deliver people from demons:

*And He said to them, "Go into all the world and **preach the gospel** to every creature."* Mark 16:15 (NKJV)

And then separately:

*And these signs will follow those who believe: In My name they will **cast out demons**; they will speak with new tongues.*
Mark 16:17 (NKJV)

## NDMC Confusion on Conversion vs. Deliverance

Most NDMC's will admit that they are a bit confused about this issue. We saw in Chapter 9 that NDMC evangelist Daniel Kolenda humbly admitted that he is. These NDMC's know that in order for their theology to work, all demons must leave a person the moment he or she is born again. The problem is, and they know it, there is nothing in the Bible that would suggest that all demons come out at the moment of conversion. Once again, for emphasis, we are not against NDMC's like Daniel Kolenda. NDMC's like Daniel Kolenda do mighty work for Jesus. Instead, we are against *Satan* for spreading the lie that conversion to Christ automatically casts out all demons.

If you ask an NDMC to show a verse that indicates that all demons leave at conversion, they will quote the ones I have already discussed in this book. They will say that light doesn't have fellowship with darkness and that we are new creations in Christ. Both of these are true, but neither proves the NDMC point. I have demonstrated this fact in this book.

As a result, the NDMC's skip over the issue of conversion and just say what makes sense to them—that born-again Christians can't have indwelling demons. In doing so, they run away from the issue of what really happens at conversion.

In this book, I want to force the NDMC to address the issue of what really does happen at conversion. I have made it clear that at conversion, we receive a new *spirit*—the Holy Spirit (John 3:3). At conversion, we are born of the Spirit. We become new creations. Everything changes in our lives.

However, our minds and bodies are not instantly and automatically cleaned out and healed. God will still need to do a work of healing in these parts. The Holy Spirit will still need to renew our minds which transforms us (Romans 12:2). This renewing and transforming will happen little by little (Deuteronomy 7:22). This is part of the process of sanctification.

God will still need to deliver us from the demons that dwell in these parts. I have made the point that salvation in Jesus Christ is not the final deliverance that a Christian will receive in his or her lifetime. Big Deliverance is the first and most important deliverance, but it is not the last.

## The Salvation-Settles-it-All Syndrome

My teacher and pioneer deliverance minister Bob Larson coined the excellent term *the Salvation-Settles-it-All Syndrome*. This term is very useful as it accurately describes the NDMC's view on deliverance. In fact, this false concept is the *foundation* of the NDMC's doctrine that Christians can't have demons.

Proponents of the Salvation-Settles-it-All Syndrome believe that at the moment of salvation, all of a person's deliverance needs are completely and instantaneously fulfilled. In other words, at the moment of conversion, all curses are broken, every ungodly soul-tie is severed, every ungodly stronghold is pulled down, and of course, every single demon is instantly expelled.

However, the concept that salvation settles it all is not supported by Scripture and is not what I or others who work in deliverance see taking place in real life either. What I see in Scripture and in everyday ministry experience is that salvation and deliverance are two separate events.

In Scripture, I see a divine order that begins with salvation. Recall the divine order from Isaiah 61 and Luke 4:

> Salvation→Healing→Deliverance

What I see happening in real life is that demonization continues beyond the born-again experience. I see that people are usually born again, and *then* they begin their journey of healing and deliverance. Being born again doesn't remove the demons. Being born again gives the individual *power and authority* over the demons—authority to resist them, bind them, and ultimately to cast them out! Being born again is the first step, not the final stop.

I even see that it is *possible* for born-again believers to get new demons after salvation. I have called this phenomenon post-conversion demonization. This can happen as a result of overt sin, passivity in the execution of Godly authority, ignorance, the embracing of Satanic thinking patterns, and others.

## *Who the Son Sets Free*

Occasionally, the NDMC will quote John 8:36 in defense of their theology that Christians cannot have indwelling demons. Essentially, this is just another way of saying that salvation settles it all. This objection to deliverance for Christians is called the *Who-the-Son-Sets-Free Argument*. Here is the verse:

> *So if the Son sets you free, you will be free indeed.* John 8:36 (NIV)

The beautiful Scripture refers to how when Jesus saves us, we are no longer "slaves to sin." We know this because, back in verse 34, Jesus said that *everyone who sins is a slave to sin.* By saying *everyone who sins*, Jesus is referring to those who are unsaved. In other words, those who sin without any care that they are sinning. The NDMC's reasoning is that if the Son sets someone free from being a slave to sin—because they now have salvation—then this person will be free from *everything* of the enemy, including indwelling demons.

This is the crux of the Salvation-Settles-it-All Syndrome, which demands that all indwelling demons must vanish at the moment of salvation. The NDMC reasons that born-again believers cannot have any indwelling demons since, after salvation, they will be and must be *free indeed*. The NDMC continues by reasoning that if one does indeed have any indwelling demons, then he or she must not have had salvation to begin with. In other words, anyone who has demons is not really born again.

It is important to return to the primary meaning of the verse. When Jesus said that we would be *free indeed*, He meant that we (those with salvation) would be free from being slaves to sin. And what is a slave to sin? A slave to sin is someone who is unsaved. It is someone with no power to overcome the influence of sin. It is someone who is held captive by their ruler, sin. Who are those that are in this state? Those that are held captive, or slaves, to sin are those who do not have salvation in Jesus Christ. Therefore, a slave to sin is someone who is not saved, or born again.

Making the jump from freedom from slavery to sin to freedom from *everything* of the enemy is reading too much into the verse. To illustrate, Paul was born again. He was no longer a slave to sin. However, he was not free from his messenger of Satan (2 Corinthians 12:7). This was the case even though he tried to get free from it (verse 8). Therefore, Paul was "free indeed," but he wasn't free from the torment of his messenger of Satan. Paul was free indeed, but he wasn't free from *everything* of the enemy.

As a secondary meaning, John 8:36 can also refer to deliverance from demons. Certainly, when Jesus sets someone free from a demon—in other words, He delivers them from a demon—

they truly are free indeed from that demon! In this way, John 8:36 can refer to deliverance from demons, or Little Deliverance.

However, and this is critical, we cannot mix the primary and secondary meanings of this verse. We cannot say that because one has received Big Deliverance (salvation), then he must have also received Little Deliverance (deliverance from demons). And likewise, we cannot say that just because one receives Little Deliverance, then he must have automatically received Big Deliverance. Therefore, the Who-the-Son-Sets-Free Argument does not prove the NDMC position.

We know this since not all the unsaved who receive deliverance from demons during Evangelistic Deliverance end up converting. It is a sad fact that some who receive Sovereign Deliverance during evangelism never truly convert.

We also know that individuals are not born again by virtue of receiving deliverance from demon spirits. Instead, Scripture teaches that people are born again when they repent of their sins and confess that Jesus is Lord. Men are saved by grace through their faith in Jesus.

## The Churches Don't Want Deliverance Ministry

Many churches can't bring the ministry of deliverance into their organizations since it represents such a radical shift in church operations. Many churches have a membership base that will not accept the radical "new doctrine" of casting out demons and other workings of the Gifts of the Holy Spirit. Their church members will ask the same questions that those in the synagogue at Capernaum asked:

> *Then they were all amazed, so that they questioned among themselves, saying,* ***"What is this? What new doctrine is this?*** *For with authority He commands even the unclean spirits, and they obey Him."* Mark 1:27 (NKJV)

They especially will not tolerate the "radical" concept that some of their own members might need deliverance from demons.

## *The Children's Bread*

In some cases, the church leadership knows that deliverance is real and that it should be taking place in their church. However, they remain silent since to do otherwise would be an affront to their denomination's tradition, catechism, or official doctrine. These leaders are aware of the fact that they could be dismissed by their Board of Directors if they were to go against their church's rules.

In other cases, the church leadership remains silent in order to submit to the will of the church members. These leaders do not want to risk offending the church members and possibly jeopardize attendance or giving. There is a lot at stake when running a church.

As an aside, most North American pastors shy away from preaching strongly against sin (showing members that they are all *personally* guilty of breaking *all* of God's moral laws). These pastors will avoid using the words "repentance" and "Hell" for the same reasons as listed above.

Still, in other cases, deliverance is shunned due to its appearances. As Pastor Sam Alcime pointed out at the beginning of this book, some people just don't care to see demonic manifestations. At my ministry office in Fort Lauderdale, Florida, we must thoroughly clean the carpet in our public meeting area once per month. This is due to the fact that when demons are expelled from individuals, spit-up and other fluids are ejected. Not all of it makes it into the trash can. The cleanup of bodily fluids may not be a pleasant topic, but it is part of the reality of delivering precious individuals from evil spirits.

When individuals come to our weekly public meetings, I tell them not to worry about what others think or see. I tell them that they are in a spiritual hospital. I assure attendees that they can let it up and let it out. Yawn, cough, vomit, scream, or spit because those things are OK in this place. Occasionally, demons must even be peed out in the bathroom. I remind attendees that when people are in the hospital, they don't worry about their image; they are there to get better!

Because of the outward appearance of deliverance

(coughing, spitting up, crying out, etc.), many churches just don't want this sort of thing taking place inside their facility. Recall the story of Reverend Mike in Chapter 3. For him, it was an embarrassment for a demon to manifest in the church.

Of course, the deep underlying reason why churches don't want deliverance ministries on their campuses is simple. They know that by doing so, they will be forced to address the question of whether a Christian can have a demon. Most churches simply aren't ready to deal with this issue.

## The Reason Why Deliverance Ministries Exist

Deliverance Ministries like ours exist precisely because all demons *do not* come out at salvation. If they did, my public meetings would be empty, and my private session calendar would have no appointments. It is unreasonable to say that *every single one* of the thousands of people who have come to my ministry to receive deliverance were really just fake Christians or false converts.

Therefore, two factors come together to create the real need for independent deliverance ministries:

1. All demons are not expelled at conversion.
2. Most churches are NDMC churches and therefore withhold the Children's Bread to the hungry believers for a variety of reasons. In other words, whole flocks are not being fed.

As a result of these two factors, God raises up ministries of deliverance like ours to fill the void and give His people the deliverance that He promises in His word. God commissions these deliverance ministries with the task of being servers of His Deliverance Bread. Therefore, the deliverance ministry will continue to be an increasingly popular spiritual supplement that Christians take since most are not getting all their spiritual, nutritional needs met at their local churches—especially in the intellectually strong churches of North America and Western Europe.

*The Children's Bread*

## *Deliverance Ministries Shouldn't Exist at All*

Actually, and this is shocking, so brace yourself—*deliverance ministries shouldn't exist at all*. Why is this? Because if the church local were obedient to the Great Commission (Mark 16:17), then there would be much less need for separate, independent deliverance ministries to begin with. Deliverance would be taking place on a wide-scale basis *in the churches*.

Until this is the case, we will continue to bless the NDMC church. I teach my deliverance ministry students that we are not to look down on the NDMC or think that we are somehow superior to them—because we are not. We do not desire that God give *us* a messenger of Satan to keep *us* from being puffed up. And let me restate something. Spiritual pride is definitely a potential legal right for demons. Every deliverance minister needs to know that.

God gave us a revelation, and we are trying to be obedient. Thankfully, many NDMC church members are now coming to our ministries. They learn about deliverance, see it taking place, and even receive it themselves. In this way, they are encouraged to really learn this ministry and take it back to their churches. By God's grace, NDMC churches are becoming ex-NDMC churches!

## *Deliverance Revival*

Things are changing. God is moving. Many NDMC churches in North America are receiving the revelation that they need to serve the Children's Bread too. And not just serve it but serve it to their own members!

Deliverance is becoming more and more accepted, and there is a revival in the area of executing the *full* Great Commission as outlined in Mark 16. As I mentioned, many NDMC churches are becoming ex-NDMC churches. God is showing them that they should be doing deliverance—within the churches. If you are involved in a church where deliverance revival is taking place, let us know. We would love to hear about it and celebrate with you!

However, until there is abundant and equal access to deliverance in the churches, ministries like Invicta Ministries will continue to rise up and meet the deliverance and healing needs of hurting Christians. God has called me to heal His Church. Many other ministers of deliverance are receiving the same call.

No doubt, while we do this, the staunch NDMC's will continue to "prove" that Christians can't have demons. The NDMC's will continue to insist that what we are doing is theologically impossible. The NDMC's will continue to say that we don't know what we are talking about, even though they themselves do no Session Deliverance and most likely no deliverance at all. As a result of the NDMC's denial, God will keep multiplying the deliverance ministries in order to fill the obvious and undeniable need.

## Radical Conversions

*Radical conversions* are those conversions where the newly born-again Christian is on fire for Jesus and begins his ministry immediately after his or her conversion. Sometimes even the day after conversion, these radically saved individuals are calling people up on the phone and praying for them! People who experience radical conversions are, as skateboarder evangelist Brian Sumner said, "Hardcore, sold-out and on-fire for Jesus." Personally, I believe that Paul the Apostle was the first Christian in the Bible who experienced a radical conversion. Radically saved people will be used mightily by God, and God will use them *immediately* after their conversions!

Many times radical conversions are accompanied by physical healing and even deliverance from demons. Once again, God is sovereign, and He determines who is delivered and when they are delivered. When deliverance from demons does occur at conversion, an example of *Spontaneous Deliverance* has happened.

## The Children's Bread

## *Spontaneous Deliverance*

Spontaneous Deliverance is a form of Sovereign Deliverance. It occurs when God forces demons to leave a person in the absence of explicit, intentional projections of Holy Spirit power such as the forceful command, "Come out in the Name of Jesus!" In other words, Spontaneous Deliverance happens when no one is consciously *trying* to cast out demons.

Spontaneous Deliverance is unplanned, and both Christians and nonbelievers alike can receive it. The key trait of Spontaneous Deliverance is that it occurs during moments of being in the strong presence of the Holy Spirit. These types of moments include:

- At radical conversion
- During Spirit-filled worship
- While hearing an anointed sermon, especially when the sermon is about repentance or fear of the Lord
- While reading God's anointed word, the Bible
- During prayer
- While being interceded for by others
- When receiving the laying on of hands
- When receiving an anointing with oil
- While fasting
- While taking Holy Communion
- While being baptized in water
- While working in the Gifts of the Holy Spirit such as speaking in tongues or prophesying
- While delivering or healing *someone else*
- While hearing the shofar being blown or other prophetic sounds
- While receiving the baptism of the Holy Spirit

Spontaneous Deliverance can occur when a demonized individual steps on blessed territory such as a particularly anointed church or home. Spontaneous Deliverance can even occur when a demonized individual comes into contact with an anointed, or blessed, *physical object*:

*Now God worked unusual miracles by the hands of Paul, so that even **handkerchiefs or aprons** were brought from his body to the sick, and the diseases left them and the **evil spirits went out of them**.* Acts 19:11-12 (NKJV)

Spontaneous Deliverance is a wonderful manifestation of God's power in our lives. I believe we should all desire to receive Spontaneous Deliverance.

However, from my understanding of the Bible and from my personal experience, I believe that *most* demons do not come out via Spontaneous Deliverance—at conversion or otherwise.

Most demons just won't give up and leave until they are *commanded* or *forced* to come out in the Name of, and by the authority of, Jesus Christ of Nazareth. And some of these demons still won't come out, either sovereignly or technically, except by prayer and fasting (Matthew 17:21).

## *Proximal Deliverance*

Proximal Deliverance is another form of Sovereign Deliverance that is frequently observed in the deliverance ministry. It occurs spontaneously and usually unexpectedly. In this sense, it is similar to Spontaneous Deliverance. However, it is different from Spontaneous Deliverance in that that it occurs sovereignly *across Godly soul-ties*, or relationship bonds. The *Godly soul-tie* is the key factor in Proximal Deliverance.

Proximal Deliverance functions like this:

1. Person A has a Godly soul-tie with Person B (for example, a husband and wife).
2. Person A receives deliverance, for example, during Session Deliverance.
3. Person B then unexpectedly receives deliverance, or healing of some kind, as a result of Person A's deliverance.
4. Person B receives this deliverance even though she was not physically present with Person A when Person A received his deliverance.

5. It is deliverance across a Godly soul-tie. It is a ripple effect. It radiates outward from Person A to those people who have Godly soul-ties, or relationships, with Person A.
6. It usually occurs unintentionally; however, it is good practice to inform the PRM that by her deliverance, those close to her may also receive healing. This is wonderful news for the PRM, who, for example, has a close family member who is unwilling to submit to deliverance or even receive Jesus as Lord. Proximal Deliverance is a wonderful way that God allows one person to be spontaneously healed through the efforts of another.

Remember, the key is that there must be a *Godly soul-tie* between the two individuals (husband-wife, father-son, friendship, etc.). Godly soul-ties are God-ordained relationships. In my ministry, Invicta Ministries, we have observed and documented the effect of Proximal Deliverance on many, many occasions. We have received many testimonies of Proximal Deliverance. Here are three examples of Proximal Deliverance that we have documented:

### Example #1

I once had a Skype Deliverance Encounter session with a 29-year-old mother from Minnesota. During her session, her husband took their four-year-old son to the mall in order to give mom privacy at home for her teleministry session. During mom's session, a powerful spirit of Fear was cast out of her. Days later, I spoke to the woman's husband. He informed me that while he was at the mall, the four-year-old had suddenly begun to make faces as if something were caught in his throat. Then the child threw up. He reported to us that he had thought to himself, *this has to be deliverance* since the child had not eaten for some time. The husband was right. The child *did* receive deliverance. By default, the child and his mother automatically have a Godly soul-tie of mother-son. When mom was delivered, this blessing crossed over to her son and provoked a deliverance response in the young child.

## Mark Chase

## Example #2

One woman from Gabon in Africa had an in-person session with our ministry. During her session, she lamented how her mother hated her and only wanted money from her. The woman also said that her mother even went to a witch doctor to send curses against her. During her session, demons of Satan, Black Panther, and Ocean Spirits were cast out of her. Some days after her session, she texted us, elated that there was a sudden softening of her mother's heart. Her mother had changed as a result of her session. Her mother had received Proximal Deliverance:

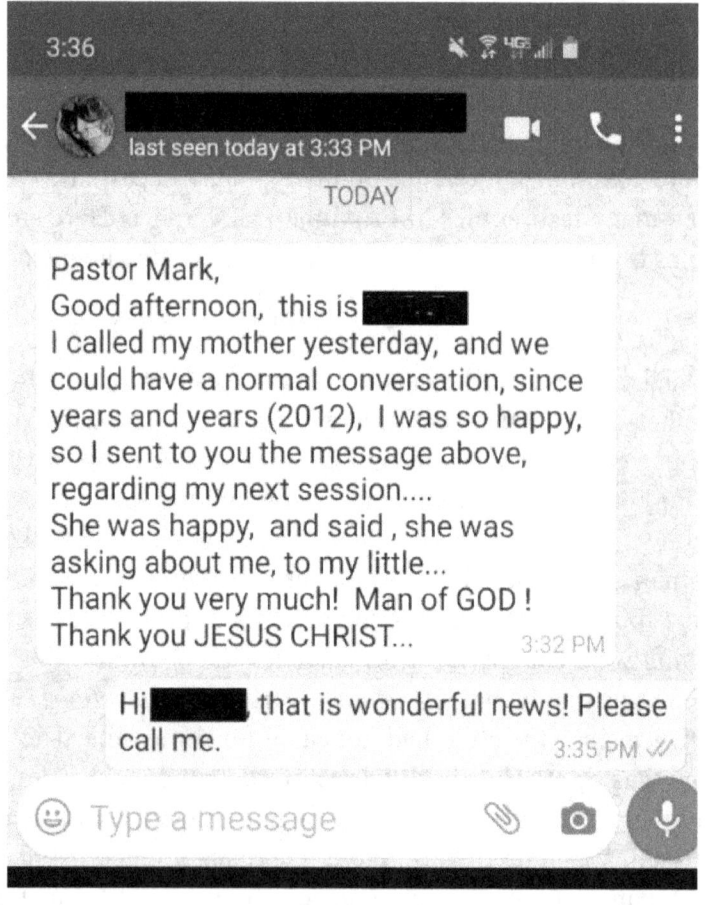

### Example #3

One married woman from Québec, Canada, had two Skype sessions with Invicta Ministries. She told us how her husband had once said the sinner's prayer but that he didn't really walk in it. In other words, he wasn't really born again. During her second session, she received deliverance from a large kingdom of demons, including spirits of Pride, Fornication, Defeat, Fear, Anger, and many others. A few months after this session, she got back in touch with us and informed us that her husband had received massive conviction of sin from the Holy Spirit and had begun to seek the Lord sincerely. This woman's blessing of deliverance crossed over to her unsaved husband and blessed him. Her Little Deliverance opened the way for Big Deliverance to take place in her husband. Her husband received Proximal Deliverance.

## Proximal Deliverance is Sovereign

Proximal Deliverance is sovereign since Person A is not *intentionally* trying to deliver person B. God just moves sovereignly to deliver Person B after Person A receives her healing.

We teach that while ungodly soul-ties can allow curses and even demons to cross over (transference of spirits), the Godly soul-tie permits *blessing* to cross over. This includes the blessing of healing and deliverance, and in the case of the woman above from Québec, even conviction of sin leading to repentance and salvation. The concept of Proximal Deliverance is taught on more in our online school, Invicta University, for those who wish to go deeper.

## Deliverance in the Developing Regions

If you are from a developing nation in the Americas, the Caribbean, Africa, or Eastern Europe, then deliverance ministry is probably not such a radical practice in your local churches. It is probably not considered a "new doctrine" or a "new teaching" (Mark 1:27). If you are from one of these regions, you may have even witnessed demonic manifestations in church. You may have even seen a Christian being delivered from demons.

Once again, I will dispel the misconception that many North American church leaders have. This misconception is that demons are more prevalent in the developing regions of the world than they are in North America and Western Europe.

As a deliverance minister, I can assure my readers that there are just as many demons here in North America as there are in Brazil, China, and Haiti. People are just as demonized in Fort Lauderdale, Florida, as they are in Lagos, Nigeria. Perhaps with different kinds of demons, different legal rights, and different levels of subtlety, but demons, nonetheless.

## Demons Do Not Manifest When They Are Not Permitted To

Demonic manifestations occur more frequently in developing regions because they are *permitted* to manifest. In most North American churches, pastors do not want demons to manifest. Recall the story of Reverend Mike O'Dwyer in Chapter 3 again. Pastors do not confront and challenge demons. Many churches prohibit the ministry of deliverance altogether. In order to understand why this occurs, one must understand that deliverance is a *miracle*. Jesus teaches us this fact in Mark 9:39.

Now, the fifth Gift of the Holy Spirit is the working of *miracles* (1 Corinthians 12:10). If the working of miracles is not tolerated in a certain church or denomination, the Holy Spirit will respect this man-made prohibition and not allow this Gift to manifest in that church. (Keep in mind that the majority of North American churches teach that the Gifts of the Holy Spirit ceased after the Apostolic age.)

God is a respecter of the will of men—even when the will of men is to reject His blessings. When Christians bind the Gifts on Earth, the Gifts will be bound in Heaven. That is the nature of God.

## *The Children's Bread*

When the miracle of deliverance is not permitted to take place in a certain ministry, demons are subsequently permitted to stay down and remain hidden in the darkness. One of the meanings of the Christian's authority to bind and loose (Matthew 18:18) is that what the leaders allow, God will allow and what the leaders disallow, God will also not allow. It is a fact that Christians have great and mighty authority in Jesus Christ.

In ministries that do not permit deliverance, God will not shine His light on demons to expose them (Ephesians 5:13). As mentioned above, God respects the will of His Church leaders. Where deliverance is prohibited, demons don't have to manifest. The (mostly) subtle demonization will continue unchallenged.

And when demons do manifest here in North America, rarely will the manifesting individual receive *enacted-on-the-spot deliverance ministry*. She will either receive the wrong kind of prayer, or she will be hidden away until the manifestation is over.

In the developing regions, the Gifts of the Holy Spirit are generally more welcomed, sought after, invited, and even coveted (1 Corinthians 12:31). As a result, demons are generally permitted to come up to manifestation. In these regions, more pastors, evangelists, and even deliverance ministers are being obedient to Jesus and confronting the demons there. They know that demons are real and that Christians can have them. They want to set people free—even if they are Christians. They are being humble and not arguing with God about who is, and who is not, allowed to receive deliverance ministry. They know that dealing with demons is an important component of the Christian faith. They are not trying to protect the impressions of the first-time visitors or remain ingratiated with the old guard church members who hold to religion, cessationism, or the Salvation-Settles-it-All Syndrome.

Churches in the developing regions realize that when God works the miracle of Sovereign Deliverance, He does it as a sign to confirm His word. They know that the Church has always needed these signs to win new converts. They know that the early

Christian Church grew so quickly because of these signs.

The writer of Hebrews teaches us:

*And God confirmed the message by giving signs and wonders and various miracles and gifts of the Holy Spirit whenever he chose.*
Hebrews 2:4 (New Living Translation)

## *Summary*

Conversion to Christ and deliverance from demons are two separate events in the Bible. There are separate Biblical stories of conversion and separate Biblical stories of deliverance from demons. There are also two separate mandates in the Great Commission in Mark 16. There is one mandate to preach the Gospel and win souls, and there is another separate mandate to cast out evil spirits. If demons all came out at conversion, why then would there need to be two separate mandates in the Great Commission?

The Bible never says that conversion is an alternative to the issuance of the forceful command. The Bible never even alludes to the notion that all demons come out at conversion. The Bible does not support the doctrine that salvation settles it all. The fact that Big Deliverance is separate from Little Deliverance is sufficient in and of itself to demonstrate that Christians can have demons.

# Chapter 16

# *The Promise vs. The Possession*

The promise vs. the possession is a major Biblical concept that runs through both Testaments of Scripture. In the Old Testament, God promised the Hebrews the land of Canaan. But it wasn't automatic. They had to cross the River Jordan, fight and conquer the pagan idolaters, and then take possession of it.

In the New Testament, God makes another promise: the promise of salvation. But, just like the Old Testament promise to the Hebrews, God's promise of salvation isn't automatic either. It must be *taken possession* of. The Gospel must be responded to.

## God's Promise to the Unsaved

The most memorized verse in the New Testament reveals both the promise of salvation and what men must do to take possession of this promise:

> *For God so loved the world that He gave His only begotten Son, that* **whoever believes in Him should not perish** *but have everlasting life.* John 3:16 (NKJV)

God promises everlasting life. This is the promise. Salvation is the promise. However, everyone in the world is not automatically saved just because Jesus went to the Cross. Instead, salvation must be *taken possession of*. Every man and woman on Earth must believe on Him in order to take possession of this promise. This is done by repenting of sin and confessing Him as Lord. This is responding to the Gospel. When man repents of sin and believes on Jesus as Lord, he takes possession of God's promise of salvation.

Only in this way can man take possession of God's promise of everlasting life and be delivered from the punishment that he rightfully deserves—the judgment fires of Hell. This is Big Deliverance. God's offer of salvation is available to the whole world, but only those who believe on Jesus are saved. In other words, there is a difference between God revealing His plan of salvation (the promise) and man actually being saved (taking possession of it). They are two separate steps. Yet another divine order: First, God reveals His plan, then man accepts or rejects it.

## God's Promise to the Born-Again Believer To Have Authority over Demons

When we are born again, God gives us *authority in Jesus Christ*. This authority legally authorizes each Christian to do not only what Jesus did but also to do even greater things. One of our many authorities in Jesus Christ is our *authority over demons*.

God promises us born-again believers that we can cast out demons in the Name of Jesus. God makes this promise to those who are His disciples. The disciple's authority over demons is stated in multiple Scriptures. Here are two examples:

> *And when He had called His twelve disciples to Him,* **He gave them power over unclean spirits**, *to cast them out, and to heal all kinds of sickness and all kinds of disease.* Matthew 10:1 (NKJV)

## The Children's Bread

And:

> *I have given you authority to trample on snakes and scorpions and to overcome all the power of the enemy; nothing will harm you.* Luke 10:19 (NIV)

Jesus gives all of His disciples the promise of being able to cast out demons in His Name. Keep in mind that the definition of His disciple is *one who abides in His word* (John 8:31). Who are those who abide in His word, post-Pentecost? It is us, the born-again Christians. Also, keep in mind that when I say, "born-again Christian," I am not referring to some evangelical denomination of North American Christianity. Jesus said that *all* men must be *born again* (John 3:3). *To be a Christian, one must be born again. No one on Earth is exempt from this requirement.*

So, God promises His disciples that they will have the power and authority to drive out demons. However, this does not mean that at the moment Jesus declared these promises to His disciples, that every demon would automatically be cast out of every Jew, Samaritan, and gentile on Earth. His disciples (we included) would still need to go out and *use* their authority and deliver the people. Using this authority is the same thing as taking possession of this promise.

Therefore, we have been promised this authority to drive out unclean spirits in the Name of Jesus. But it doesn't just happen automatically. We need to take possession of this promise. We believers need to go out and get the job done. If we don't, God's promise of giving us authority over demons goes unfulfilled. If we don't, we never take possession of this promise.

Deliverance ministers walk in this authority daily. I can attest to this. I can feel the authority I have when I confront demon spirits. But I know that my authority is not from me, nor is it for me. It is the Lord's. This authority is inside of me because the Holy Spirit resides in me. In this way, God uses me to carry out His work of proclaiming freedom for the captives (Isaiah 61:1).

Mark Chase

## *The Formula for Freedom*

*Submit yourselves, then, to God. Resist the devil, and he will flee from you.* James 4:7 (NIV)

James, the brother of Jesus, teaches about yet another promise of God. I call this promise the "Formula for Freedom." It takes the previous authority-over-demons promise one step further. In the previous section, we saw that Christians have been promised by God to have spiritual authority to drive out demons.

Now, James shows how the *one with the demons* (the PRM, the one that needs to be delivered) is promised by God that she can have authority over her own demons and make them flee.

The promise of the Formula for Freedom has two levels of meaning. The first level of meaning refers to freedom from the fires of Hell, which is Big Deliverance. If man would submit to God (repent and confess Jesus as Lord) and resist the devil (renounce his old god Satan), he or she can rest in God's eternal salvation. He will be freed from his previous slavery to sin.

The second level of meaning of the Formula for Freedom refers to deliverance from demons. This is Little Deliverance. In this section about the Formula for Freedom, we will focus on this second, deeper level of meaning. When the Formula for Freedom refers to Little Deliverance, it is a formula that is given to the *believer* who desires to be set free from demons.

Like all Scripture, the Formula for Freedom is a *law* of God that Satan must obey. It is a law that the deliverance minister may quote to Satan's face during Session Deliverance if needed. The Formula for Freedom promises the believer that he or she can be set free from the hold of demons. However, in order to take possession of this promise, this believer must take two legally binding *action* steps:

1. Submit to God
2. Resist the devil

*The Children's Bread*

**Submitting to God** at its deepest level means choosing to do the will of God and forsaking one's own will. It involves thinking, believing, and doing things that go against the grain of the carnal man's prideful, self-sufficient, self-righteous, and fleshly natures. Truly submitting to God is something that only Christians can do since it requires the help of the indwelling Holy Spirit.

Submitting to God can be summed up by the following: *coming into right relationship with God by surrendering to Him.* Submission to God involves an individual doing some or all of the following:

- Admitting that he has transgressed *every one* of God's laws—whether in the heart or with the hand. For example, he admits that he has committed adultery, whether by looking with lust (Matthew 5:28) or committing actual physical adultery. The same with murder, etc. He has stopped trying to justify himself by claiming that he hasn't committed certain sins
- Admitting that before knowing Jesus, he worshiped the wrong god
- Repenting of sin
- Confessing sin
- Confessing that Jesus is Lord (being born again).
- Reading the word (the Bible)
- Walking in the forgiveness of Christ
- Forsaking sin
- Taking refuge in Jesus only
- Dying to self
- Inviting the Holy Spirit
- Consulting the Holy Spirit
- Living for His glory
- Giving instead of receiving
- Forgiving instead of retaining the sins of others
- Being obedient to His commands, including the Great Commission

- Praying to God
- Worshiping God
- And many others…

**Resisting the devil** means actively coming out of agreement with the enemy as well as actively and forcefully beating him back and casting him out. Like submission to God, resisting the devil can only be done by a Christian since resisting the devil requires the authority to do so. Resisting the devil is done in the Name and authority of Jesus. Man cannot resist the devil on his own authority. Only Christians can lawfully speak in the Name and authority of Jesus Christ to resist and cast out demon spirits.

In addition, it is only the Christians who are *commanded* to resist the devil in the Great Commission (Mark 16:17). No other group is mandated by God to carry out the labors of deliverance. Neither Muslims, Hindus, nor even Jews (referring to those Jews who have rejected Yeshua as Messiah) have the license or authority to resist the devil. Resisting the devil is only for those who have the indwelling Holy Spirit. And in this age, it is only the Christians who have God's Spirit residing in them. Resisting the devil includes the following:

- Renouncing the devil and all his gifts
- Binding the devil
- Loosing the devil
- Breaking his curses
- Pulling down ungodly strongholds
- Severing ungodly soul-ties
- Tormenting and weakening the devil
- Interrogating the devil (*What is your name?* etc.)
- Commanding the devil to go

Resisting the devil can be summed up by the following: *breaking and removing specific legal rights and casting out the demons.*

The Formula for Freedom outlined in James 4:7 is a recipe for spiritual freedom. It is a recipe that only believers can follow. The deliverance minister guides the PRM in following this recipe.

The Formula for Freedom strongly points to *Technical Deliverance*, whereby something is required on the part of the receiver of deliverance (the PRM) before God forces the demons to flee. This something is submission and resistance. Technical Deliverance is focused on the breaking and removing of legal rights before demons are confronted and cast out.

One final note about submitting to God and resisting the devil: Ultimately, submitting to God and resisting the devil cannot be defined with such precision. This is because by submitting to God, one is also resisting the devil. And by resisting the devil, one is also submitting to God. In this sense, there is overlap between the two. However, it is profitable as well as practical for the student of deliverance ministry to conceptualize the two concepts in the manner outlined above.

## The Seven Sons of Sceva Did Not Have The Authority to Speak in the Name of Jesus

In Acts 19, there is a story of a group of non-Christians who attempted to resist the devil unlawfully. These individuals were known as the Seven Sons of Sceva. Sceva was a Jewish chief priest, and his seven sons tried to resist the devil by utilizing the forceful command without having the authority in Jesus Christ to do so. None of them personally knew Jesus as Lord, and therefore, none of them walked in His authority:

> *Then some of the itinerant Jewish exorcists took it upon themselves to call the name of the Lord Jesus over those who had evil spirits, saying, "We exorcise you by the Jesus whom Paul preaches."*
> Acts 19:13 (NKJV)

The Seven Sons of Sceva were not followers of Jesus, nor did they have the indwelling Spirit of Jesus. As such, they were attempting to do something that was spiritually illegal, improper, and unauthorized. As a result, the demons were able to exploit this illegality. Instead of being forced to flee, the demons were permitted to attack and even injure the Seven Sons:

> *Then the man who had the evil spirit jumped on them and overpowered them all. He gave them such a beating that they ran out of the house naked and bleeding.* Acts 19:16 (NIV)

The Seven Sons of Sceva attempted to walk in an authority that God had not given them. However, we, as born-again Christians, *do* walk in this authority. The indwelling Holy Spirit inside of us is the seal of this authority. This authority permits us to resist the enemy *as if we were Jesus Himself.* This is God's plan. We are to act in His stead. In other words, this authority, which is our authority in Jesus Christ, allows us to do what Jesus did—and even to do greater things.

When the PRM is ministered to during Session Deliverance, he or she needs to be taught to walk in this authority as well. The PRM needs to be able to repeat the deliverance minister's RAM prayer with spiritually binding legal authority. In order to do this, he or she must have the indwelling Holy Spirit. If the PRM is not born-again, he or she technically can't speak the deliverance minister's RAM prayer as a spiritually legally binding confession. Speaking the deliverance minister's RAM prayer without the authority of Christ might annoy the demons, but it won't bind them on Earth or in Heaven.

However, even if a non-born-again PRM can't speak in the authority of Christ, he or she can still receive deliverance during Session Deliverance. I have seen this many times. But instead of the PRM receiving deliverance by way of Technical Deliverance, he or she will receive it through sovereign Power Encounter. Recall from the definitions in Chapter 1 that Sovereign Deliverance, such as Power Encounter Deliverance, does not consider legal rights. God can and does move to expel demons even when they have legal right. God can and does do this according to His good pleasure during Sovereign Deliverance.

The well-trained and anointed deliverance minister should be able to move effectively in both the technical and sovereign deliverance realms. The Invicta-Certified Deliverance Minister (those deliverance ministers who have completed Level 2 or 3 of our online school, Invicta University) are comfortable ministering both technically and sovereignly.

## *Repentance*

There is one special way that Christians submit to God that is critical in the process of being set free from demons. This special thing is *repentance*. Repentance is a grace that God gives men. Repeat, God gives men repentance. Men cannot repent on their own. Men can choose to receive repentance from God. When man receives this repentance from God, it becomes his.

Repentance means to turn from sin and turn back to God. It is a change of heart that leads to a change in behavior. Repentance is the foundation of both Little Deliverance and Big Deliverance. Without repentance, the Bible says that we cannot have salvation or be set free from demons.

When God showed me the following verse, I knew that His will was for me to make repentance the foundation of my deliverance ministry. The Apostle Paul positively correlates repentance with deliverance. The *Escape-from-the-Snare Verse*:

**24** *And a servant of the Lord must not quarrel but be gentle to all, able to teach, patient,* **25** *in humility correcting those who are in opposition,* ***if God perhaps will grant them repentance****, so that they may know the truth,* **26** *and that they may come to their senses and* ***escape the snare of the devil****, having been taken captive by him to do his will.*   2 Timothy 2:24-26 (NKJV)

In other words, Paul is teaching us that if a person has repentance (which is given to him by God), he can then escape from the trap of the demons. We can also extrapolate and affirm the opposite. We can say that if an individual does *not* have repentance, he *cannot* escape from the snare of the devil.

For this reason, in my own ministry, we are unwavering in our declaration that repentance is foundational in order to be set free from demons. Therefore, and without apology, I have made repentance the spiritual core of my deliverance ministry. If you ever attend my public meetings of deliverance, or if you schedule a private Deliverance Encounter with my ministry, you will hear the message of repentance proclaimed with boldness and urgency.

I have seen that if people are not truly repentant, Satan can continue to keep them trapped in his snare. In practical terms, this means that demons might not be cast out even at the forceful command in the Name of Jesus.

I have had people come to my public deliverance meetings who were unable to be delivered. When it came time for me to issue the forceful command of expulsion, "Out in the Name of Jesus!" the demons held their ground and didn't budge. What happened on those occasions? Was the demon stronger than the Name of Jesus on that day? Was Jesus not willing to heal? No and no.

Then I find out the real reason why their deliverances didn't work. I ask the question: "Are you currently in some sin that hasn't been dealt with?" The individual then comes clean about her current or recent sin, saying, "I was just fornicating with my boyfriend this weekend." Or he admits, "I was just watching porn last night." Or she says, "Yeah, I smoked weed this morning for my anxiety. I knew I was coming for deliverance, so I was really nervous." And keep in mind there can be a lack of repentance with regards to much more subtle sins such as unforgiveness, anger, fear, self-justification, self-reliance, self-sufficiency, or pride.

These people could not escape the snare of the devil because they lacked repentance. They hadn't yet admitted and turned from their sin. They were still *in* their sin. And Satan knew it. When Satan knows that his victim is not walking in repentance, he will hold on tenaciously and resist the Holy Spirit by any means. And most times, unless God elects to override the demons' legal right of lack of repentance through an act of Sovereign Deliverance, the demons will not come out.

Satan knows God's law, and Satan will hold God to His own law. Satan will tell God, "I have a right to be here. You, God, say that he needs to have repentance in order to escape my snare. He doesn't have repentance. Therefore, I will not let him out of my snare." And God usually honors this.

## *Deliverance Is Not a Substitute for Obedience*

I have teaching entitled, "Deliverance Is Not a Substitute for Obedience." In this lesson, I talk about how many people don't want to really submit to God. They do not want to go through the steps of the Formula for Freedom. They just want all the badness, heaviness, fear, rage, poverty, failure, pain, sickness, torment, and darkness to go. They say, "I don't want to have to take up my cross and follow Jesus. I don't want to give up my porn which I like so much. I don't want to really give my life to Jesus. Can you please just make my bad spirits go away?"

Many people have a lack of interest in submitting to God and resisting the devil. This is because they don't want to do the *work* that is involved in submitting to God and resisting the devil. Submitting to God and resisting the devil is not easy.

First and foremost, they don't want to exercise self-control and forsake sin. They adore their darling sins and have no will to stop doing them. They don't want to cut off the toxic, abusive, controlling, sinful, and lustful relationships that they are involved in. They don't want to stop taking refuge in their favorite sin strongholds. They don't want to stop worshiping their favorite idols. They don't want to seek first His Kingdom (Matthew 6:33).

Instead, they just want someone to wave a Bible in front of them and make all their demons go away. They don't want to make the personal sacrifice that submission to God and resisting the devil requires.

Especially when it comes to Christians, getting set free

from demons requires work, and work is never easy. Satan always sets out to hinder God's people from submitting to Him. And Satan ferociously attacks those who purpose to resist him. The deliverance process is not easy. Ultimately, the Christian way itself is not easy, and only a few find it. Only a few are willing to take the time to enter through the narrow gate (Matthew 7:14).

People who aren't willing to put in the work that submission to God requires prefer that someone else submit for them. They prefer that someone else resist the devil for them. I can spot these people immediately because they are the ones who call our ministry and ask, "Are you strong enough or anointed enough to cast out my demons?" To which I respond, "No, I am not [look of shock on their faces] ...But God is. If you submit to Him and resist the devil, He can deliver you and make your demons go."

Or they ask, "Do I have to become a Christian for you to cast out my demons?" Or, "Do I really have to give up fornicating/smoking weed/watching porn/my lifestyle for you to cast out my demons?"

The Formula for Freedom teaches us that getting delivered from demons is not a substitute for obedience to God's word. One cannot choose the short route of having a deliverance minister command the demons to leave without the individual himself having to put in the hard work of submission to God and resisting the devil.

Finally, it needs to be added that submitting to God and resisting the devil is obedience to God. We are commanded to submit to God and resist the devil. By not doing it, one is in sin.

## *Where Sovereign Deliverance Ends And Technical Deliverance Begins*

Those who don't want to submit may ask, "Well, what about Sovereign Deliverance? In Sovereign Deliverance, God just overrides legal rights and heals people according to His good pleasure. Can't you just make God sovereignly deliver me without me having to do all that submitting?"

The answer is NO. No man can force the hand of God. The reason why it is called "Sovereign Deliverance" is because God, not man, sovereignly decides how and to whom it is dispensed.

Of course, God does do this sovereign delivering. He does it even when there is still legal right. It happens during different forms of Sovereign Deliverance, such as Evangelistic Deliverance.

But the moment you begin to *seek* deliverance because God has brought your spiritual issues to your attention, you leave the sovereign realm and enter the technical realm. You will now need to submit and resist. This involves repentance, being born again, renouncing sin, breaking and removing legal rights, etc.

By bringing your need for deliverance to your attention, God is showing you that He desires that you submit to Him and resist the devil *first* before he is willing to move in your life to make your demons flee.

The primary anointing over my ministry is that of Technical Deliverance. Therefore, nine times out of ten, when individuals are led by the Holy Spirit to the doors of my ministry, I already know that God wants to deal with them on some issue before He delivers them.

## The Deliverance Minister Guides the PRM In the Process of Submission

While the deliverance minister cannot do the PRM's job of submitting to God for her, he does help the PRM by guiding her through the process of submission. This is where good Deliverance Counseling comes in.

The deliverance minister might first do this by preaching the Gospel of repentance to the PRM if needed (and I have found that it is needed more often than not). In my own ministry, I have found that most Christians are gravely deficient in the area of repentance and general fear of the Lord.

The deliverance minister may even need to show the PRM specific areas of her life that are not submitted to God. These are the undealt-with sin areas. Of course, Satan will fight back by accusing the deliverance minister of "judging," but the deliverance minister ignores these accusations. The deliverance minister knows that God expects His servants to gently and lovingly show others their sins (John 4:18, Mark 10:21, etc.).

Once the PRM is ready, the deliverance minister then leads the PRM in a process of submitting to Jesus through a series of surgically precise RAM prayers. And make no mistake about it, this submitting to Jesus through RAM prayer is completely inefficacious if the PRM merely parrots the words of the deliverance minister. The PRM must be convicted in her heart of what she is declaring and understand the authority by which she is declaring it.

If the PRM is unwilling to really submit to God, the deliverance minister will be limited as to how much he can help her through the ministry of Session Deliverance.

When the PRM demonstrates an unwillingness to submit to God, the deliverance minister will many times go ahead and conduct Sovereign Deliverance. He will pray forceful command prayer anyway. If demons are cast out in this situation, it is likely that God decided to move sovereignly and expel demons through Power Encounter. Hopefully, as a result of this Power Encounter, the PRM will then be convicted to submit to Jesus after her deliverance.

## *Deliverance for Nonbelievers Doesn't Make Sense*

Recall that repentance is foundational in both Big Deliverance and Little Deliverance. Repentance is foundational in submitting to God. Therefore, without repentance, one cannot submit to God. And without submission to God, one cannot resist the devil. And without resisting the devil, the devil will unlikely flee.

Who is the best candidate to receive deliverance ministry? Is it the unrepentant, hard-hearted unregenerate sinner? Or, is it the born-again Christian believer who has turned from sin?

Of course, the born-again believer is the best candidate to

## The Children's Bread

receive deliverance from demons. She is the one who has repentance! She is the one who can submit and resist. In fact, the very reason why she is born again is that she *has* submitted to God by repenting of her sin. If she hadn't repented, she wouldn't be born again, to begin with. Jesus said in Luke 13:3 that *...unless you repent you will all likewise perish.*

Unless God sovereignly decides to expel demons from an unrepentant, nonbeliever in order to confirm His word, which He can and does do during miracles of Sovereign Deliverance, delivering nonbelievers, doesn't even make sense. This is additional evidence that believers can have demons.

## Two Candidates for Deliverance

Consider the following scenario. You are a deliverance minister. Two people come to you to receive deliverance. Who would you most likely be convicted to pray deliverance prayer for, Candidate A or Candidate B?

### Candidate A

Candidate A tells you, "I'm tormented in my sleep, and I hear voices telling me to commit suicide. BUT I don't need Jesus, and frankly, I think religion is for weak people. I love my porn and my weed too. Weed is legal where I live. So, are you going to *judge* me and tell me I need to stop smoking it? Doesn't your Bible tell you not to judge? Anyway, I am tired of these ugly spirits harassing me. I see them in my house. They really scare me. Can you just do me a favor and use your powers to make them go?

### Candidate B

Candidate B says to you, "I'm tormented in my sleep, and I hear voices telling me to commit suicide, but I am *finished* with my old sinful ways. I am trying so hard to stop the porn, and I don't want to smoke weed anymore. I see how it is messing up my mind. Last month, I repented of my sins, and I confessed Jesus to be my Savior. I am born again, I want to follow Jesus, but I need help."

## Who Would You Pray Deliverance Prayer For?

Out of these two candidates for deliverance, who would you most likely take the time to pray deliverance prayer for? Yes, it is possible that the Lord might convict you to pray forceful command over Candidate A, but I doubt it. I believe you would be more convicted to first preach the Gospel to this individual. With Candidate A, you would most likely spend time doing serious Deliverance Counseling first.

On the other hand, Candidate B is ready to receive. He knows he needs it, and he doesn't want sin anymore. He wants to submit and resist. He is ready to receive God's healing.

*Delivering nonbelievers from demons doesn't make sense since nonbelievers do not and cannot have repentance. In 2 Timothy 2, Paul said that repentance is necessary for deliverance. He made it clear that there is a positive correlation between repentance and deliverance.*

This means that delivering Christians makes far more sense than delivering non-Christians. Christians are the best candidates for deliverance from demons because they have repentance, and Paul said that one must have repentance in order to escape the snare of the devil.

Now, of course, God can and does do things that "don't make sense" to our rational minds. For example, God puts the last first. He says it is better to give than receive. He says to bless those who persecute. God's perfect mind is far above man's rational, carnal mind. This is true even when we don't understand why He does what He does.

He even casts out demons from unrepentant sinners like Candidate A as a sign to confirm His word. He does this through acts of Sovereign Deliverance. We cannot box God in and demand that everything He does "make sense."

Ultimately the deliverance minister must be led by the Holy Spirit on the issue of who to pray forceful command for and who to preach the Gospel to. I often say that *some people don't need deliverance; what they really need is repentance.* Just because a person *says* they need deliverance doesn't mean they are ready to receive it. It is like a patient telling his doctor which surgery he needs and when. The Spirit-filled deliverance minister will know what to do because the Holy Spirit will direct his ministry.

Recall that the definition of the deliverance minister is that he is "anointed and highly trained." His anointing comes from the Holy Spirit. He will therefore use both his anointing and his training to make these critical ministry decisions.

## Can a Nonbeliever Walk in His Deliverance?

There is an additional question that arises when it comes to casting out demons from nonbelievers. If a nonbelieving, unrepentant individual, such as Candidate A, is delivered from demons, will he be able to *walk* in his deliverance? In other words, will he be able to forsake future sins that would give new legal rights for future demons to enter? Or will he go back to his habitual sins and then be demonized even worse than before he was delivered? Will a sinner return to his own vomit?

Pastor Paul Cooprider made this point at the beginning of this book. He said that if a nonbeliever is delivered and returns to sin, his demonization will be worse afterward than it was before. We call this concept the *demonic reentry clause*. Pastor Paul was making reference to the words of Jesus:

> *Then he goes and takes with him seven other spirits more wicked than himself, and they enter and dwell there;*
> *and* **the last state of that man is worse than the first.**
> *So shall it also be with this wicked generation.*
> Matthew 12:45 (NKJV)

The Apostle Peter also teaches about this issue by quoting the Proverb:

> ..."*A dog returns to his own vomit,*" and, "*a sow, having washed, to her wallowing in the mire.*"   2 Peter 2:22 (NKJV)

Yes, God delivers even the unrepentant, nonbelievers according to His good pleasure through Sovereign Deliverance. He does this as a sign to confirm His word and to demonstrate who He is—that He is all-powerful and worthy of worship and Satan is not.

I also believe that when God delivers an unrepentant sinner through Sovereign Deliverance, He also gives them the revelation that they need to repent. He gives them the revelation that they need the Savior Jesus.

The deliverance minister needs to be sensitive to the conviction of the Holy Spirit in order to know what to do when individuals like Candidate A come to his ministry. However, *in general*, I see the need for individuals to first repent and be saved before receiving deliverance. Especially deep deliverance. This follows Isaiah's divine order:

Salvation→Healing→Deliverance

## The Purpose of the Miracles

When God performs a miracle of either healing or deliverance with the unsaved, it is to demonstrate His power and to confirm who He is. It is to move them to repent and follow Him. This is the purpose of Sovereign Deliverance.

Jesus and the disciples, and later the early Church, didn't do miracles just to pass the time. They did them to force people into making a decision one way or another for Christ.

Yale University history professor Ramsay MacMullen in his book, *Christianizing the Roman Empire* (1984), wrote that deliverance served the purpose of showing the people the superiority of the "the Christian's patron power" (God) over the *daimones* (demons). This, in turn, would convince people in the audience that their other gods were not worth worshiping:

*The manhandling of demons—humiliating them, making them howl, beg for mercy, tell their secrets, and depart in a hurry—served a purpose quite essential to the Christian definition of monotheism: it made physically (or dramatically) visible the superiority of the Christian's patron power over all others. One and only one was God. The rest were daimones demonstrably, and therefore already familiar to the audience as nasty, lower powers that no one would want to worship anyway.* (page 28)

In other words, the original disciples and the early Christians did the signs and wonders so that the people would turn from the gods ("the lower powers") of the world and convert to the One True God.

I believe that when God sovereignly delivers the unsaved from demons, it is because He has predestined that they be saved in the future—hopefully, that very day that they are delivered! Therefore, if I deliver an unbeliever sovereignly, I will exercise best practice and give them an opportunity to respond to the Gospel at that time.

People who are delivered through Sovereign Deliverance may not consciously know it, but they *are* God's people. God has predestined them to know Him. We know this because:

### *God delivers those who belong to Him*

Since we as men do not know who has and has not been predestined to know the Lord's salvation, we will evangelize everyone that God brings to us. In the same way, we will be willing to deliver anyone who God brings to us to be delivered. If the Holy Spirit convicts us, we will confront their demons and cast them out. We will do this even with individuals like Candidate A if the Spirit moves us.

However, most individuals that God sends to the deliverance ministries to be delivered will be true born-again believers that He has ordained to be set free from demons. However, He wants to deal with them regarding some issue of sin first before He delivers them. Remember that Technical Deliverance (breaking and removing legal rights before casting out the demons) exists because God desires to deal with His people before He delivers them.

If the NDMC would just start *doing deliverance*, he would quickly find this out for himself. He will quickly see that it is not the pagans who will come to him for help. It will be his fellow brothers in Christ!

## The Promised Land of Canaan

I want to continue to study the Biblical pattern of the promise vs. the possession by examining two examples in the Old Covenant. By relating these stories to our lives as New Covenant believers, we see that we are not delivered by God's *promise* of being set free from demons. Instead, we are delivered when we *take possession* of the promise by submitting to God and resisting the enemy.

In the beginning, God promised the land of Canaan to Abraham:

*Also I **give to you** [this is the promise] and your descendants after you the land in which you are a stranger, all the land of Canaan, as an everlasting possession; and I will be their God.*
Genesis 17:8 (NKJV)

Then, after God led the Hebrews out of Egyptian slavery, and after they had spent forty years in the desert, God spoke to Moses and told the Hebrews to take possession of their Promised Land:

*See, I have set the land before you; **go in and possess the** **land** [this is the command to take possession of the promise] which the Lord swore to your fathers—to Abraham, Isaac, and Jacob—to give to them and their descendants after them.*
Deuteronomy 1:8 (NKJV)

## The Children's Bread

God had *already* given the Promised Land to His people. But they still had to cross the Jordan River and *take possession* of it. And this taking possession of Canaan would require hundreds of years of difficult struggles, battles, and temptations to commit spiritual adultery.

Joshua and the Hebrews crossed the River Jordan in the year 1406 BC. However, the peaceful United Kingdom of Israel with its capital in Jerusalem under the rule of King David didn't happen until around 1000 BC. This means that it took the Jews some 400 years before they were able to *fully* take possession of the Promised Land!

The Hebrews' taking possession of their Promised Land certainly didn't happen all at once. God's people had to fight, resist, and overcome many enemies. They had to defeat the Hittites, Girgashites, Amorites, Canaanites, Perizzites, Hivites, and Jebusites (Deuteronomy 7:1-2) and many others before they could fully possess the Promised Land.

The fact that they would not be able to take the Promised Land all at once was not a surprise to God's people, though. God explicitly told the Hebrews that they wouldn't be able to do it. Instead, it would be a *process* of conquering *little by little*. Here is the Little-by-Little Verse once again:

*The LORD your God will drive out those nations before you,* **little by little***. You will not be allowed to eliminate them all at once, or the wild animals will multiply around you.*
Deuteronomy 7:22 (NIV)

This is God's pattern of deliverance. In most cases, He delivers *little by little*. Therefore, I tell people who come to our ministry that their deliverance will most likely not happen all at once. I tell the PRM that it will be a *process*. It will be little by little. Just as the Israelites did not conquer the Promised Land all at once, the PRM's deliverance will not all take place in one public meeting or in one private session.

Do you see how God's promise to the Hebrews relates to

our lives under the New Covenant? There is a beautiful correlation here:

| Old Testament | New Testament |
|---|---|
| God's promise of the Promised Land to the Hebrews | Our Predestination of Being God's People |
| Crossing the Jordan River into the Promised Land | Being born again |
| The Old Testament-New Testament Warfare Shift ||
| Taking possession of the Promised Land by overcoming the enemies (the Hittites, Philistines, Amorites, etc.) one kingdom at a time. This was the Israelites' process of taking possession of Canaan | Taking possession of one's spiritual Promised Land by overcoming the enemies (Satan, Fear, Jezebel, etc.) one demonic kingdom at a time. This is the deliverance process of every born-again believer |

Just like God promised Abraham the land of Canaan, He has also promised us the Promised Land of salvation in Jesus Christ. It has been promised to us because He has predestined us for it. And by our free will, we choose whether we will leave the world, cross the river, and take possession of this wonderful promise.

God has also promised us spiritual freedom from demons. But once again, we must take possession of this promise through the Formula for Freedom (James 4:7). We submit to God, resist the devil, and *then* the demons will flee. We force the demons to flee by commanding them to go in the Name of Jesus.

And they will flee. But it will be a process. If it took the Hebrews more than 400 years to subdue Canaan, it could surely take even a lifetime to achieve full spiritual and emotional freedom.

So just like the Hebrews had to fight and overcome the enemies that had previously dwelled in the land that God had promised them, we Christians must now fight and overcome the holdover demons that have been dwelling in our minds and bodies since before we were converted. New demons may have even entered after salvation (post-conversion demonization). These demons are there because they were let in by sin. All of these demons have been assigned to block us from enjoying the milk and honey blessings that God has already ordained for us in each of our own Promised Lands.

Therefore, our battles with the Amorites, the Canaanites, and Philistines are our *resistance* to the enemy. This is our deliverance process. The Amorites, Canaanites, and the Philistines are emblematic of our spiritual enemies, the demons. And these will have to be resisted and overcome *little by little* until we have taken full possession of our Promised Lands—our total spiritual freedom. Our spiritual enemies didn't start attacking us last week. They have been there for decades, maybe back to our childhoods and perhaps even back to when we were in the womb. Overcoming these enemies won't happen all at once. We will need to be patient, faithful, submit to God, resist our enemies, and let the Lord work to make these devils flee.

I try to create proper expectations with those that I minister to. I tell them that they will likely spend the rest of their lives on Earth taking possession of their spiritual Promised Land. It won't all be casting out demons. It will also involve overcoming fear, anger, unforgiveness, and other ungodly emotions. It will involve the healing of the heart, which is inner healing. It will involve reigning in the lust of the eyes, the lust of the flesh, and the pride of life. The Christian life is hard work, but it is the best life. The Christian way is not easy, but it is the only way that brings true peace. Serving under our Commander-in-Chief Jesus is the best life that I have ever known. There is no other life in which we can walk in such awesome power and authority and have so much hope!

What is the Promised Land for us? It is our progressive process of sanctification. Philippians 2:12 says, "working out our salvation with fear and trembling." Working out our salvation is the progressive process of becoming more like Jesus. And this process includes our healing and deliverance. This is the process of taking possession of our individual Promised Lands.

Our deliverance is the spiritual war that Paul talks about in Ephesians 6. It is the spiritual war that deliverance ministers like me help fellow Christians fight every time we minister Session Deliverance. We do this at our public meetings and when we sit with people during private deliverance appointments.

## *The Battle of Jericho*

Another Old Testament story that demonstrates the promise vs. the possession is the battle for the Canaanite city of Jericho. God told Joshua that the city was theirs. This is the promise:

*And the Lord said to Joshua: "See!* ***I have given Jericho into your hand****, its king, and the mighty men of valor.*   Joshua 6:2 (NKJV)

Nonetheless, Joshua and his men still needed to *take possession* of Jericho. This would involve hard work. God gave Joshua specific instructions on how they would do this work:

**3** *You shall march around the city, all you men of war; you shall go all around the city once. This you shall do six days.* **4** *And seven priests shall bear seven trumpets of rams' horns before the ark. But the seventh day you shall march around the city seven times, and the priests shall blow the trumpets.*   Joshua 6:3-4 (NKJV)

This is exactly how God gives the Christian instructions today. Except that the Christian's specific battle instructions are not found in the Book of Joshua but in the Formula for Freedom outlined in James 4:7. These instructions are to submit to God, resist the devil, and then the devil will flee.

James wrote his epistle to *Christians*. This makes sense since only Christians can follow his Formula for Freedom. This is so since it is only the Christian who can truly submit to God. Only Christians have the spiritual authority to resist the devil.

*The Children's Bread*

We cannot miss this subtlety. The James 4:7 formula can only be followed by *Christians*. Only Christians can submit to God and resist the devil because only Christians have the Helper, the Holy Spirit, to *equip* them to submit and resist. Forgiving others' sins is one way in which a Christian submits to God.

Only Christians can truly forgive others since they have been forgiven by God. Nonbelievers cannot truly forgive others. *Christian forgiveness*, which is true forgiveness, is a foreign concept to those who have not been forgiven by God. True forgiveness is about canceling a debt, not about a transitory emotional state. Christian forgiveness is founded on repentance, while apologies are founded on feelings. Christian forgiveness is an important subject area of Deliverance Counseling.

If God gave us the Christians the Formula for Freedom, it is because we Christians have a need to obtain this freedom. Christians need freedom not just from the power of sin and death but also from the heaviness of indwelling demonic spirits.

Joshua and his army followed God's instructions, and God delivered the enemy city into their hands. They supernaturally overcame their Canaanite enemies and took possession of God's promise. The walls of Jericho fell:

*So the people shouted when the priests blew the trumpets. And it happened when the people heard the sound of the trumpet, and the people shouted with a great shout, that the wall fell down flat. Then the people went up into the city, every man straight before him, and **they took the city**.* Joshua 6:20 (NKJV)

## *Summary*

In the Name of Jesus and by the power of His Spirit, we, like Joshua, supernaturally overcome our enemies. Joshua and his men overcame the Canaanite city of Jericho. We overcome the demons. We will take city after city, demonic kingdom after demonic kingdom, until the entire Promised Land is ours. God has promised us the land, but we still need to *take possession* of it. It won't be automatic, though. In order to take possession of it, we will need to do the hard work of submitting and resisting.

Only Christians are capable of submitting to God, and only Christians are capable of resisting the devil. If the only ones God made capable of submitting and resisting are the Christians, then that means that the Christians have a *need* to submit and resist. Christians have a need to submit and resist because Christians can have demons.

I now call on the NDMC to crush the prideful and intellectually superior attitude that Christians don't need spiritual healing. I call on the NDMC to shatter the Satanic thinking pattern that Christians don't need deliverance. I call on the NDMC to reject the concept that salvation settles it all. I call on the NDMC to see the Biblical pattern that God delivers those who belong to Him. I call on the NDMC to *just start doing deliverance* and let God show you His truth—that He may even be calling *you* to bring deliverance to His Church.

I call on the NDMC to join the resistance against the demons that wage Satanic war inside the minds and bodies of the precious members of His Church.

## Chapter 17

# Six Challenge Questions Posed to the NDMC

### Question #1

You say that a nonbeliever can have demons but that a born-again Christian cannot have demons.

**Question:** What happens to all a nonbeliever's demons the moment that he is born again?

Please provide Scriptural references to support your answer.

### Question #2

**Question:** Do you think that the doctrine that Christians can't have demons might benefit Satan in some way?

## Question #3

This book makes the assertion that all deliverance ministers know that Christians can have demons.

**Question:** Can you locate a single deliverance minister who believes otherwise? In other words, can you locate one individual who sits with individuals to cast out demons *and* who believes that Christians *can't* have demons?

The ministry should be a well-documented and transparent ministry of deliverance. It must be a ministry that sits with people to cast out demons during private deliverance session appointments and or scheduled public meetings of deliverance.

## Question #4

On behalf of every deliverance ministry, I invite you, the NDMC, to attend a public deliverance meeting. There, you will see firsthand Christians (and perhaps some non-Christians too) being delivered from demons. After their deliverances, you will see some praising God, others speaking in tongues, others quoting Scripture, and others in quiet contemplation. When you witness this, ask the Holy Spirit to show you what you saw.

**Question:** What did the Holy Spirit show you?

*The Children's Bread*

## Question #5

This question is to be answered *after* you have visited a public deliverance meeting and witnessed deliverance taking place firsthand.

**Question:** Do you have the spiritual confidence to approach one of these individuals, whom you just observed receiving deliverance, and tell them, to their face (not online), the following?

*I am a born-again believer in Jesus Christ. I am saved. But since I just saw you receive deliverance from demons, that means that you are not and cannot be born again.*

## Question #6

Put your Christians-Can't-Have-a-Demon Doctrine to the test. Challenge yourself by inaugurating your own public deliverance meeting. Let everyone know that you will be confronting demons and casting them out. Do not say that it is only for born-again Christians (or any other subgroup). Just invite everyone. Advertise it on your website and on your social media. Let everyone know that you will be doing deliverance just like they do in the Bible—by ordering demons to go in the Name of Jesus. Then, at your meeting, do what Jesus did and begin to drive out demons according to Mark 16:17.

**Questions:** Who showed up to your meeting seeking deliverance? Were they mostly Christians, or were they non-Christians? Out of whom did you cast out more demons—out of Christians or out of nonbelievers?

*Mark Chase*

## *A Note on Supersessionism*

Throughout this book, I have made it very clear that *God delivers those who belong to Him*. I have used this fact as the primary evidence that Christians can have demons. But who exactly are *those who belong to Him*?

Those who belong to God are His children. I have stated that the children of God under the New Covenant are those who have called on Jesus as Lord. This is true. However, there is more to this story. Therefore, I am convicted of clarifying some important points for this Second Edition.

The Jews are the natural heirs of the blessing of Abraham. They are the natural children of God. They are the natural branches. We gentiles are the adopted sons and daughters. We gentiles are the grafted-in branches. However, those Jews who have rejected Yeshua as Lord have willingly cut themselves off from God's blessing of salvation. I do not believe that any Jew of today can be saved by an attempted adherence to the Mosaic Covenant. In fact, I would say that the dual covenant concept is a false one as no one can come to the Father except by the Son. In addition, no Jew who has rejected Jesus can speak in the Name and authority of Yeshua.

The Jews who have rejected Jesus are akin to the prodigal son. The Father loves them, yearns for their return, and when they do return, He will run toward them, welcome them, and restore them. After the Cross and the Outpouring at Pentecost, the Jews who reject Yeshua are God's children genetically but not salvifically. However, **the Jews are still His chosen people**. They are still the apple of His eye. One is still cursed if one curses Israel, and one is still blessed if one blesses Israel. This is the reason why the United States of America has been so prosperous historically. And God continues to deliver His people, the Jews. A wonderful modern example of this is Israel's miraculous victory during the Six-Day War of 1967.

## *The Children's Bread*

I do believe that deliverance from demons is also for the unsaved Jews—even though they themselves cannot speak in the Name of the Messiah. In this way, deliverance is for the Jews as much as it is for the Christians. However, as I see it, the Jews will be delivered via Sovereign Deliverance, and the Christians will, for the most part, be delivered via Technical Deliverance. The Christian believers are the only children of God who can speak in the Name of Jesus.

Am I a supersessionist? In other words, do I believe that the New Covenant has superseded, or replaced, the Old Covenant? I am, only in the sense that—and read this sentence to the end—the New Covenant replaces the obsolete Old Covenant **as being the *best* covenant**. The New Covenant is better than the Old Covenant as it is established on better promises (Hebrews 8:6). Before the Cross, the Old Covenant was the best covenant, but not after.

Has the Old Covenant been abolished? No, not at all! However, the New Covenant is now the better covenant. It is the only covenant that is mediated by Jesus Christ. And once again, no one can come to the Father except by the Son. For this reason, it is critical that we, just as did Paul, preach the Gospel to God's natural children, the Jews. In order to be saved, the Jews *must* hear and receive the Good News of Yeshua Ha'Mashiach.

Finally, does the Church replace Israel? Absolutely not! God is not done dealing with His land, Israel, or His natural children, the Jews—even the prodigal Jews who are in rebellion for having rejected the Son. We also know from Scripture that the Jews play a key eschatological role. In the end times, there will be a mass return of Jews to the land of Israel, and the Jews will recognize Jesus as their Messiah. Do the Jews belong to Him? Yes. Do the Christian believers belong to Him? Yes. Does God deliver those who belong to Him? Yes!

Mark Chase

# Index

abortion clinic analogy, 69-70
*aggelos* (Gk. for angel), 261-262
Alcime, Sam, 12-15, 220, 291
Ananias & Sapphira, 181-183
angel, 56, 183, 215, 261-262, 270-271, 281
angelic assistance, 96, 281
Annacondia, Carlos, 50
Argument, Body-is-the-Temple, 167-174
Argument, Christians-Can't-Be-Possessed, 187-212
Argument, Light-Can't-Dwell-with-Darkness, 123-138
Argument, New-Creation-in-Christ, 175-186
Argument, Who-the-Son-Sets-Free, 288-290
armchair quarterbacks, 96-97
Asa, King, 90-91
Assemblies of God, 217-218
assertions, 93-99

assignments, demonic, 63, 68, 72, 78, 193, 253
authority of Scripture, 227
authority over demons, 33, 84, 98, 155, 266, 280, 286, 304-306
authority in Jesus Christ, 29-31, 33-36, 39, 73, 84-85, 96. 155, 163, 301, 304, 308-310
authority, bind and loose, 33, 36, 96, 181, 275, 277, 288, 300-301, 308, 310
authority, spiritual authority to act, 38, 91-92
Authority to Act Deliverance, 31, 37-38
authority to bind & loose, 36, 301
authority to do greater things, 34, 186, 304, 310

backslidden believer, demonization of, 157
baptism, water, 60-61, 75, 141
baptism of the Holy Spirit, 124, 218, 295
Bartlett, Jay, 18-19, 61
battlefronts, 71-72, 111

Big Deliverance (deliverance from Hell), 57, 76, 108, 220, 235, 285, 287, 290, 299, 302, 304, 306, 311, 316
bind and loose, 33, 36, 96, 301
bipartite, (dichotomous nature of man), 145-148, 162
blessed objects, 265, 295
body, 144-165
body as "house," 133, 135, 138, 154, 160-161, 168, 218, 220
Body-is-the-Temple Argument, 167-174
Bonnke, Reinhard, 41, 45, 62, 218-219, 254
born again, (man's spiritual rebirth), 7, 35-37, 39, 43, 56-57, 101, 108, 137, **152**-153, 157, **160**-161, 163, 171, **177**-181, 288, 290, 304-305, 307, 317, 324
Bottari, Pablo, 50, 99, 226

Canaan, God's promise, 303, 322-326
cessationism, 74, 103, 228, 300-301
children vs. descendants of Abraham, 247-249
children's Bread, 59, 196, 233-242, 292-293

Christ for All Nations (CFAN), 62, 218-220
Christian can have a demon, summary of how, 161-162
Christians-Can't-Be-Possessed Argument, 187-212
Christians-Can't-Have-a-Demon Doctrine, 220, 228, 331
Church Deliverance Stories, 243-249
*Codex Sinaiticus*, 189, 199
*Codex Vaticanus*, 199
Cooprider, Paul, 24-25, 61, 319
confirm His Word, the purpose of the miracles, 6, 40-41, 53, 103, 214, 226, 239, 301-302, 317-318, 320
conversion & deliverance are separate, 81, 163, 285-302
Covenant, New, 52, 76, 167-169, **234-235**, 237, 254, 322, 324
Covenant, Old, 167, 169, 234, 236, 238, 243, 245, 249, 322
cover, book meaning, 185

*daimonizomai*, 189. **200**, 203, 206
Daughter of Abraham, 215, 243, 245-249, 276-277

David teaches who God delivers, 251-253
decision-making process, Christian, 227-228
deliverance & conversion are two separate events, 81, 163, 285-302
deliverance is a miracle, 34, 50, 300-301, 317, 320
Deliverance Counseling, 33, 36-**37**, 68, 79, 107, 131-132, 135, 159, 315, 318
Deliverance Session, Deliverance Encounter, 29, 60, 312
Deliverance Session, group public meeting, 29, 35, 28, 43-44, 61, 77, 246
deliverance is for Christians & nonbelievers, 37, 103, 239
deliverance is taking possession of our Promised Land, 254, 303-305
deliverance minister, 38-39
deliverance minister, five distinguishing traits, 39
deliverance process, 31, 68, 79, 134-135, 180-181, 185, 287, 311, 314-316, **316-317**, 323-326
deliverance revival, 293-294

denomination, 45, 60, 77-78, 84-85, 98, 103-104, 111, 112, 164, 213-229
demonic reentry clause (Matthew 12:43-45), 319
demonic sexual harassment and violation (DSHV), 85, 196-197
demonization, **45**, 130-131, 135, 150-151, 153, 162, 280
demonization, as spiritual sickness, 14, 80, 83-86, 90, 98-99, 102, 206, 210, 222-223
demonization, subtle, **192-193**, 195, 206-208, 264, 275, 301
de Souza Ferreira, Ezequiel, 22-23, 59
disciple of Jesus, definition of, 54-55, 98, 304-305
disciples of Jesus, the ones who are delivered, 54-55
disputable matters of faith, **74-77**, 83
divine order, God reveals plan & man accepts or rejects it, 304
divine order, Passover, 53-54
divine order, prayer then doctors, 90-91
divine order, preach-heal-deliver, 52-53, 288, 320

divine order, tripartite, 144
doctrine, 213-214, 216-217
dual covenant, 232

*Echó*, 201, 203, 206
Escape-from-the-Snare Verse (2 Timothy 2:24-26), 311
Evangelistic Power Encounter (Evangelistic Deliverance), 37, 39-40, 41, **42**, 43-45
Evangelistic Power Encounter, five distinguishing features, 43

familiar spirits, 78, **135-136**
Figueras, Omar, 20-21
forceful command, 30, 32, 39-41, 43-44, 68, **72**, 73-74, 79. 96, 109, 244 254, 266, 276, 295, 302, 309, 312, 316, 318-319
Formula for Freedom (James 4:7), **306**, 307-309, 313-314, 324, 326-327
forgiveness, Christian, 327
free will, 56, 69, 324

Gary, Pastor, 114-115, 224
Gavin's dad, 115-116
get behind me, Satan, 273-282
Gifts of the Holy Spirit, 74, 100, 102-103, 228, 290, 295, 300-302
God delivers those who belong to Him, OT & NT examples, 51-52, 118, 215-216
Godhead, 140-142, 150
gotquestions.org, 84, 94
Great Commission, 47, 50, 52, 82, 85, 206, 214, 223-225, 264, 286, 293, 302, 307-308
groundwork, 68

Hammond, Frank & Ida Mae, 61
Hays, Edra, 10-11, 61, 83
holdover demons, 81, 111, **152-153**, **159-160**, 184, 270, 285, 325
Holy of Holies, 167-174
Holy Place, 169-170
Holy Spirit, blasphemy of, 71, 85
hospital analogy, 222-223, 291

inner healing, 35-**37**, 53, 65, 138, 140, 142-143, 256, 325
inside or outside, demons can be, 63-66, 269

Jericho, God's promise, 326-327
Juan, the ex-witch, 108-110

Kolenda, Daniel, 45, 62, 218-219, 286
King James Bible, 187-189, 200-202, 204-205

Larson, Bob, 5, 61, 143, 180, 287
Larsonian Tripartite Model, **143**, 150-151, 165
legal right, 29-31, 35, 39, 65, **66-69**, 70-71, 78-79, 92, 105-108, 131-132, 156, 159, 264, 276
legal right, unbelief in the presence of demons, 78-79, 106-108
Leeper, Elizabeth Ann, 60
light & darkness cannot dwell in the same vessel, 123
Light-Can't-Dwell-with-Darkness Argument, 123-138
Little Deliverance (deliverance from demons), 57, 76, 220, 235, 285, 290, 299, 302, 306, 311, 316
Little-by-Little Verse (Deuteronomy 7:22), 186, 287, 323
loaded questions, 207

MacMullen, Ramsay, 320
*malak* (Heb. for angel), 261
Man in the Synagogue, 243

Messenger of Satan, Paul's, 259-271
minor exorcism, 60
miracle, deliverance is, 34, 50, 296, 300-301, 317, 320
misconception, if a person has a demon, he cannot be saved, 162-163, 190

new creation in Christ can't have a demon, 175
New-Creation-in-Christ Argument, 175-186
Non-Deliverance Ministry Christian (NDMC), **44-47**, 58-62, 70, 74, 77, 79-81, 86-87, 93-97. 101, 117, 162, 164, 205, 208, 210, 219
Non-Deliverance Ministry Christian (NDMC), six distinguishing features, 45
Non-Deliverance Ministry Christian (NDMC), solution to demonization: claim deficits in one's Christian walk, 61-62, 95-96, 126, 165, 198
Non-Deliverance Ministry Christian (NDMC), solution to demonization: claim that one is being punished by God, 62

Non-Deliverance Ministry Christian (NDMC), solution to demonization: claim that one is blaming too much on the devil, 62, 95

Non-Deliverance Ministry Christian (NDMC), solution to demonization: claim that one is not really saved, 45, 162-163, 94-95, 281

Non-Deliverance Ministry Christian (NDMC), solution to demonization: medical science, 88-91

non-disputable matter of faith, 263

Non-Evangelistic Power Encounter, 42, 43-44

no right, never challenged (NRNC), 70-71

obsession, 64

*Ochleó*, 201-202, 203

Oklahoma, pastor from, 116-117

O'Dwyer, Reverend Mike, 113-114, 300

Old Testament-New Testament Warfare Shift, **254**, 324

omnipresence, God's, 161

Outer Court, 169-174

Paul's Messenger of Satan, 259

Penn-Lewis, Jessie, 146, 165

person receiving ministry (PRM), **29**-30, 33, 36-37

Personal Spiritual Profile (PSP), 107

Pharisaic Reasoning, 58-59, 80, 107, 214, 221

*pneuma* (spirit), 144

point of entry, 66, 68, 71, 97, 159, 163, 279

possession & possessed, 64, 84, 94, 187

possessed, a Christian can't be, 187

possessed, Bible translations without, 207

post-conversion demonization, 153-157, 288, 325

poverty spirits, 107, 313

Power Encounter Deliverance, 37-39, 41, **42**, 43-44, 46, 100, 103, 278, 310

predestination, 56, 226, 240, 321, 324

Prince, Derek, 55, 61, 224

project Holy Spirit power, 30, 39, 44, **72-74**, 96, 109, 276, 278, 280, 295

promise vs. the possession, 303, 322, 326

Proximal Deliverance, **42**, **296-297**, 298-299
Psalms of David, 251
*psuché* (the soul), 144-145, 148-149, 178
public spectacle, 41, 246

radical conversions, 178, **294-295**
rebirth, spiritual (born again), 152, 185-186
repeat after me (RAM) prayer, **29**-30, 33, 35-36, 40, 68, 79, 131-132, 159, 310, 316
repentance, the foundation, **57**, 311-312, 316
resisting the devil, 69, 96, 132, 153-154, 281, 288, 306, **308**, 309-310, 313-315, 322, 325-328
Rick, Pastor, 157, 195-199, 204, 224, 275
Rob, Pastor, 110-113, 152, 163, 211

saint, definition of, 262-263
salvation, can it be lost? 158-159
Salvation-Settles-it-All Syndrome, **287-288**, 289, 301-302
Samantha's neck injury, 63
*sarx*, 144, 149

Satanic thinking patterns (STP), 78, 92, 105, 107, 119, 154, **156-157**, 161-162, 164, 185, 199, 275, 288, 328
Sebastian's sexual dysfunction, 64
Self-Deliverance, 31-**32**, 37, 266
semantic change, 203-204
Session Deliverance, 29-31, 32, 33-39, 44-47, 53, 57-58, 60, 66, 68, 71, 79, 86, 93-94, 96-97, 104, 131, 140, 150, 153, 159, 175, 229, 274-275, 310, 316
Session Deliverance, excellently suited for Christians, 30, **32**, 35-36
Session Deliverance, Jesus alludes to, 33
Session Deliverance, non-Christian PRM, 36-37
Session Deliverance, seven distinguishing features, 35-36
Seven Sons of Sceva, 309-310
sickness, demonically induced, 63, 71, 83, 85, 91, 98-99, 164, 193, 222, 246, 261, 268-269, 304
sickness, idiopathic, **85**, 91
Simon the Sorcerer, 184-185

sin, dealt with & not dealt with, 65, 67, 105, 153, 316
*soma* (body), 144, 149
soul (the mind), 53, 142-150
soul-tie, 29, 33, 65, 296-297, 299
soul-spirit, secular definition, 148
Southern Baptist Convention, 218
Sovereign Deliverance, 41, **42**, 43-46, 73, 79, 99, 223, 290, 310-311
Sovereign Deliverance, where it ends & where Technical Deliverance begins, 314-315
Sovereign Deliverance, five forms of, 44
Sovereign Deliverance Graphic, 42
Sovereignty of God (God's good pleasure), 41, 56, 67, 79, 108-109, 168, 178-179, 239, 265, 320
spirit, human, 142-144, 151-152, 169
spiritual authority to act, 38, 91-92
spiritual technician, 38
Spontaneous Deliverance, 44, 294, **295-296**

submitting to God, 69, 153-154, 181, 306-308, 309, 311, 313-317, 327-328
summary of how a Christian can have a demon, 161
Sumner, Brian, 294
Sumrall, Lester, 61, 80-81
Supplicatory Deliverance, 44, 265-267
Supersessionism, 332-333
Syrophoenician Woman's Daughter, 196, 233

Technical Deliverance, 31, **32,** 35, 37-38, 57, 69, 73, 309-310, 314-315, 322
Technical Deliverance Graphic, 32
technician, spiritual, 38
teleministry, 233, **240-241**, 297
Temple, God's in Israel, 169-170
Territorial Deliverance, 31, 37, **38**
thorn, Paul's, 259-261, 267-269
tradition, church, **223-224**, 227, 241, 291
Trinity, Holy, 141, 150, 185
tripartite (triune, or trichotomous) nature of man, 137-138, **140**, 168, 171, 178, 185, 219

Tyndale Bible, 187-189,
 199-200, 203-205, 209

unbelief does not change
 reality, 82
unknown exorcist, 34
*upage satana*, 276

vexation, 64
Vic, Pastor, 123-126, 134,
 162
virtual session, 240

warfare shift, OT-NT,
 254, 324
who the Son sets free
 (John 8:36), 288-290
Who-the-Son-Sets-Free
 Argument, 288-290
Williams, Donnie, 16-17
witchcraft (WC), 86,
 108-109, 153, 155,
 **183**, 184, 225, 264
Wycliffe Bible, 188,
 199-200, 209

yoked (equally &
 unequally), 127-134
yoked together, legally
 binding human
 relationships,
 127-130
yoked, referring to having a
 demon, 131-132

www.ingramcontent.com/pod-product-compliance
Lightning Source LLC
Chambersburg PA
CBHW050311120526
44592CB00014B/1860